Index

RESTRUCTURING INDIA'S MILITARY
OUT OF BOX OPTIONS

Restructuring India's Military Out of Box Options

A.P. Revi

GYAN

Restructuring India's Military: Out of Box Option

ISBN : 978-81-212-1161-1

Published in 2012 in India by
Gyan Publishing House
23, Main Ansari Road, Daryaganj,
New Delhi - 110002
Phones : 23282060, 23261060
Fax : (011) 23285914
E-mail: books@gyanbooks.com
website: gyanbooks.com

Laser Type Setting : Rajender Vashist, Delhi
Printed at : Chawla Offset Printers, Delhi

I dedicate this book to the
memory of my
mother in law - Sarojini.
She was the silent inspiration
to my writings.

Contents

Tele : 23014864

Marshal of the Air Force Arjan Singh D.F.C.

★★★★★

7-A, Kautilya Marg
New Delhi - 110021

Foreword

I knew Wing Commander Murkot Ramunny ever since he got his commission in the Air Force in 1941. During the partition, he served in the Cabinet Secretariat and oversaw the Air Force assets being divided between the two countries. He was a great proponent of the concept of joint operations and a prolific writer. He was the first Chief Instructor of the Joint Services Wing of the National Defence Academy at Clement Town, Dehra Dun. At that time, Rear Admiral A.P. Revi, his son-in-law, was a cadet at JSW. I am pleased to note that Revi has taken upon himself to carry forward Ramunny's ideas.

Revi has obviously done extensive research and indepth survey of the global scenario on Higher Defence Management. In the book he has come out with some very innovative / unorthodox solutions to meet the ever so complicated defence management structure. One may not agree with all his findings and recommendations but they will give food for thought to most readers. The book is primarily targeted as a reference book on Higher Defence Management, to military professionals, research scholars, academicians, and defence / political analysts, students of management / social sciences, service institutions, think-tanks and professional libraries. These issues are always of great concern to our nation.

Arjan Singh

30 Sep 11 — Marshal of the Air Force Arjan Singh, DFC

Preface

Researching and writing of this book has been a unique learning experience for me. I was deeply distressed with the slow rate of progress in our so badly needed restructuring exercise. In January 1999, Shri. George Fernandes, the former Defence Minister, had declared that within three months, he would integrate and restructure the Defence Ministry and Service – headquarters. Thirteen years down the line – India still does not have a clear road map – in spite of a Cabinet Committee on National Security (CCS) approval to the GOMs recommendations given in February 2002.

Global survey clearly showed that India was not alone in this predicament. All nations had a hard time going through such a phase. And without exception, in all cases, the changes had to be pushed through with determination by the political leadership. Turf war was a universal phenomenon. The Russian case is about the worst – in both depth and magnitude. Compulsions of financial / economic melt-down combined with the political and social upheaval - gave the necessary incentive to the political leadership to ram it through. Not being embedded in a classic democratic frame work – facilitated the actions. Still, their *perestroika* / restructuring are a long way from over.

In the case of India – this exercise is equally challenging, due to the historical baggage that goes along with it. The political, bureaucratic and military establishments are deeply entrenched in their respective stands. India's advantage is that this exercise is taking place in an environment of stable financial / social conditions and within a democratic framework. It is certainly not advisable or feasible for India to attempt to leap-frog into the 21st century structure without first ironing out the basic underlying fault line between the stake-holders. The interim near / mid term *out of box* option suggested here is to facilitate the final objective in the shortest period and with least pain. Notwithstanding, which option is chosen – my considered view is that unless the issues of Logistic reform and C^4I^2SR structure is *taken by the horn* and pushed through on priority vigorously with all the determination and persistence that one can muster - all our efforts on creating Chief of Defence Staff (CDS) and unified theatre commands etc will fail in the final test on the battlefield. This affects the Army the most and holds back the Navy and the Air Force considerably. A mind set change is called for. This by no means, belittles the urgent need for the appointment of CDS.

The first four chapters of the book discuss in depth the foremost global models of Higher Defence Management systems and the trauma they went through in their process of restructuring. The most optimal and pragmatic solution for India has been suggested. The model offered – envisages triple function architecture i.e. Staff, Operation and Support. This would be a long term option and in conformity with National Security Council (NSC) directive of 2001 also. Appointment of CDS is a necessity but per force has to await fulfilment of the indicated essential conditionality that is likely to take time. As a stop gap measure, an interim out of the box option is recommended – taking the present CCS approved solution forward. The emphasis is on building a sound joint / unified service concept and a focused effort on reforming the logistics frame-work to meet all the future battle contingencies. Ultimately, which ever route one may take – these are essential and unavoidable elements. The illustrations used in the book are mostly Navy oriented but are equally applicable to other services also. The comparatively new areas of National Coastal Security, National Disaster Management architecture have also been covered in brief.

Naresh Chandra Committee has been apprised of the findings and recommendations at Chapter 10.

In this venture, the long stint with the Royal Navy (British) during the initial stages of my career was a great help. I served on board the RN Air Craft carriers HMS *Eagle and Ark Royal* and participated in NATO exercises in the North Atlantic and cross operation between HMS Ark Royal and USS Forrestal in the Mediterranean. Later in my career, I worked closely with the Soviet Navy for almost twenty years. I was the Naval Attache at Moscow from 1981 to 1985. During that period, I had the good fortune of personally interacting with such legendary soviet military leaders as:

(a) Defence Minister - Marshal of the Soviet Union DF. Ustinov.
(b) Chiefs of the General Staff - Marshal of SU. NV. Ogarkov and Akhrameiv.
(c) Naval Chiefs - Admirals of the Fleet of the SU, SG. Goroshkov and VN. Chernaven.
(d) Ministers of Ship Building - Mr. MV Yegorov and Belausev.
(e) Engineer Admirals - PG Kotov (in charge of Nuclear s/m construction) and VG Novikov (equivalent of India's Chief of Material).

The author introducing CNS Admiral Dawson to the Soviet Chief of General Staff, Marshal of the Soviet Union Ogarkov and the Soviet Naval Chief, Admiral of the Fleet of the SU Gorashkov

In the course of the research – amongst others, I also had one to one informal discussions / interaction with the following. I am greatly indebted to their inputs. The views expressed, observations made and conclusions drawn are, however, my own:

(a) The UK Minister of Defence in charge of DES&T. Mr. Peter Luff and separately with the First Sea Lord Admiral Sir Mart Stanhope and the Military and Air Attachés at the UKHC at Delhi.
(b) Mr Duncan Lang a member in the Department of US Under Secretary of Defence (AT&L).
(c) Lt. Gen (Armament) Alain Costes. DGA France.
(d) Prof. Gred Becham. Head of the US Defence Acquisition University.
(e) Admiral Arun Prakash. In his capacity at the time as CNS and CJCSC.
(f) General Deepak Kapoor. In his capacity at the time as COAS.
(g) General V.K. Singh. In his capacity as the COAS.
(h) V. Adm. D.K. Dewan. In capacity as COP.
(i) V. Adm. Shekar Sinha. In his capacity at the time as CIDS.
(j) Lt Gen. S.S. Dhillon. In his capacity at the time as MGO.
(k) Lt. Gen. B.S. Nagal. In his capacity at the time as DGOL.
(l) V. Adm. Ganesh Mahadeavan. In his capacity at the time as COM.
(m) Air Marshal Rama Sunderam. In his capacity at the time as AOM.
(n) Lt. Gen. A.K.S. Chandela. In his capacity at the time as DGEME.
(o) Lt. Gen. B.S. Sisodia. In his capacity at the time as DGORD.
(p) AVM. Sharma. S.K. In his capacity at the time as ACAS (Logistics).
(q) Maj. Gen. A.S. Lamba. In his capacity at the time as ADGOL.
(r) R. Adm. S. Madhusudanan. Flag Officer (PV and AOD).
(s) Brig. Khosla. In his capacity at the time as CICP.
(t) Brig. Sareen. In his capacity at the time as PD Standardisation.

Acknowledgements

I am deeply indebted to my immediate family for their unflinching support given to me, on this venture. My wife Yeshoda took the brunt of my idiosyncrasies and the odd working hours. My son Aromar presented me with a PC – on which I did most of my writings. My younger son Amitabh kept me on my toes intellectually. Wing Commander Murkoth Ramunny my mentor, father in law and a prolific writer – set me a difficult example to emulate. Many of my complex illustrations were conceptualised on his computer, in the serene environment at *Bitra*, during my vacations at Dharmadam in Kerala.

Here, I have drawn on my previous articles published in India Defence Review, Journals of Indian Ocean Studies, United Services of India and my thesis for M.Phil submitted to National Defence College, Madras Univeraity. I am greatly indebted to them for permitting me to use the same material in my current book.

"Last but not least – I am grateful for the professional manner in which the publisher has taken on this task. I am particularly appreciative of the meticulous job done by the editorial members and those who took on the task of assimilating / incorporating the intricate graphics into the document".

A.P. Revi

List of Illustrations

List of Abbreviations

Chapter 1

1.	ABM	: Anti Ballistic Missile.
2.	ACF	: Acquisition Career Field.
3.	ACQ	: Acquisition.
4.	AE	: Acquisition Executive.
5.	AMC	: Air Mobility Command.
6.	AOR	: Area of Responsibility.
7.	ASCOM	: Armed Support Command.
8.	ASCOM	: Army Combined Arms Support Command.
9.	ASD	: Assistant Secretary Defence.
10.	ASD (P&L)	: ASD (Production and Logistics)
11.	ASD	: Assistant Secretary Defence.
12.	ASN (RD&A)	: Assistant Secretary Navy (Research, Development and Acquisition).
13.	ASN	: Assistant Secretary Navy.
14.	BE	: Bachelor of Engineering.
15.	BES	: Budget Estimate Submission.
16.	BMDO	: Ballistic Missile Defence Organisation.
17.	C in C	: Commander in Chief.
18.	C^2	: Command and Control.
19.	C^4I	: Command, Control, Communication, Computer and Intelligence.
20.	CCDR	: Combat Commander.
21.	CCNS	: Cabinet Committee on National Security.

22. CENTO : Central Treaty Organisation.
23. CFE : Treaty on Conventional Force in Europe.
24. CIA : Central Intelligence Agency.
25. CIA : Central Intelligence Agency.
26. Civ : Civilian.
27. CMS : Chief of Marine Services.
28. CNO : Chief of Naval Operation. US Naval Chief.
29. CO Army : Chief of Army Staff. COAS.
30. COAF : Chief of Air Force.
31. COAS : Chief of Army Staff.
32. COCOM : Combat Command.
33. COMCDR : Combat Commander.
34. COS : Chief of Staff.
35. CTBT : Comprehensive Test Ban Treaty.
36. DAB : Defence Acquisition Board.
37. DCI : Director of Central Intelligence.
38. DDG : Guided Missile Destroyer.
39. DDOC : Deployment and Distribution Centre.
40. DDS : Deputy Secretary of Defence.
41. Dep't : Department.
42. DG : Defence Guidance Statement.
43. DHS : Department of Homeland Security.
44. DIA : Defence Intelligence Agency.
45. Dir : Director.
46. DLA : Defence Logistics Agency.
47. DOD : Department of Defence.
48. DP&RB : Defence Planning and Resource Board.
49. DPG : Defence Planning Guidance Statement.
50. DSB : Defence Science Board.
51. DSD : Deputy Secretary Defence.
52. DSPO : Defence Supply Process Owner.

53.	DSRPO	: Defence System Readiness Process Owner.
54.	Dy	: Deputy.
55.	DyAS	: Deputy Assistant Secretary.
56.	EA	: Executive Agent.
57.	FAA	: Federal Aviation Agency.
58.	FAR	: Federal Acquisition Regulation.
59.	FBI	: Federal Bureau of Intelligence.
60.	FM&P	: Force Management and Personnel.
61.	FYDP	: Future Year Defence Programme.
62.	GNA86	: Gold Water Nicholls Act 1986.
63.	GOI	: Government of India.
64.	GOM	: Group of Ministers.
65.	HDM	: Higher Defence Management.
66.	HLS	: Homeland Security.
67.	HLSC	: Homeland Security Council.
68.	HRD	: Human Resource Development.
69.	IAIP	: Directorate of Information Analysis and Information Projection of Homeland Security.
70.	INR	: Bureau of Intelligence Research of State Department.
71.	IPL	: Integrated Priority List.
72.	JCS	: Joint Chiefs of Staff.
73.	JCSC	: Joint Chiefs of Staff Committee.
74.	JDPO	: Joint Deployment Process Owner.
75.	JFCOM/JFC	: Joint Force Command.
76.	JFSCC	: Joint Force Support Component Command.
77.	JIEP	: Joint Intelligence Estimate Plan.
78.	JITF-CT	: Joint Intelligence Task Force – Combating Terrorism.

79. JLE : Joint Logistics Environment.
80. JLOC : Joint Logistics Centre.
81. JMIP : Joint Military Intelligence Programme.
82. JPAM : Joint Programme Assessment Memorandum.
83. JRMB : Joint Requirement Management Board.
84. JSCP : Joint Strategic Capability Plan.
85. JSPD : Joint Strategic Planning Document.
86. JTLC : Joint Theatre Logistics Command.
87. LPD : Landing Ship Dock.
88. ME : Master of Engineering.
89. Mil : Military.
90. MIT : Massachusetts Institute of Technology.
91. NATO : North Atlantic Treaty Organisation.
92. NAVAIR : NAVSEA - Air Systems.
93. NAVFAC : NAVSEA - Facilities.
94. NAVSEA : US Navy Material Command - Sea Systems.
95. NAVSUP : NAVSEA - Supply Services.
96. NCA : National Command Authority.
97. NCC : National Command Centre.
98. NCTA : National Commission on Terrorist Attack.
99. NCTC : National Counter - Terrorism Centre.
100. NGA : National Geospatial Agency.
101. NIC : National Intelligence Centres.
102. NMCC : National Military Command Centre.
103. NMMC : National Military Command Centre.
104. NMS : National Military Strategy.
105. NORAD : North American Aerospace Defence Command.
106. NPT : Non Proliferation Treaty.
107. NRO : National Reconnaissance Office.

108. NSA : National Security Adviser.
109. NSA : National Security Agency.
110. NSA (47) : US National Security Act 1947.
111. NSC : National Security Council.
112. NSC : National Security Council.
113. NSDD : National Security Decision Directive.
114. NSLC : Naval Sea Logistics Centre.
115. NSS : National Security Strategy.
116. NSWC : Naval Surface Warfare Centre.
117. NUWC : Naval Under-Water Warfare Centre.
118. OMB : Office of Management and Budget.
119. OPLAN : Operation Plans.
120. OSD : Office of Secretary of Defence.
121. OT&E : Operational Test and Evaluation Group.
122. P&L : Production and Logistics.
123. PAD : Product Area Director.
124. PBD : Programme Budget Decision.
125. PDM : Programme Decision Memorandum.
126. PDP : Programme Decision Package.
127. PE / PEO : Programme Executive.
128. PM : Programme Manager.
129. PM : Programme Manager.
130. POM : Programme Objective Memorandum.
131. PPB&E : Planning, Programming, Budget and Execution.
132. PPB&S : Planning, Programming and Budget System.
133. PPBS : Planning Programming and Budgeting System.
134. QDR : Quadrennial Defence Review.
135. QDR : Quadrennial Defence Review.
136. QM : Quarter Master.

137. R&D : Research and Development.
138. R&E : Research and Engineering.
139. R&T : Research and Technology.
140. RDT&E : Research Development, Test and Engineering.
141. SAE : Service Acquisition Executive. Secretary (Navy).
142. SCN : Shipbuilding Conversion Navy.
143. SDDC : Surface Deployment and Distribution Command.
144. SDR : Strategic Defence Review.
145. SEATO : South East Asia Treaty Organisation.
146. SECNAV : Secretary Navy.
147. Secy Navy : Secretary Navy.
148. Secy of Def : Secretary of Defence.
149. SF : Special forces.
150. SIG : Senior Inter-Departmental Group.
151. SLBM : Submarine Launched Ballistic Missile.
152. SOC : Special Operations Command.
153. SOP : Standard Operation Procedure.
154. SPAWAR : Space and Naval Warfare.
155. SSBN : Ballistic Missile Nuclear Submarine.
156. START : Strategic Arms Reduction Treaty
157. STRATCOM : US Strategic Command.
158. TA : Technical Authority.
159. TIARA : Tactical Intelligence and Related Activities.
160. TSC : Theatre Sustainment Command.
161. TTIC : Terrorist Threat Integration Centre.
162. U/S : Under Secretary.
163. UK : United Kingdom.
164. USA : United States of America.

165. USAF : US Air - Force.
166. USD : Under Secretary of Defence.
167. USD (ACQ) : USD Acquisition.
168 USD (AT&L) : USD (Acquisition, Technology and Logistics).
169. USMOD : US Ministry of Defence.
170. USN : United Services Navy.
171. USSR : Union of Soviet Socialist Republic.
172. VC of JCS : Vice Chief of JCS.
173. VP : Vice President.
174. WC : Warfare Centre.
175. WMD : Weapons of Mass Destruction.
176. WWII : Second World War.

CHAPTER 2

1. ACDS : Assistant Chief of Defence Staff.
2. AG. : Adjutant General.
3. AEW : Aircraft Early Warning.
4. AOM : Air Officer In charge Maintenance.
5. ASW : Anti Submarine Warfare.
6. CAS · Chief of Air Staff.
7. CCS : Chief of Corporate Services.
8. COL : Chief of Logistics.
9. CDL : Chief of Defence Logistics.
10. CDM : Chief of Defence Material.
11. CDS : Chief of Defence Staff.
12. CGS : Chief of General Staff.
13. CJO : Chief of Joint Operation.
14. CJO : Commander Joint Operations.
15. CNH : CinC Naval Home..
16. CNS : Chief of Naval Staff.
17. COM : Chief of Material.

18. COO : Chief Operations Officers.
19. COS : Chiefs of Staff.
20. CSA : Chief Scientific Adviser.
21. CST : Customer Support Team.
22. CWP&A. : Controller of Warship Production and Acquisition.
23. DCSA : Defence Commercial Service Agency.
24. DDP : Department of Defence Production.
25. DE&SA : Defence Equipment and Support Agency.
26. DE&ST : Defence Equipment and Science Technology.
27. DGFIN : DG finance.
28. DGL : Director General Logistics.
29. DGND. : Director General of Naval Design.
30. DLB : Defence Logistics Board.
31. DLO : Defence Logistics Organisation.
32. DMB : Defence Management Board.
33. DPA : Defence Procurement Agency.
34. EinC. : Engineer in Chief.
35. FM : Foreign Minister.
36. GOSPLAN : USSR State Planning Commission.
37. HDM : Higher Defence Management.
38. IPT : Integrated Project Team.
39. MGO : Master General of Ordnance.
40. MOD : Minister of Defence.
41. NATO. : North Atlantic Treaty Organisation.
42. NCS(I) : National Security Council India.
43. PM : Prime Minister.
44. PSO : Principal Staff Officer.
45. PUS : Permanent Under Secretary.
46. QMG : Quarter Master General.
47. RAF : Royal Air Force.

48. RFA : Reserve Fleet Auxiliary.
49. RML : Revolution n Military Logistics.
50. RN : Royal Navy.
51. SDR : Strategic Defence Review.
52. SOD : Secretary of Defence.
53. STC : Strike Command.
54. TLB : Top Level Budget.
55. UK : United Kingdom.
56. USSR : Union of Soviet Socialist Republic.
57. VCDS : Vice Chief of Defence Staff.

CHAPTER 3

1. ABM : Anti Ballistics Missile.
2. AF : Air Force.
3. ASV : Army Aviation.
4. ASW : Anti Submarine Warfare.
5. C of S : Chief of Staff - Chiefs of respective Service.
6. CGS : Chief of General Staff.
7. CinC : Commander in Chief.
8. CMNS : Chief of Main Naval Staff.
9. CPSU : Communist Party Soviet Union.
10. DA : Long Range Aviation. Strategic Aviation. Strike Force. LRA
11. DM : Defence Minister.
12. EW : Early Warning.
13. FA : Tactical Aviation.
14. FSB : Domestic Intelligence Agency.
15. FSB : Domestic Intelligence Agency.
16. GF : Ground Force.
17. GKO : State Committee for Defence. Defence Council.
18. Glavkom : Service Chiefs.

19. GOSPLAN : State Planning Commission.
20. GOU : Military Operation Directorate.
21. GRU : Military Intelligence Directorate.
22. GS : General Service.
23. HDM : Higher Defence Management.
24. Lakh : 1,00,000.
25. M&SDF : Missile and Space Defence Force.
26. MAD : Mutual Assured Destruction.
27. MD : Military District.
28. MID : Ministry of External Affairs.
29. MOD : Ministry of Defence.
30. MVD : Ministry of Interior Affairs.
31. NATO : North Atlantic Treaty Organisation.
32. NCP : National Security Concept.
33. NTVS : Logistics Services. Rear Services.
34. NW : Nuclear Weapon.
35. PM : Prime Minister.
36. RF : Russian Federation.
37. RFSC : Russian Federation Security Council.
38. RSVN : SRF - Strategic Rocket Force.
39. SAM : Surface to Air Missile.
40. SCRF / RFSC : Russian Federation Security Council.
41. SORT : Strategic Offensive Reduction Treaty.
42. SSS : Strategic Deterrence Force.
43. STO : Council of Labour and Defence.
44. SU : Soviet Union.
45. SV : Ground Forces.
46. SVR : Foreign Intelligence Service.
47. TVD : Theatre Military Operation.
48. USA : United States of America.
49. USSR : Union of Soviet Socialist Republic.

50. VGK : Supreme High Command.
51. VMF : Navy.
52. VP : Vice President.
53. VPVO : ADF - Air Defence Force.
54. VTA : Transport Aviation.
55. VVS : Air Force.
56. WMD : Weapons of Mass Destruction.
57. WW : World War.

CHAPTER 4

1. A&N : Andaman and Nicobar.
2. ABM : Anti Ballistic Missile.
3. AMS : Academy of Military Sciences.
4. ASAT : Anti-Satellite.
5. ASW : Anti Submarine Warfare.
6. C[4]ISR : Command, Control, Communication, Computer, Intelligence Surveilance and Reconnaissance.
7. CC : Central Committee.
8. CCP : China's Communist Party.
9. Cdr : Commander.
10. CDS : Chief of Defence Staff.
11. CGS : Chief of General Staff.
12. CMC : Central Military Commission.
13. CNP : Comprehensive National Power.
14. CR : Cultural Revolution.
15. CYL : Communist Youth League.
16. DWP : Defence White Paper.
17. EM : Electro- Magnetic.
18. FE : Far East.
19. GAD : General Armament Department.
20. GF : Ground Force.
21. GLD : General Logistics Department.

22. GOM : Group of Ministers.
23. GPD : General Political Department.
24. GPL : Gang of Prince-lings.
25. GSD : General Staff Department.
26. HRD : Human Resource Development.
27. IT : Information Technology.
28. KMT : Kuomintang.
29. LR : Long Range.
30. MD : Military District.
31. MND : Ministry of National Defence.
32. MOOTW : Military Operations Other Than War.
33. MP : Military Police.
34. MR : Military Region.
35. NCO : Non Commissioned Officer.
36. NDU : National Defence University.
37. NMC : National Military Commission.
38. NPC : National Peoples Congress.
39. PAP : Peoples Armed Police.
40. PB : Politburo.
41. PLA : Peoples Liberation Army.
42. PLA : Peoples Liberation Army.
43. PLAAF : PLA Air Force.
44. PLAN : PLA Navy.
45. PRC : Peoples Republic of China.
46. RF : Russian Federation.
47. RHQ : Regional Head Quarters.
48. RMA : Revolution in Military Affairs.
49. RML : Revolution in Military Logistics.
50. SC : Standing Committee of NPC.
51. SIIS : Shangai Institute of International Studies.
52. SLBM : Submarine Launched Ballistic Missile.

53. SLC : Sea Lane of Communication.
54. SSBN : Ballistic Missile Nuclear Submarine.
55. SSN : Nuclear Powered Attack Submarine.
56. UK : United Kingdom.
57. USA : United States of America.
58. USSR : Union of Socialist Soviet Republic.
59. UVV : Unmanned Under water Vehicle.

CHAPTER 5-6

1. A&NC : Andaman and Nicobar Command.
2. ABM : Anti Ballistic Missile.
3. AC : Allied Countries.
4. ACCS : Artillery Combat C^2 System.
5. ACF : Acquisition Career Field.
6. ACIDS : Assistant CIDS.
7. ACNS (P&P) : ACNS (Policy and Plans).
8. ADA : Aircraft Development Authority.
9. ADC&R : Air Defence Control and Reporting System.
10. ADG : Assistant DG.
11. AECM : Airborne Electronic Counter Measure
12. AEW&C : Airborne Early Warning and Control A/C.
13. AFNET : IAF Network System.
14. AG : Adjutant General.
15. AHSP : Authority Holding Sealed Particulars.
16. AJT : Advanced Jet Trainer.
17. AMC : Air Mobility Command.
18. AMC : Army Medical Corps India.
19. AMC : Annual Maintenance Contract.
20. AOC : Army Ordinance Corp.
21. AOM : Air Officer in Charge Maintenance.
22. AON : Approval of Necessity.

23. AOR : Area of Operations.
24. APCC : Acquisition Plan Categorisation Committee.
25. ASC : Army Supply Corps.
26. ASEAN : Association of South East Asia Nations.
27. ASMACS : ASC Stores Monitoring and Control System.
28. AWAC : Airborne Warning and Control A/C.
29. BARC : Bhabha Atomic Research Centre.
30. BDL : Bharath Dynamics Ltd.
31. BEL : Bharath Electronic Ltd.
32. BMS : Battle Management System.
33. BSF : Border Security Forces.
34. BSS : Battlefield Surveillance System.
35. C o S : Chief of Staff.
36. C^3IS : Command, Control, Communication, Intelligence and Surveillance.
37. C^4ISR : Command, control, Communication, Computer, Intelligence, Surveillance and Reconnaissance.
38. CAC : Central Air Command.
39. CALS : Computer Aided Acquisition and Logistics Support.
40. CAS : Chief of Air Staff.
41. CC : Central Command.
42. CCS : Cabinet Committee on Security.
43. CDD : Capability Development Document
44. CDM : Chief of Defence Material.
45. CDS : Chief of Defence Staff.
46. CFA : Competent Financial Authority.
47. CGS : Chief of General Staff.
48. CICP : Computer Inventory Control Project.
49. CIDS : Chief of Integrated Defence Staff.

50. CIDSS : Command Information Decision Support System.
51. CJCS : Chairman Joint Chief of Staff .
52. CJO : Chief of Joint Operations.
53. CLMA : Command Logistics and Maintenance Officer.
54. CNO : Chief of Naval Operation.
55. CNS : Chief of Naval Staff.
56. COAS : Chief of Army Staff.
57. COCOM : Combat Commander.
58. COD : Central Ordinance Depot.
59. COL : Controller of Logistics.
60. COM : Chief of Material.
61. COP : Chief of Personnel.
62. COS : Chiefs of Staff. COAS, CNS, CAS.
63. CRPF : Central Reserve Police Force.
64. CSL : Cochin Shipbuilding Yard.
65. CST : Customer Support Team.
66. CWP&A : Controller of Warship Production and Acquisition.
67. DAAQ : Directorate of A/c Acquisition..
68. DAB : Defence Acquisition Board.
69. DAC : Defence Acquisition Council.
70. DAE : Department of Atomic Energy.
71. DCDS : Deputy CIDS.
72. DCIDS(PP&FD): Deputy CIDS (Policy, Plans and Force Deployment).
73. DCN : Defence Communication Network.
74. DCN Inter Service Defence Communication Grid.
75. DCOAS(P&S) : Deputy COAS (Planning and Systems).
76. DCSA : Defence Commerce Service Agency.

77.	DDG	: Deputy DG.
78.	DDP	: Department of Defence Production.
79.	DDPO	: Distribution Process Owner.
80.	DE&SA	: Defence Equipment and Support Agency.
81.	DEE	: Directorate Electrical Engineering.
82.	DEF STAN	: Defence Standards.
83.	DGACQ	: DG Acquisition.
84.	DGAI	: DG Air Intelligence.
85.	DGATV	: DG Advanced Technology Vessel.
86.	DGEME	: DG Electrical and Mechanical Engineering.
87.	DGIS	: DG Information Systems.
88.	DGMI	: DG Military Intelligence.
89.	DGMIS	: DG military Intelligence Service.
90.	DGMO	: DG Military Operations.
91.	DGMS	: DG Medical Services.
92.	DGND	: DG Naval Design.
93.	DGOL	: DG Operational Logistics.
94.	DGQA	: DG Quality Assurance.
95.	DGST	DG Supply and Transport.
96.	DGWE	: DG Weapon and Engineering.
97.	DHAQ	: Directorate Harrier A/C Acquisition.
98.	DIPAC	: Defence Imagery Processing and Analysis centr.
99.	DLO	: Defence Logistics Organisation.
100.	DLS	: Directorate of Logistics Services.
101.	DMDE	: Defence Machinery Development Establishment.
102.	DNA	: Director ate Naval Architecture.
103.	DNAM	: Directorate Naval Air Material.
104.	DNAS	: Directorate Naval Air Staff Division.
105.	DND	: Directorate of Naval Design.
106.	DNI	: Director Naval Intelligence.
107.	DOD	: Department of Defence.
108.	DOFA	: Defence Off-set Facilitating Agency.
109.	DoS	: Department of Standardisation.

110. DOT : Department of Telecommunication.
111. DPA : Defence Procurement Agency.
112. DPM : Defence Procurement Manual.
113. DPP : Defence Procurement Procedure.
114. DPSU : Defence PSU.
115. DRDO : Defence R&D Organisation.
116. DS&DA : Defence Storage and Distribution Agency.
117. DSA : Director of S/M Arms.
118. DSAQ : Directorate of Ship Acquisition.
119. DSB : Defence Science Board.
120. DSDG : Directorate of S/M Design Group.
121. DSMAQ : Directorate of S/M Acquisition.
122. DSP : Directorate Ship Production.
123. DSPRO : Defence System Readiness Process Owner.
124. DWE : Directorate Weapon Engineering.
125. Dy Def Secy : Deputy Defence Secretary.
126. E in C : Engineer in Chief.
127. E&L : Engineering and Electrical Branches.
128. EAC : Eastern Air Command.
129. EC : Eastern Command.
130. ECCMA : Electronic Commercial Code Management
131. EMERALD : EME Reliable Availability Delivery System.
132. ENC : Eastern Naval Command.
133. EOTD : ECCMA Open Technical Dictionary.
134. FA (DS) : Financial Adviser (Defence Services).
135. FGFA : Fifth Generation Fighter A/C.
136. FINAS : Future Infantry Soldier as a System.
137. FMS : Foreign Military Supply.
138. GOM : Group of Ministers.
139. GRSE : Garden Reach Ship Yards Ltd.
140. GSL : Goa Ship Yard Ltd.
141. HAL : Hindustan Aeronautical Ltd.
142. HDM : Higher Defence Management.
143. HF24 : Hindustan Fighter A/C 24.

144. HQIDS : HQ Integrated Defence Staff.
145. HSL : Hindustan Shipyard Ltd.
146. HUMINT : Human Intelligence.
147. IAC : Indigenous A/C Carrier.
148. IAF : Indian Air Force.
149. IB : Intelligence Bureau.
150. IDR : India Defence Review.
151. IDSA : Institute of Defence Studies and Analysis.
152. ILMAS : Integrated Logistics Management System.
153. IMMOLS : Integrated Materials Management System.
154. IN : Indian Navy.
155. IPL : Illustrated Parts Lists.
156. IPMT : Integrated Project Monitoring Team.
157. ISO : International Standards Organisation.
158. J3 : Operations Division.
159. J4 : Plans Division.
160. J5 : Logistics Division
161. JCO : Junior Commissioned Officer.
162. JCSC : Joint Chief of Staff Committee.
163. JDPO : Joint Deployment Process Owner.
164. JFCOM : Joint force Command.
165. JFSCC : Joint Force Component Command.
166. JTF : Joint Task Force.
167. JTLC : Joint Theatre Logistics Command.
168. LCA : Light Combat A/C.
169. LCH : Light Combat Helicopter.
170. LOGOPS : Operational Logistics.
171. LRMR : Long Range Maritime Reconnaissance A/C
172. LTIPP : Long Term Integrated Perspective Plan.
173. LTPP : Long Term Perspective Plan.
174. MBT : Main Battle Tank.
175. MDL : Mazagon Dock Ltd.
176. MES : Military Engineering Service.
177. MGO : Master General of Ordinance.

178. MIS : Management Information system.
179. MoD : Ministry of Defence.
180. MoS : Minister of State.
181. MoU : Memorandum of Understanding.
182. MMRCA : Medium Multi Role Combat A/C.
183. MTC : Machinery Test Centre.
184. NAL : National Aeronautical Laboratory.
185. NASD : Naval Armament Stores Depot.
186. NATGRID : National Information Grid.
187. NATO : North Atlantic Treaty Organisation.
188. NAVAC : Naval Academy.
189. NC : Northern Command.
190. NC^3I : National C^3Information Grid. (IN / CG).
191. NCO : Non Commissioned Officer.
192. NCS : NATO Codification System.
193. NIA : National Intelligence Agency.
194. NSA : National Security Advisor.
195. NSAB : National Security Advisory Board.
196. NSC : National Security Council.
197. NSD : Naval Stores Depot.
198. NTRO : National Technical Research Organisation.
199. OEM : Original Equipment Manufacturer.
200. OFB : Ordinance Factory Board.
201. OPV : Offshore Patrol Vessel.
202. OSD : Office of Secretary Defence
203. PAK-F : Russian FGFA prototype.
204. PENRAD : Peninsular Radar System.
205. PGD : Power Generation and Distribution.
206. PM : Programme Manager.
207. PM : Prime Minister.
208. PMB : Programme Management Board.
209. PPP : Public Private Partnership.
210. PRC : Peoples Republic of China.
211. PSCD : Parliamentary Standing Committee on Defence.
212. PSO : Principal Staff Officer.

213. PSU : Public Sector Undertaking.
214. PUS : Permanent Under Secretary.
215. QMG : Quarter Master General.
216. QR : Qualitative Requirement.
217. R&D : Research and Development.
218. R&R : Research and Referral.
219. RAW : Research and Analysis Wing.
220. Rev.Int : Revenue Intelligence Services.
221. RM : Defence Minister.
222. RMA : Revolution in Military Affairs.
223. RML : Revolution in Military Logistics.
224. RN : Royal Navy (British)
225. ROD : Regional Ordinance Depot.
226. SAC : Southern Air Command.
227. SATNAV : Satellite Navigational System.
228. SAW : Service Acquisition Wing.
229. SBC : Ship Building Centre.
230. SC : Southern Command.
231. SCAPCC : Service Capability Acquisition Plan Categorisation Committee.
232. SCAPCHC. : Service Capability Acquisition Plan Categorisation Higher Committee.
233. SDDC : Surface Deployment and Distribution Command.
234. Secy Navy : Secretary Navy.
235. Secy (DPS) : Secretary Defence Production and Supply.
236. SFC : Strategic Force Command.
237. SHQ : Service HQ.
238. SMA : S/M Operation Authority.
239. SMSO : Senior Maintenance Staff Officer.
240. SNC : Southern Naval Command.
241. SOD : Secretary of Defence.
242. SPG : Special Planning Group.
243. SSA : Special Secretary Acquisition.
244. SSK : S/M to S/M Killer.

245.	STEP	: Standard for Exchange of Product model data.
246.	SW	: Strategic Wing.
247.	SWAC	: SW Air Command.
248.	SWC	: South Western Command.
249.	TAG	: Technical Coordination Group.
250.	TAS	: Torpedo and Anti Submarine.
251.	TMB	: Technical Management Board.
252.	TOT	: Transfer of Technology.
253.	TPCR	: Technology Perspective and Capability Road map.
254.	TRANSCOM	: Transport Command.
255.	US	: United States Of America.
256.	US	: Under Secretary.
257.	USI	: United Service Institute of India
258.	USN	: United State Navy.
259.	USSR.	: Union of Soviet Socialist Republics.
260.	VCDS	: Vice Chief of Defence Staff.
261.	VCDS	: Vice Chief of Defence Staff.
262.	VCNS	: Vice CNS.
263.	VCOAS	: Vice Chief of Army Staff.
264.	WAC	: Western Air Command.
265.	WC	: Western Command.
266.	WED	: Weapon Equipment Depot.
267.	WNC	: Western Naval Command.

CHAPTER 7

1.	AIS	: Automatic Identification System.
2.	AWACS	: Airborne Warning and Control System.
3.	C^4ISR	: Command Control Communication Computer Intelligence, Surveillance and Reconnaissance.
4.	CCS	: Cabinet Committee on Security.
5.	CG	: Coast Guard.
6.	CISF	: Central Industrial Security Force.
7.	CNS	: Chief of Naval Staff.
8.	COP	: Common Operation Picture.

9. CPS : Coastal Police Station.
10. CSG : Coastal Security Group.
11. CSS2005 : Coastal Security Scheme 2005.
12. DAE : Department of Atomic Energy.
13. DG : Director General.
14. DGLH : DG Light House.
15. EEZ : Extended Economic Zone.
16. ETD : Electronic Tracking Device.
17. FPV : Fast Patrol Vessel.
18. HUMINT . Human Intelligence.
19. IN : Indian Navy.
20. IPV : Inshore Patrol Vessel.
21. IR : Infrared.
22. ISPFS : International Ship and Port Facility Security.
23. JOC : Joint Operation Centre.
24. JPT : Joint Coastal Patrol.
25. MDA. : Maritime Domain Awareness.
26. MHA. : Ministry of Home Affairs.
27. MPF : Marine Police Force.
28. NC^3IN : National Command Control Communication and Intelligence.
29. NCSMCS : National Committee on Strengthening Maritime and Coastal Security.
30. OPV : Offshore Patrol Vessel.
31. RCC : Regional Control Centre.
32. ROC : Regional Operation Centre.
33. ROS : Remote Operation Sensor.
34. SOP : Standard Operation Procedure.
35. TN : Tamil Nadu.
36. UAV : Unmanned Airborne Vehivle.
37. UID : Universal ID card.
38. VTSM : Vessel Traffic Management System

Chapters 8-10

1. A&N. : Andaman and Nicobar.
2. ADA. : Aircraft Development Agency.

3. AEC. : Atomic Energy Commission.
4. BSF. : Border Security Force.
5. CCS : Cabinet Committee on National Security.
6. CDS. : Chief of Defence Staff.
7. CICP. : Computerised Inventory Control Project.
8. CIDS. : Chief of Integrated Defence Staff.
9. CISF. : Central Industrial Security Force.
10. CJCSC. : Chairman Joint Chiefs of Staff Committee.
11. COAS. : Chief of Army Staff.
12. COM. : Chief of Material.
13. COS. : Chiefs of Staff, Chiefs of Service.
14. CRPF. : Central Reserve Police Force.
15. CSF. : Coastal Security Force.
16. CSS. : Coastal Security System.
17. CWP&A. : Controller of Warship Production and Acquisition.
18. DC. : Defence Council.
19. DDMA. : District Disaster Management Authority.
20. DGCG. : DG Coast Guard.
21. DGLH. : DG Light House.
22. DGND. : Director General Naval Design.
23. DGOL. : Director General Operational Logistics.
24. DOD. : Department of Defence.
25. DPP. : Defence Procurement Procedure,
26. DRDO. : Defence Research and Development Organisation.
27. FGFA. : Fifth Generation Fighter Aircraft.
28. FMS. : Foreign Military Supply.
29. GOM. : Group of Ministers.
30. HAL. : Hindustan Aeronautical Limited.
31. HDM. : Higher Defence Management.
32. HRD. : Human Relations Department.
33. IAF. : Indian Air Force.
34. IDSHQ. : Integrated Defence Services HQ.
35. IMMOLS. : Integrated Material Management on Line System.
36. IN. : Indian Navy.

37. ISO. : International Standards Organisation.
38. ITBF. : Indo Tibetan Border Force.
39. JCSC. : Joint Chiefs of Staff Committee.
40. JV. : Joint Venture.
41. KGB. : USSR State Committee for National Security. Soviet Intelligence Agency.
42. LCA. : Light Combat Aircraft.
43. LSPSC. : Lok Sabha Parliamentary Standing Committee.
44. MDA. : Maritime Domain Awareness.
45. MEA. : Ministry of External Affairs.
46. MES. : Military Engineering Service.
47. MHA. : Ministry of Home Affairs..
48. MRTAC. : Multi-Role Transport Aircraft.
49. NAL. : National Aeronautical Laboratory.
50. NCS. : NATO Codification System.
51. NCSMCS. : National Committee on Strengthening Maritime and Coastal Security.
52. NDMA. : National Disaster Management Act.
53. NDRF. : National Disaster Response Force.
54. NEC. : National Executive Council.
55. NSA. : National Security Advisor.
56. NSC. : National Security Council.
57. PM. : Prime Minister.
58. PSC. : Parliamentary Standing Committee.
59. PSO. :Principal Staff Oficer.
60. RM. : Raksha Mantry, Defence Minister.
61. SDMA. : State Disaster Management Authority.
62. SEC. : State Executive Committee.
63. SF. : Strategic Forces.
64. SGATV. : Director General ATV Project.
65. SHQ. : Service Head Quarters.
66. US. : United States of America.
67. USI. : United Services of India.

1

US Higher Defence Management (HDM) Organisational Structure

In the context of this study, the US HDM organisation structure is being viewed as a typical model under a Presidential form of democratic governance.

Various institutions involved in US HDM are discussed sequentially.

As a historical milestone, the organisation as originally envisaged under the US National Security Act 1947 (NSA-47) is illustrated at Fig. 1.1.

It comprised three Departments – one for each Service - under a dedicated Service Secretary (not a bureaucrat but a Presidential appointee duly approved by the Senate). The Secretary of National Defence was overall in-charge – being advised by the War Council, the Munitions Board, the R&D Board and the Joint Chiefs of Staff. The National Security Resource Board and the National Security Council worked directly under the President.

CALENDAR OF EVENTS - MILE-STONES CROSSED

In 1945 – President Truman recommended to Congress a unified Defence structure. After two years of Congressional debate and negotiations – the NSA-47 as shown in Fig. 1.1 emerged.

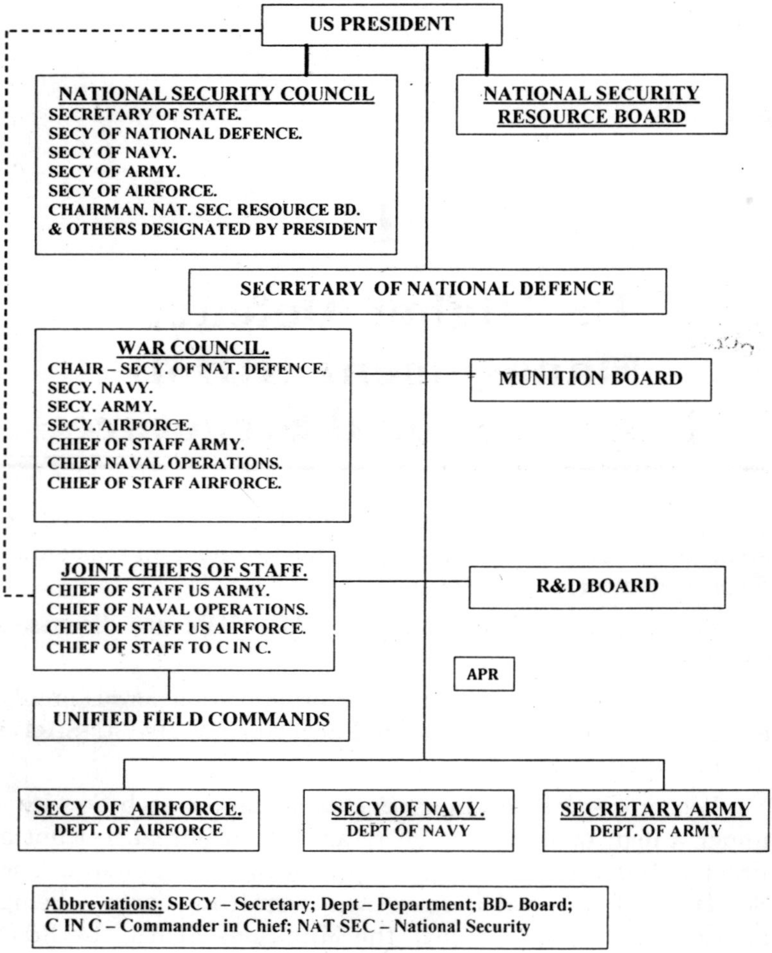

Fig. 1.1. US National Security Act of 1947

To give a historical perspective - some of the important events that have intervened since then and have substantially contributed towards the evolution of the present structure are listed below, chronologically. These have been subsequently elaborated:

(a) US National Security Act 1947 (NSA-47) – was formulated as an outcome of Second World War (WW. II) experience on HDM. This did not fully come up to President Truman's expectations. Instead of one unified department – a Secretary of Defence was created, empowered to exercise general authority and control over three separate service departments. And the Congress retained its right to question each Service separately about its expenditure.

(a) NSA.47 created Central Intelligence Agency (CIA).

(c) In 1949, Amendment to NSA.47 was adopted – which required :

(i) Merger of Service Departments into Department of Defence (DOD).

(ii) Creation of Chairman Joint Chiefs of Staff Committee (CJCSC) – to preside over JCSC meetings. He was however, not expected to give independent advice to the Secretary of Defence but act essentially as spokesman of JCSC consensus.

(iii) US Congress cleared the Act with two caveats - the services to be separately administered and centralised defence planning to be under Office of Secretary of Defence (OSD).

(d) Cold war - formation of North Atlantic Treaty Organisation (NATO) / Central Treaty Organisation (CENTO) / South East Asian Treaty Organisation (SEATO) etc.

(e) In 1958 President Eisenhower confirmed the authority of the Secretary of Defence (SOD) over defence policy and allocation of funds. And created the National Security Adviser (NSA). It must be remembered here that in the case of USA – the Secretary of Defence is equivalent to India's Defence Minister and not the bureaucrat Defence Secretary.

(f) Korean War – 1950 to 1977.

(g) Department of Defence (DOD) Reorganisation Act 1958. – created / stipulated the following :

(i) Unified Command for specific geographic areas.

(ii) Strategic Air Command as a functional Command.

(iii) Orders to Commanders in Chief (C in Cs) of Combat Commands (CCDR) to be conveyed through CJCS.

(iv) The President is the Supreme Commander but Congress retained powers to declare war.

(v) Presidential appointment of key officials - subject to advice and consent of the Senate.

(h) During the 1960s President Kennedy's regime – the inter-service rivalry over resource allocation continued. To insulate planners from parochial thinking of service departments – McNamara, the Secretary of Defence introduced his own style of active management. He brought in the PPBS (an output budgeting system) as a new management system and technique.

(i) The Planning Programming and Budgeting system (PPBS) - required the Joint Chief of Staff (JCSs) to submit their strategic plan to the Secretary of Defence – so that a preliminary guidance for five years force-structure and financial programme could be formulated, on which the annual defence budget would be based.

(j) McNamara also established the Defence Intelligence Agency (DIA).

(k) Vietnam War > 1965.

(l) In 1968, President Nixon inherited a highly centralised decision making system. He introduced the so called - *participatory management.* The JCS was required to develop force structure within stated monitory ceiling. Accordingly, initiation in planning process once again passed back to the Services.

For resource allocation purposes – the National Security Council (NSC) was enlarged. A Defence Programme Review Committee was created. Decisions not only on Defence Budget but also on major programmes became the responsibility of this inter Agency forum.

(m) The War Power Act 1973, was an out come of Korean and Vietnam experience. It introduced a restraining legislation. Sixty days limit was put on the President for authorising deployment of forces in an emergency – unless Congress formally voted, to extend it or declare war.

(n) The formal structure for coordination and policy planning did not evolve until 1981. During President Reagan's Presidency – Bundy, Kissinger and Brzezinski, his Assistants for National Security Affairs, did not have the cabinet status nor did they directly report to the President. During his tenure – the NSC Secretariat comprised of about fifty professionals [i.e. (one third military + one third civil servants inclusive from CIA, Commerce Department and Treasury + one third Academicians)].

(o) In 1981 - President Reagan also set up Senior Inter Departmental Groups (SIG) – for policy coordination framework.

(p) In 1982 - press release promulgating formal structure of NSC was issued.

(q) In 1983 – Packard recommended to the Senate Armed Forces Committee that each service should restructure to have two clearly defined and separate career path for officers :

(i) One of them will train personnel as commanders of Military Forces.

(ii) The other as managers in procurement.

(r) In 1984 – the Congress passed legislation requiring a minimum four years tenure for Programme Managers.

(s) Some of the highlights of the 1986 - David Packard Commission Recommendations / Blue Ribbon Commission on Defence Management are listed below:

(i) Established Under Secretary (U/S) of Defence for Acquisition, Technology and Logistics [USD (AT&L)].

(ii) On issues of acquisition - the USD (AT&L) was given precedence over Service Secretaries.

(iii) Created Service Acquisition Executives (SAE) in each service. SAEs were given dual responsibility - both to the new DOD U/S and the respective Service U/S reporting to the Secretary of Defence. This is further elaborated at Fig.1.2.

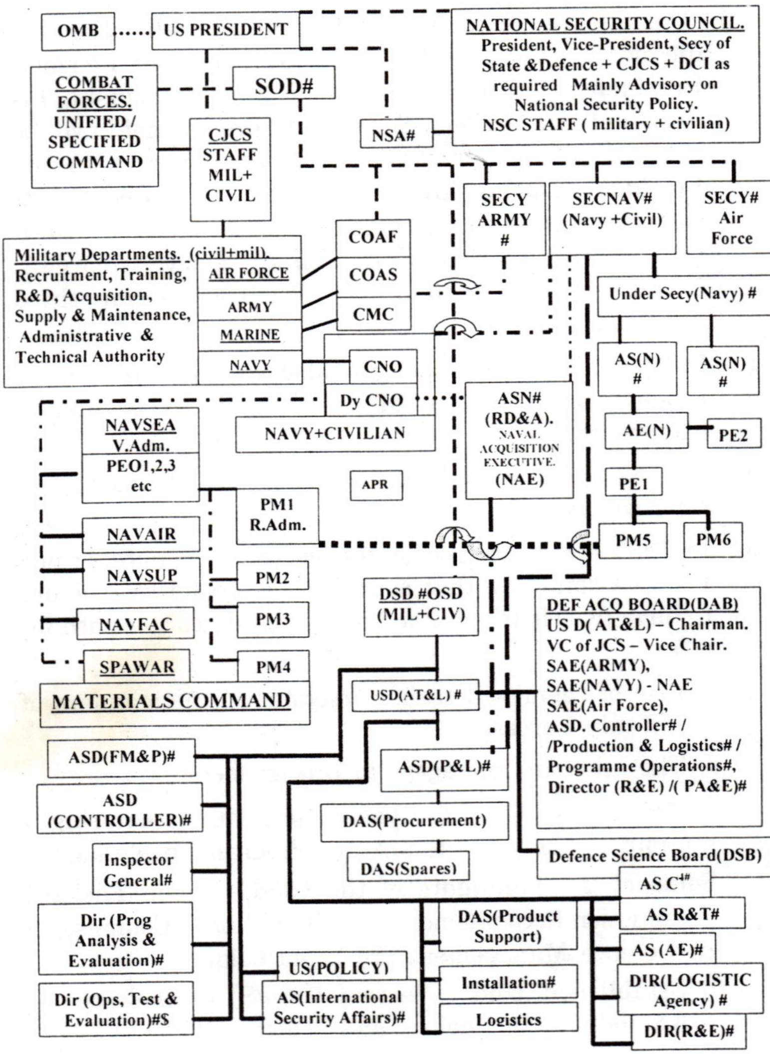

Fig. 1.2 : USDOD Acquisition Navy- Organisation Tree.

(iv) It also created Programme Executive Officer (PEO) reporting directly to AEs. Each PEO was required to oversee a group of Programme Managers.

(v) It gave the CJCS more authority and created a Vice Chairman – who along with the new U/S was to be a part of Joint Requirement Management Board (JRMB)/ Defence Acquisition Board (DAB). DAB was also assigned the task of establishing requirements for new weapons and approve or reject them at each stage along the path of production.

(t) In April 1986 - the Gold Water Nichols Act (GNA-86) – a water-shed Act was enacted. The GNA-86 included the following:

(i) The functional demarcation of responsibilities between the process owners was clearly defined.

(ii) The authority and responsibility of CJCS to provide advice to President, NSC and Secretary of Defence was enhanced.

(iii) The CJCS was empowered to over-see activities of Unified and Specified Command.

(iv) The responsibility and authority of CinCs (CCDR) over their respective Commands was clarified. Also, they were given full authority on administration and support functions necessary to accomplish mission.

National Command Authority (NCA) – USA.

The functional organisational structure of US Defence Command and Control, as has now evolved, after Goldwater Nichols Act 1986 (GNA86), is illustrated at Fig. 1.3. As an illustration, this basically focuses on the Naval Chain.

The President assisted by his Secretary of Defence form the NCA. The operational chain of command flows from the NCA, through the Chairman Joint Chiefs of Staff Committee (CJCSC) to the Unified Command and down the line to the Component Commanders, Type Commanders and finally to the Unit Commander. The operational chain of command could also be exercised by the NCA directly after keeping the CJCS informed.

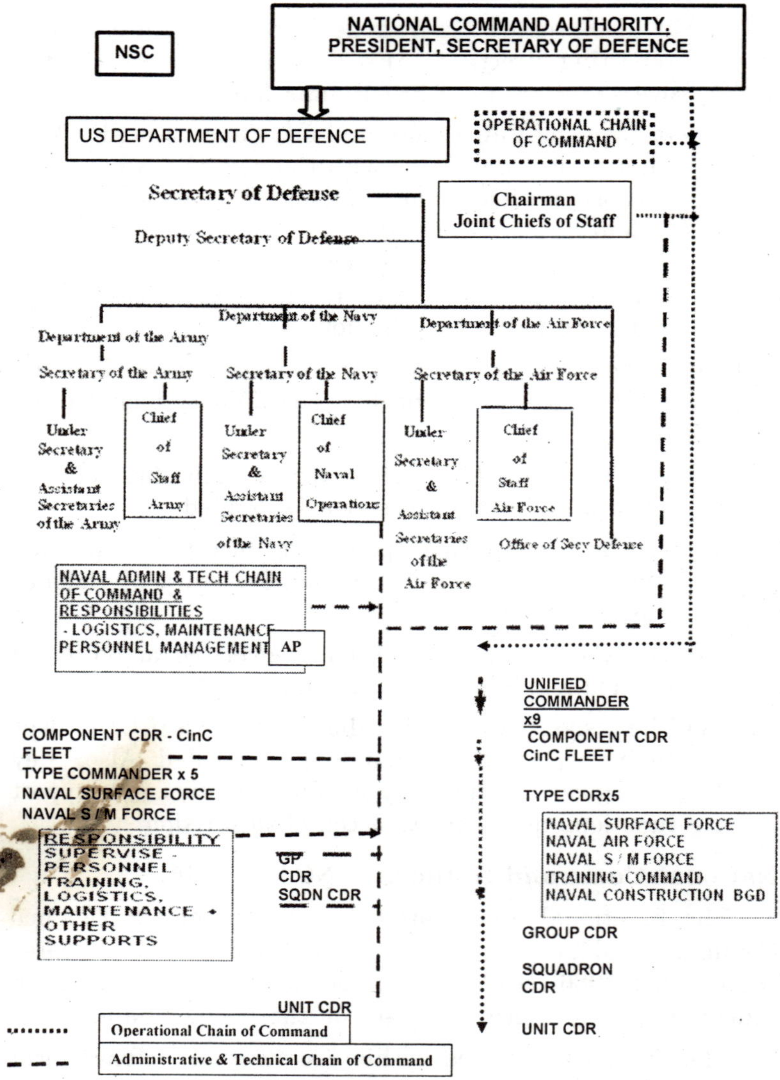

Fig. 1.3. US Operational / Administrative Command

It may be observed that the Chief of Naval Operations (CNO) has no direct operational control over the Fleet Commanders. As shown, he has down the line administrative and technical chain of command. He is responsible for logistics, maintenance, personnel management, procurement, supply and

R&D. The allocation of forces to each Unified and Specified Commands is made by JCSC. The Naval Chief is required to ensure that they are made available for deployment on time, in quantity and quality envisaged. The same applies to the other chiefs of services as too.

US National Security Council (NSC)

The functional flow chart of NSC is illustrated at Fig. 1.4. The NSC comprises the President, Vice President (VP),

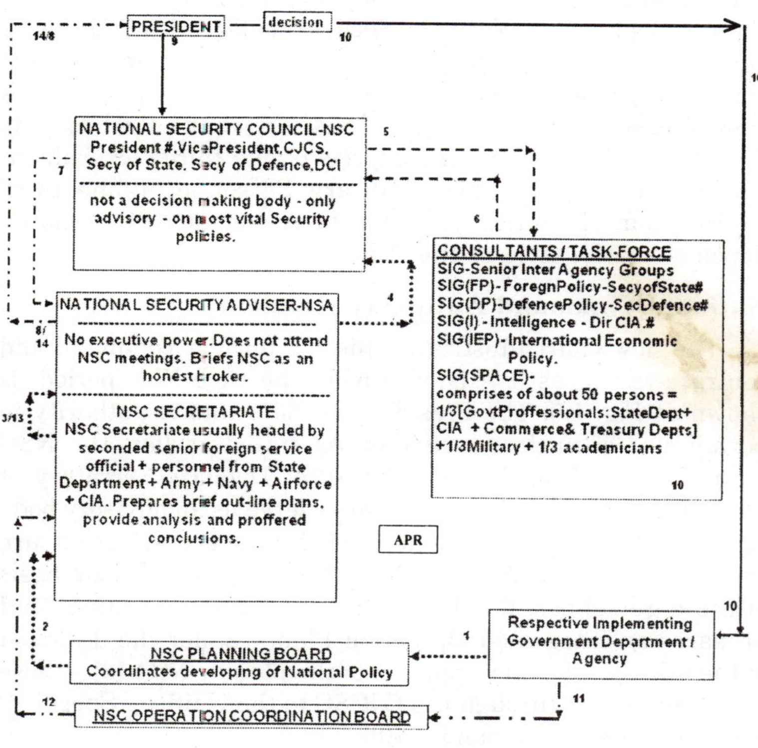

NOTE:- *Emphasis varies with style of functioning of the President particularly on details though - Institutional arrangements continue.*

SYMBOL/CODE :- *# - chairman.*

Fig. 1.4. Typical Sequential Functional Flow Chart - National Security Council - USA. As Represented by Arrangement during Late Twentieth Century.

Secretary of Defence (S O D), Chairman Joint Chiefs of Staff Committee (CJCSC) and Director Central Intelligence (DCI). It is an advisory body to the President on security policy issues. The final decision is taken by the President. The National Security Adviser (NSA) has no executive powers nor is he /she a member of the NSC. He is the primary security adviser to the President and serves as an honest broker. He also heads the NSC secretariat – manned by senior officials from the State Department, DOD, Army, Navy, Air force and the CIA. They prepare outline plans, provide analysis and proffer conclusions on proposals submitted by respective Government departments / agencies. The NSC Planning Board coordinates the development of National Security policies. And the NSC Operation Coordination Board – monitors / coordinates - the execution process. The Senior Inter Agency Groups (SIG), as shown, assist the NSC on specific issues when called upon to do so. The SIG secretariat comprise of one third Government Professionals + one third Military Personnel + one third Academicians. Historically, the functioning of the NSC primarily depends on the style of the President.

National Command Authority (Nuclear)

The flow chart illustrating the US nuclear command and control system, as it existed during the Cold War period, is shown at Fig. 1.5. The President is the ultimate authority to permit use of nuclear weapons. As stated earlier, the NSC with the Vice President, Secretary of Defence, Secretary of State, CJCSC and DCI as members - serve as an advisory body to the President. The guide-lines for target selection are specified by the NCA [1] on the advice of NSC. On the basis of these guidelines, the Joint Strategic Target Planning Staff prepares an integrated Operation Plan – under the direction of the CJCSC [2]. After approval of the plan by NCA [6] – these are promulgated through the CJCSC to the Unified / Specified/ Strategic Force Commands [10].

On the basis of surveillance reports – the Space Command conveys a *nuclear attack warning* to [7] NCA / CJCS / STRATCOM etc. NCA is required to take the final decision and convey - *strike orders* [9] through CJCSC to Unified Command / STRATCOM / Launch Control Centres. The NCA

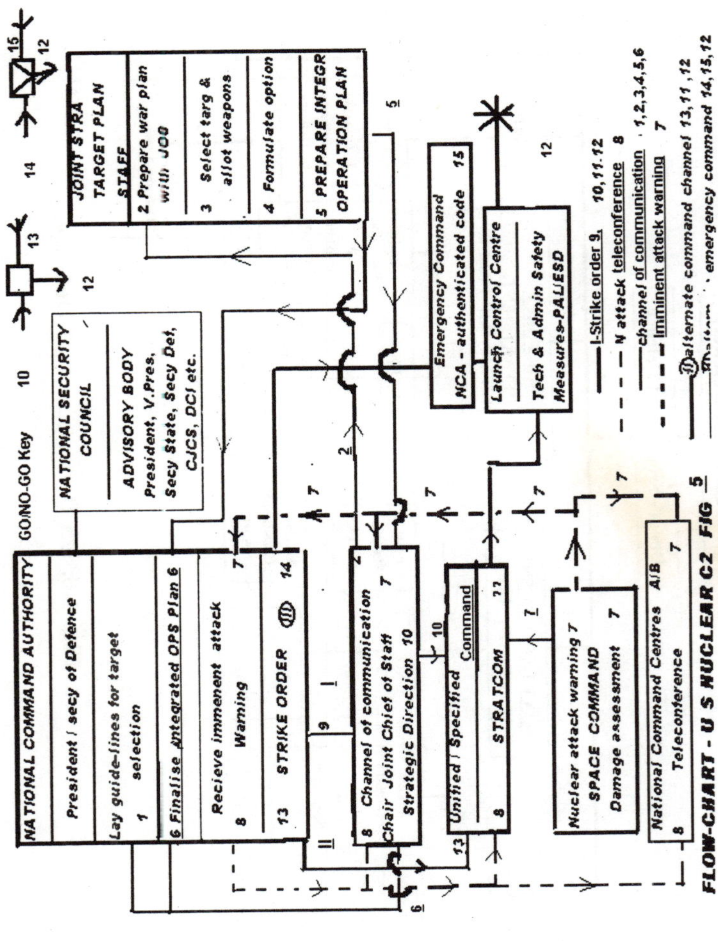

Fig. 1.5. US Nuclear Command and Control Flow-chart.

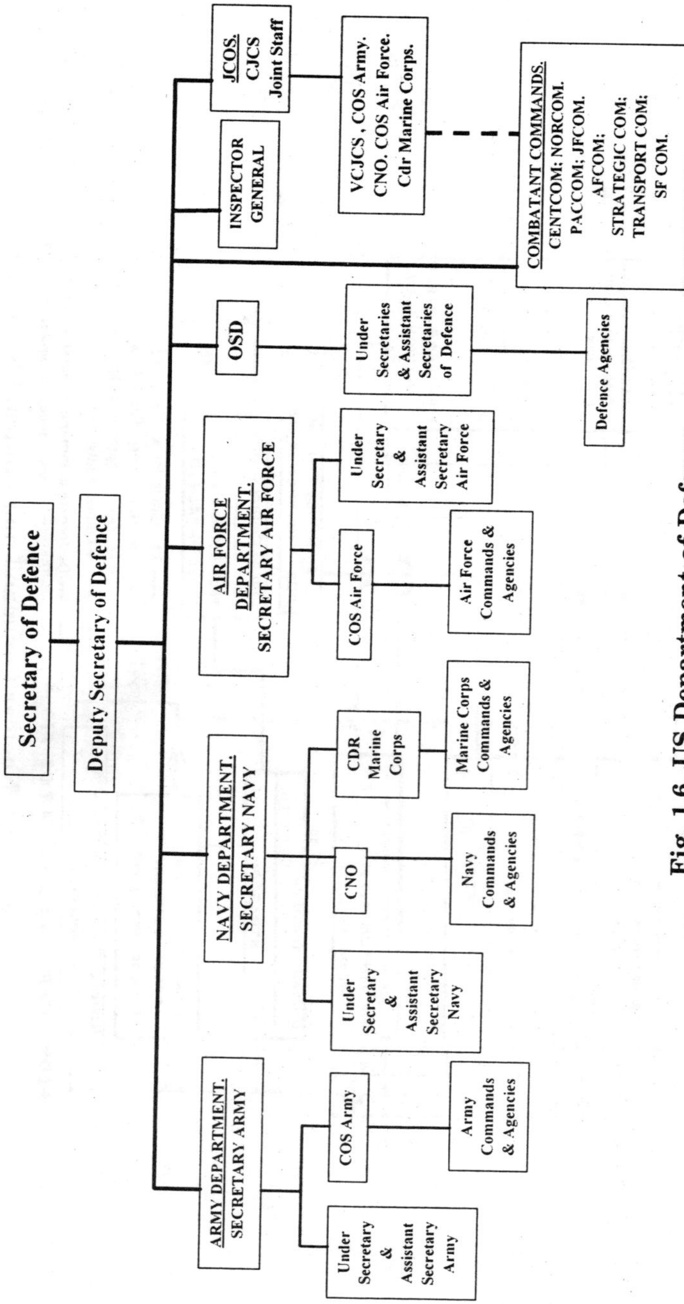

Fig. 1.6. US Department of Defence.

could convey the strike order directly to Unified Command / Launch Centres [13] keeping CJCSC informed or in an emergency directly to the launch centres via duly authenticated code system [14] / [15].

The present overall DOD organisational structure is illustrated at Fig. 1.6.

DEFENCE ACQUISITION SYSTEM

Classical acquisition process emanates from National Aims – from which emerges National Security Interest. Thereafter, super imposition of environmental and threat analysis - leads to formulation of the Grand Strategy and National Security Objectives / Joint Military Strategy / Doctrine etc.

The GNA (86) compels the US government to formulate and present a National Security Strategy (NSS) annually. On the basis of that, the JCSC formulates and presents the National Military Strategy (NMS) – from which follows the doctrine / service objective / perspective plan and finally the budgetary allocation and the acquisition process.

Quadrennial Defence Review is also undertaken regularly.

The US Defence Acquisition System consists of three primarily overarching and interlinked elements:

(a) The Requirement Assessing Process – Joint Capability Integration and Development System (JCIDC). Requirements are formally generated with bottom up inputs from respective individual Service. JCIDC was developed and implemented in 2003 – to produce fully integrated joint war-fighting capabilities in which programme and budgets are developed in response to Programme Guidance Document (PG) issued by SOD.

(b) PPB&S process – a closed loop system designed to allocate resource within DOD. This will be discussed in greater detail in the next paragraph.

(c) Defence Acquisition Process. – is governed by DOD 5000 series directives. A key aspect of DOD 5000 instructions are the programme life cycle structure. It also defines the decision-points for approvals, necessary for moving from one phase to another. The most significant change in the instructions involved the introduction of an evolutionary acquisition (EA) approach.

THE US BUDGETING PROCESS

The US Budget process is an enormously complex and protracted procedure. It is drawn up within the Executive Branch and then sent to the Congress for review and approval.

The outline of the process is briefly discussed in the folowing paragraphs. It is a long drawn process – consuming at least three years from the beginning of planning stage to the enactment of a Congressional Bill for any fiscal year. In USA, by law, the President must submit the budget by the first Monday in February. The fiscal year begins from October. At any given time – there may be four fiscal year *submissions* in some stage of the PPB&S system. One may be at the Budget Phase. Another one may be at the Congressional Review stage. The third one, being reviewed by the DOD. And the last one, going through the Programme Phase – at different Commands and Military Departments.

The process starts in the Executive Branch and involves the *Planning, Programming and Budget System* (PP&BS) – which was one of the innovations brought in by (SOD) Robert McNamara in 1961. This is a closed loop system to allocate resources within the DOD. To give a feel of the process involved – essence of the same, as it existed, before 2003, is illustrated at Fig. 1.7.

The DOD Authorisation Act of 1986 required the submission of a two year budget. But the Congress continues to authorise and appropriate DOD funds on an annual basis. It comprised four iterative phases. The characteristics of each phase is enunciated below, sequentially:-

(a) PHASE I – Planning Phase

(i) The planning stage focus is on *Defence Planning Guidance Statement* (DPG). This process throws up an assessment of military requirements along with the material and financial resources available for the purpose.

(ii) The period allotted for the process to proceed from

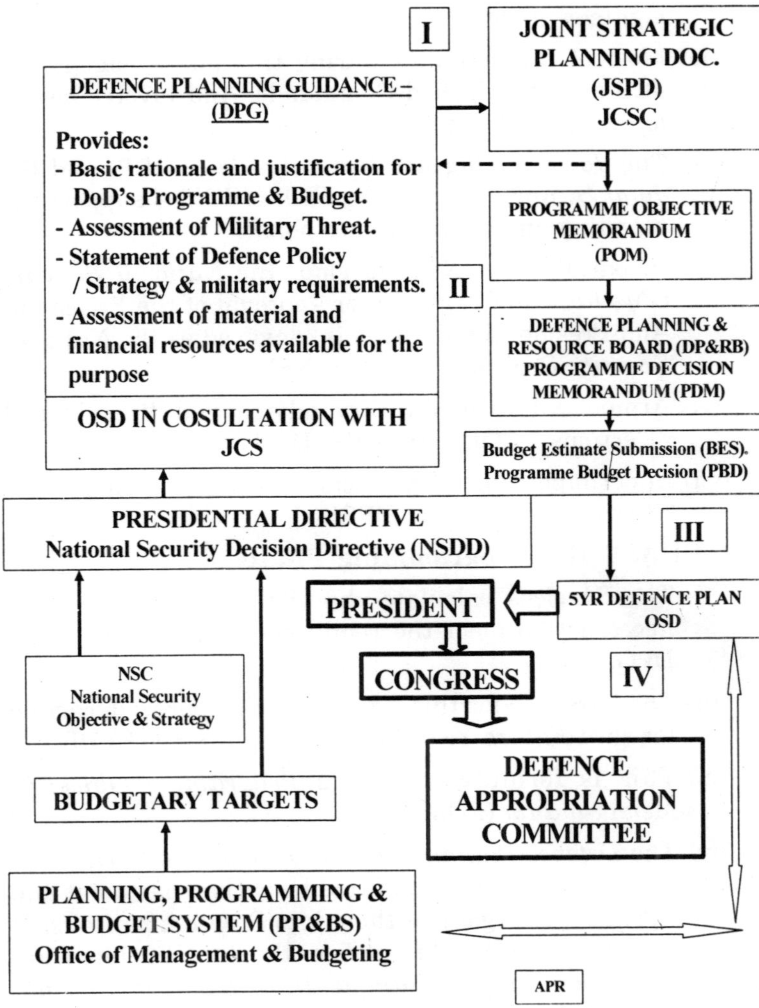

Fig. 1.7. US Budget Process Functional Chart.

the JCSC commencing activities on preparation of *Joint Strategic Planning document* (JSPD) to submission of SOD's *Defence Planning Guidance* document (DPG) is eighteen months.

(iii) Most of the activities during this phase engage the JCS and the Unified Commands. And involve both a *top-down* and *bottom-up* process.

(iv) The *Joint Intelligence Estimate Plan* (JIEP) and the *Joint Strategic Capability Plan* (JSCP) – support the planning and programming phase.

(v) In parallel, the NSC develops the *National Security Objectives and Strategy* for approval of the President. And Presidential decision is conveyed as the *National Security Decision Directive* (NSDD).

(vi) Armed with the military advice and Presidential directions - SOD issues the DPG.

(vii) Superimposition of the fiscal constraints - bring in the Programme Phase of PPBS.

(b) PHASE II – Programming Phase

(i) The Services calculate the size and type of forces necessary to meet the requirements specified in the DPG.

(ii) The base line for this activity is the approved, carried forward *Future Year Defence Programme* (FYDP).

(iii) This is formulated into a *Programme Objective Memorandum* (POM).

(iv) The *Defence Planning and Resource Board* (DP&RB) reviews the POMs submitted by each department and Agencies. Reorganises them into *Programme Decision Packages* (PDP) and formalises the decisions into what is termed the *Programme Decision Memorandum (PDM)*. The PDP outlines the resources required to implement the programme (manpower, equipment and material etc).

(v) This provides the basis for the next phase - *Budgeting*.

(vi) Meanwhile the JCS issues its Joint Programme

Assessment Memorandum (JPAM) which evaluates the risks in the military service POMs and offers risk diminution measures.

(vii) The DP&RB comprise of the following members:

- Deputy Defence Secretary (DDS) – Chairman.
- Service Secretaries.
- CJCS.
- Key USDs and ASDs.
- Representative from OMB.
- Ballistic Missile Defence Organisation (BMDO).
- Operational Test and Evaluation Group (OT&E).
- Service Chiefs attend as non-members.

(viii) In the DP&RB process - the Combat Commander (COMCDR)s have been empowered to:

- Intercede by challenging any issue through an *issue paper*.
- Independently submit, their *Integrated Priority List* (IPL) covering all the *Components* in their respective *Unified Commands*.

(c) PHASE III – Budgeting Phase

(i) Defence Department and the Agencies rework their respective POMs based on the DP&RB decisions and resubmit the POMs as a *Budget Estimate Submission* (BES).

(ii) Final decisions are conveyed as *Programme Budget Decisions* (PBD).

(iii) The financial requirement is vetted by the Office of Management and Budgeting (OMB). And after incorporation of inflation data etc - the requirements are processed through the DOD and through the President to the Congress.

(d) PHASE IV – The Congressional Review takes place in four stages

(i) First Stage. A funding ceiling is formulated in the form of First *Concurrent Budget Resolution.*

(ii) Second Stage. Results in the *Authorisation Bill* - which defines the scope and authorises the funding levels. The Armed Forces Committee in both the House of Representative and the Senate considers the same. No budgetary authorisation is made at this stage.

(iii) Third Stage. The Bill is finally passed by the *Appropriation Committee – Defence and Military Construction Subcommittee.*

(iv) Fourth Stage. If the House and Senate clear different versions of the authorisation and appropriation legislation – then a *Conference Committee* has to sit and reconcile the issues.

Since 2003, PP&BS has been superseded by *Planning, Programming, Budgeting and Execution* (PPB&E) system. This has brought about - the following important changes to the PPBS practice, discussed earlier. PPB&E is still an evolving, ongoing process:

(a) Added an emphasis on *Execution.*

(b) Rationalised the overall budget process to dove-tail into the four year Presidential term.

(c) PPB&E process has a two year iterative budget cycle.

(i) First year considers – *the review and refinement* of previous administration's strategy and plans.

(ii) Second year includes a full PPB&E review and a Quadrennial Defence Review (QDR).

(iii) Third year focuses on execution of QDR and the previous years DPG.

(iv) In the fourth year – full DPG is prepared to refine the alignment between the President's strategy and DOD's programme.

(d) From 2005, the annual POM and BES was to be reoriented to a biannual cycle.

(e) During the *off-year:*

(i) DOD to use *Budget Change Proposal* (BCP) instead of BES.

(ii) Rather than the use of POM - use Programme Change Proposals. This would accommodate the changed realities on the ground in keeping with the requirement to meet the contingency alignment of Defence Programme with the altered defence strategy.

The functional organisation tree for the OMB is illustrated at Fig. 1.8.

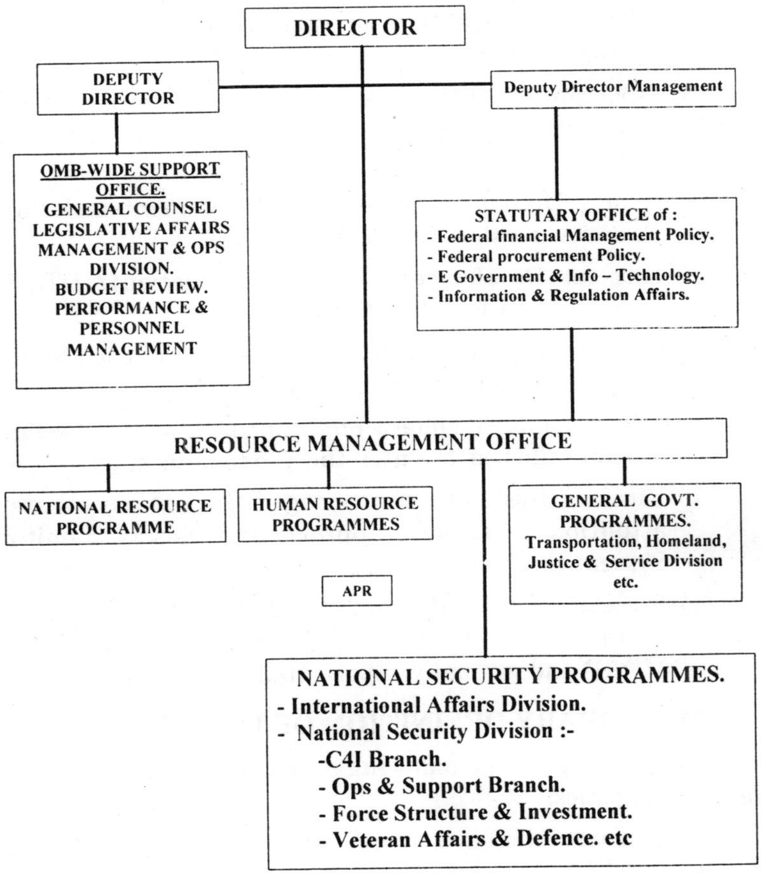

US - Office of Management and Budgeting (OMB)
Fig. 1.8. Functional Organisational Chart

US WEAPON SYSTEM ACQUISITION REFORMS ACT OF 2009 (WSARA)

To address some of the shortcomings observed in the execution of the Acquisition process –WSARA 2009 has called upon the system to re-focus and pay particular attention in the following areas:

(a) CCDRs to be given more say in the weapon requirements.

(b) The following key Directors have been brought directly under SOD / DSOD. And their thrust redirected as indicated:

(i) Director (CAPE) – A new Department of Cost Assessment and Programme Evaluation (CAPE) was created.

(ii) A new Director (Performance Assessment and Root Cause Analysis) / (PARCA) created.

(iii) Director (Development, Test and Evaluation) / (DT&E) – directed to focus on the task of :

- Review, approve, and monitor testing of each Major Defence Acquisition Programmes (MDAP).
- Laying more emphasis on testing new weapons before being allowed to enter the production stage.

(iv) Director (Systems Engineering) / (SE) - to pay greater attention to review, approve and closely monitor System Engineering practices.

(v) Director (Defence Research and Engineering) / (DR&E) – to periodically assess the chronological maturity of MDAP and annually report finding to Congress.

CONTEMPORARY DEFINITION OF LOGISTICS

One USJCS gave the following contemporary definition for Defence Logistics:

"In its comprehensive sense, those aspects of military operations which deal with:

(a) Design, development, acquisition, storage, movement, distribution, maintenance, evacuation and disposition of material.

(b) Movement, evacuation, hospitalisation of personnel.

(c) Acquisition, construction, maintenance, operation and disposition of facilities.

(d) Acquisition and furnishing of services."

CHIEF OF NAVAL OPERATION (CNO) AND NAVAL SEA COMMAND (NAVSEA)

The NAVSEA Command is the Material Command of the Navy – under the CNO. As will be elaborated later – the Materials Command is under dual control and works in an intimately cross linked environment – being closely overseen by ASN (RD&A). Break down of the NAVSEA organisation structure, since early 21st century, is shown in the functional chart at Fig. 1.9. This needs to be looked at along with Figs.1.2, 1.3 and 1.6.

The Command comprises over fifty thousand civilian and military personnel. Their responsibilities stretch to engineer, build, buy and maintain USN's ships and combat systems from concept design to final disposal (*womb to tomb).* To enable implementation of its task – it has five Programme Executive Officers (PEOs), four Naval Ship Yards, and two Warfare Centres (WCs).

NAVSEA Command is a subset of the overall USMOD structure, under CNO as illustrated at Figs. 1.2 and 1.6. The operational naval sub-set under NCA is represented at Fig.1.3.

As per US statute - DOD's charter divides *providers* from *user establishments*. Only the Secretary of Defence is responsible for both operational chain of command and the provider establishment.

The NAVSEA Command is a military organisation comprising five lines of activities, as illustrated at Fig. 1.10:

(a) Engineering.

(b) HRD

(c) Industrial.

(d) Technical Support.

(e) Business Support.

As shown at Fig. 1.2 - the Commander NAVSEA has formal

partnership with NAVSUP (SUPPORT) for fleet logistics support and NAVSPAWAR for C[4]I etc. As illustrated at Fig. 1.9 - the Command is divided into ten departments and is supported by the PEOs and designated Field Support Organisation as listed:

(a) NAVSEA 01 - CONTROLLER. His mission is to provide financial policy, advice and service to their customers.

(b) NAVSEA 02. Contracts.

(c) NAVSEA 03. Human Resource Development (HRD).

(d) NAVSEA 04. Logistics, maintenance and repairs. Coordinates public and private naval ship maintenance / modernisation facilities.

(e) NAVSEA 05. Ship design integration and engineering.

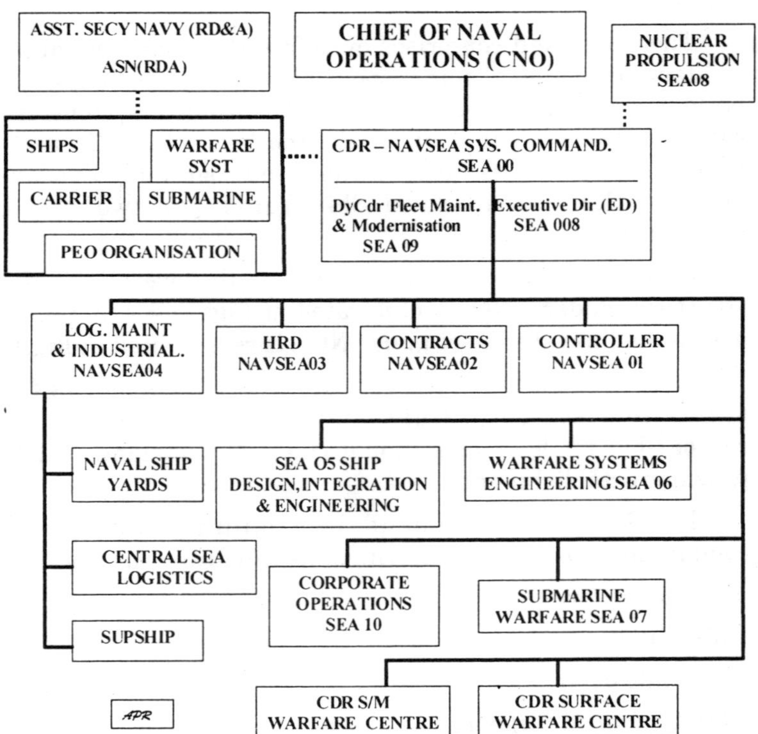

Fig. 1.9. CNO Organisation Chart.

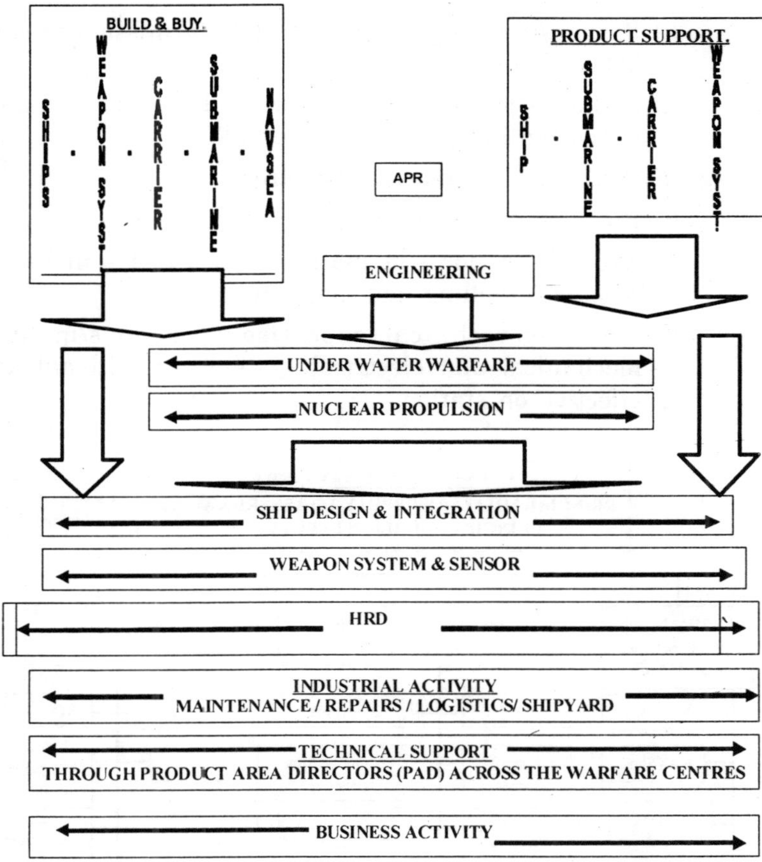

Fig. 1.10. NAVSEA Functional Activity Matrix.

(i) Establishes and maintains technical standards through life cycle of ships.

(ii) Evaluates new ship concepts, formulates and develops ship design goals / requirements. And supervises ship design process.

(iii) Is the Technical Authority (TA) for hull, mechanical and electrical systems?

(iv) Directs design process during modernisation and oversees in service engineering during ship system operation.

(f) NAVSEA 06. Warfare System Engineering.

(i) Responsible for deployment of fully mission-capable battle groups to sea.

(ii) Is the TA for weapons, sensors and combat systems – supported by Warfare Centres (WC).

(g) NAVSEA 07. Submarine Warfare.

(i) Provides integral service to in service s/m Force.

(ii) Executes major s/m maintenance cycle - including reactor refuelling and major refits.

(iii) Provides technical expertise to keep s/m hull, mechanical and electrical system – functional and effective on station.

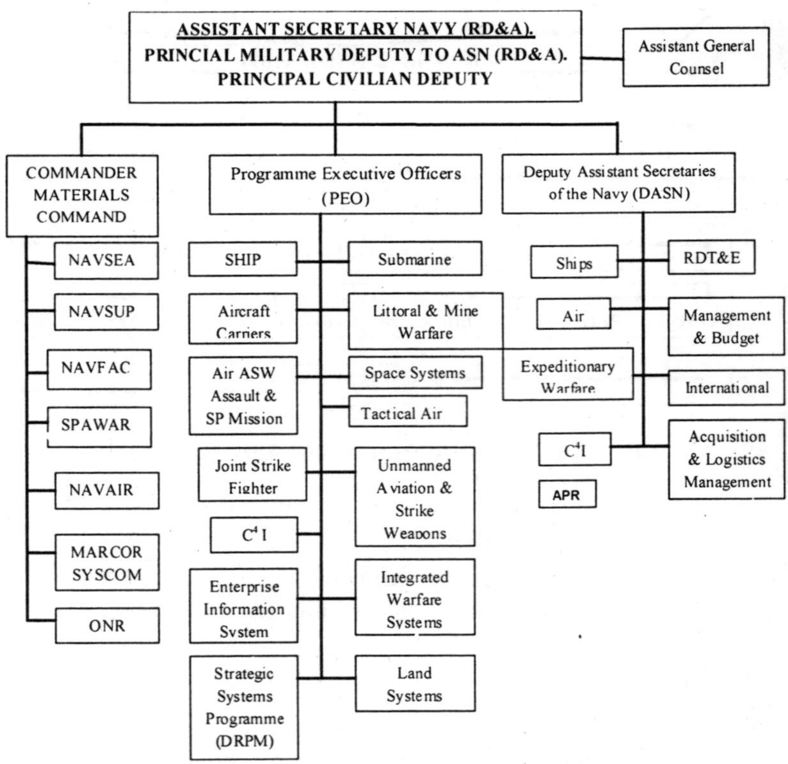

Fig. 1.11. USN (RD and C) Organisation Tree.

(iv) S/M escape and rescue programmes.

(v) Provide centralised life cycle support to s/m.

(h) NAVSEA 08. Nuclear Propulsion.

(i) NAVSEA 09. Vice Commander. Responsible for coordinating Fleet Maintenance and Modernisation.

(j) NAVSEA 10. Corporate Functions.

The horizontal linkage with ASN (RD&A) the PEO organisation is clearly shown at Figs. 1.2 and 1.11.

PROGRAMME EXECUTIVE OFFICER (PEO)

PEOs are responsible for all aspects of life cycle management of their respective programmes i.e. Ship, S/M, Carrier, Integrated Warfare Systems etc. In this context Fig. 1.2 also refers.

NAVSEA provides PEOs:

(a) With total ship system engineering.

(b) Establishes and coordinates technical policy and procedures.

(c) Delivers integrated Logistics.

PEOs report directly to two authorities:-

(a) Assistant Secy. to the Navy for Research Development and Acquisitions [ASN (RD&A)].

(b) COMMANDER NAVSEA – for planning and execution of in service support.

FIELD SUPPORT ORGANISATIONS

SUPSHIP has the following multiple - responsibilities:

(a) Is MoD's designated contract administrator for ships - including construction and is located near private ship yards.

(b) Acts as NAVSEA's onsite technical, contractual and business agent.

(c) Brings out new ships from design to fleet and ensures serviceability through ship's life.

(d) Provides Navy's water front leadership.

NAVAL SEA LOGISTICS CENTRE (NSLC)

NSLC provides integrated logistics, engineering and information technology expertise.

NAVAL SURFACE AND UNDERSEA WARFARE CENTRES.(NSWC / NUWC)

(a) Each centre is headed by several Production Area Directors (PAD).

(b) They provide appropriate technology, capability and specialised R&D facilities to support all aspects of Surface and Underwater warfare.

SHIP ACQUISITION PHASE

The next logical stage, after obtaining budget allocation, is project implementation. To illustrate this process a typical naval example has been chosen. For a Destroyer class of ships – this process used to take anything up to thirteen years from a concept design stage to lead ship production.

For illustration purposes a typical break down of the process for DDG51 class of Destroyers is listed below:-

(a) Concept Design.
(b) Preliminary Design.
(c) Contract Design.
(d) Lead ship Detail Design.
(e) Keel laying.
(f) Lead ship launch.
(g) Lead ship Delivery.

In USN jargon, changes in configuration to the hull within the basic ship class concept are termed 'flights' and changes in combat system for the same class are termed 'base line'. In the case of the sixty two planned DDG51 class of Destroyers – three hull flight changes and several base line changes; adding war fighting capability in an incremental fashion were incorporated in the series.

Due to several conceptual changes incorporated during the evolution process – the USN's 21st century Destroyer DD(X) / DD21 has taken a much longer period. Twenty five ships of this class were originally planned.

The next generation of Littoral Combat Ships – by adopting, an innovative approach and more comprehensive modular construction technology – considerable time was expected to be saved. However, due to changes in budget allocations – this objective could not be satisfactorily met. As a concept, it has been highly successful.

Since the risk factor from the concept design stage to lead ship building is very high – in the US system of budgeting - funding up to the lead ship is provided for - under what is termed as Research and Development, Test and Engineering [RDT&E] funding. For the same reason, payment for this phase is assessed on cost (+) basis. Series production, thereafter, is catered for under USN budget Shipbuilding Conversion Navy [SCN] head. The price in this case is normally negotiated with the builders on fixed cost basis.

It has also been the US policy to keep two ship yards loaded on a project – both to introduce an element of competition and to keep adequate ship building capacity going. And generally, up to the lead ship delivery the cost is based on cost plus basis. Series production is based on fixed price with escalation provided for.

AN INDIAN PARADOX OVER DIVISION OF LABOUR IN FIELD OF MILITARY ACQUISITION

A quandary exists in the Indian context, as to how much role need be assigned to the military visa-vis the generalist civil servant, on military acquisition management. The political role in decision making and the political control over military is quite clear. There are however, some serious concerns over the generalist civil servants in India, hijacking and perpetuating a strangle holds, over the military acquisition process. In the Indian context, he neither has the expertise nor accountability. Selective statistical data from global models is often quoted to justify continuation of such a situation. This controversy needs to be addressed squarely, pragmatically and rationally. A holistic understanding of the main global models – would by itself – provide the answers to the paradox. The following elaborations of the US Defence Acquisition Cadre model, read together with the earlier discussions on linked subjects– should put to rest some of the misconceptions on the issue. This will be further substantiated with examples of other global models in the subsequent Chapters.

U.S. DEFENCE PROCUREMENT CADRE

Till late 20th century, the US defence procurement agency did not have a dedicated cadre for the purpose of defence procurement. Service officers, interspersed, at junior levels with large civilian components, predominantly manned the Agency at higher levels. The civilian personnel comprised cost accountants, contract specialists, technicians, logisticians, programmers, economists and in rare cases, junior managers. As stated earlier, the Packard Commission in 1984 recommended that the US military be divided into two streams. One for combat stream and the other for procurement management stream. Later, the Gold Water Nichols Act of 1986 firmly converted this concept into reality.

An outline of US Acquisition organisational chart, as existed in late 20th century, with focus on naval functions, is represented at Fig.1.2. Some of the relevant characteristics of the system, are discussed briefly in the following paragraphs.

The procurement process is governed by the Federal Acquisition Regulations (FAR). Current US DOD Instructions on acquisition management have been promulgated under DODI 50000.01 and 50000.02 of 08 December 2008. As discussed earlier – the US Materials Command is fully involved in the process under the *womb to tomb* concept for each acquisition. This can be clearly seen by the institutional cross linkages shown at multi-levels at Fig. 1.2.

All acquisition related policy decisions and apex level programme monitoring of major projects are undertaken by the Defence Acquisition Board (DAB). The USD (AT&L) is the chairman and as will be demonstrated later – he is no civil servant bureaucrat. The JCS is also given appropriate representation in the Board – by having the Vice Chief of JCSC as the Vice Chairman of the DAB. In addition, the DAB also provides an opportunity for the Combat Commanders (COMCDR) to influence the acquisition plans. In any case, at the working level – service institutions e.g. the Material

Command, play a predominant role in keeping the *womb to tomb* commitment going for each programme.

As brought out earlier, at the budget formulation stage also – the Services are well represented in the DP&RB with due weightage being given to CCDR too.

The Secretariat of each Military Department includes two or more Assistant Secretaries (AS). They are required to provide - over sight to the departments acquisition activities. In the case of the Navy – there are meant to be two Assistant Secretaries - one for *ship building and logistics* and the other for *research, engineering and systems*. Today, this is combined into the ASN (RD&A). The Secretary Navy (SECNAV) is their immediate superior. He also represents the Navy (CNO) with the Legislators and share responsibilities with ASD (P&L).

To encourage, an integrated approach - the National Security Council (NSC) secretariat and the supporting staff with Chairman Joint Chief of Staff (CJCS), Chief of Naval Operation (CNO), SECNAV, Office of Secretary of Defence (OSD), Defence Acquisition Board (DAB) and Defence Science Board (DSB) etc are all manned by military and civilian personnel.

In addition, institutionalised horizontal linkages are provided between the Navy and Department of Defence (DOD) - at least at two levels, as indicated at Fig. 1.2. The process and the institutions involved in acquisition decision making has been elaborated earlier. In this context attention is drawn to illustrations at Figs. 1.7, 1.8, 1.9 and 1.10. Cross linkages of the ASN (RD&A) with NASEA / PEO / DASN have been further elaborated as a sub set of Fig. 1.2 at Fig. 1.11.

As stated earlier, the Under Secretary (Acquisition) / USD (AT&L) is not a civil servant (bureaucrat) but a Presidential appointee, duly approved by Senate and enjoying statutory powers and responsibilities over Procurement, Production and R&D Divisions.

In addition, the civil servants in the DOD spend at least ten to fifteen years on the job. Hence they are an important source of continuity.

Over two decades ago - induction to the Acquisition cadre in USN was initiated at two levels i.e. Ensign / Midshipman and Lieutenant Commander / Commander, with the object of introducing a dedicated service cadre, as opposed to ad hock assignments hitherto.

At first glance, of the US Defence Organisation Chart at Fig.1.2 - one gets an impression of a predominantly bureaucrat controlled military organisation. This, in the Indian context, is taken to justify the present stranglehold of the generalist civil servant over the military. A deeper look at the US organisational structure - soon dispels this misnomer. It would be seen that overwhelming majority of the senior civilian officials shown are not bureaucrats but are Presidential nominees duly cleared by the senate for their specific task. For ease of identification, these individuals have been earmarked # on the Organisation Chart at Fig. 1.2.

The above observation should be superimposed on the fact that all acquisition personnel (both military and civilian) in the US system are now required to be officially certified at the appropriate level by Defence Acquisition University before being employed on any acquisition tasks. For this purpose the uniformed personnel are classified into following streams, commonly referred to as Acquisition Career Field (ACF):

(a) Programme Manager - ACF A.

(b) Contracting. - ACF C.

(c) Systems Planning, Research, Development and Engineering, Science and Technology Management. - ACF-S.

(d) Information Technology. - ACF-R.

(e) Testing and evaluation. - ACF-T.

Further, a military officer in the acquisition cadre is expected to develop functional expertise in a minimum of two ACFs and broaden his experience and knowledge through exposure to several different assignments. An officer can at any stage in his career decide to opt to join the acquisition stream. In the Navy, experience has shown better suitability for the acquisition assignments - among the restricted entry officers. And Engineer Officers are preferred both due to their competence for the task and availability. The supply officer was found better suited for financial, contractual and administrative duties.

To obviate frequent transfer of service officers assigned to acquisition – strict statutory obligations prevent such occurrences. By legislation, the Programme Manager (PM) is to have a minimum of four years assignment. Exceptional cases require written exemption from the Service Chief and the Service Secretary concerned.

Besides the above safeguards in the system – what needs to be noted, in addition, is that every single person involved in the acquisition system is a specialist in specific area linked to defence acquisition and life time support of the product involved. Also, the person concerned is committed to the profession, as a full time career. There is no place for any generalist civil servant in the organisation, except in areas of common administration. To emphasise this point and highlight the significance of such stringent stipulations – the career profile of seven key incumbent officials in the Naval Acquisition Chain are illustrated below. By no stretch of imagination could these incumbents be equated with any generalist civil servant:

(a) Mr. Robert Gates. The Secretary of Defence (SOD). He is the equivalent of Defence Minister / (Raksha Mantry) and not of the Indian bureaucrat Defence Secretary, as some time insinuated by Indian Civil Servants. He is also in the President's Cabinet.

(b) Mr William J Lynn III Deputy Secretary Defence (DSD): 12 February 2009.

Nominated by the President and approved by the Senate and accorded statutory powers and responsibility. He has held wide range of defence assignments. His brief academic and career profile is as follows:

(i) Graduate from Dartmouth College.

(ii) Law Degree - Cornell Law College.

(iii) Executive Director - Centre for Strategic and International Studies.

(iv) Senior Fellow – Strategic Nuclear Forces - National Defence University.

(v) ASD (Budget).

(vi) OSD.

(vii) USD (Controller)

(c) Mr. Ray Mabus : The Secretary of Navy (SECNAV). Nominated by the President and approved by the Senate in May 2009. Accorded statutory powers and responsibility. He has had hands on naval experience and was:

(i) In Naval Service. – 1970 -1972.

(ii) Governor of Mississippi. – 1988-1992.

(iii) US Ambassador to Saudi Arabia. – 1994 – 1996.

(d) Dr Ashton Carter. The Under Secretary of Defence (Acquisition, Technology and Logistics) USD (AT&L). Nominated by the President and approved by the Senate in April 2009.Accorded statutory powers and responsibility. He has over riding powers over the Secretary Navy on acquisition matters. He has had over twenty years of distinguished defence related career. His career profile is as follows:

(i) A Physist from Yale and Oxford University.

(ii) Served five years as member Defence Science Board. – 1991-1993.- 1999-2001.

(iii) Four years in the Defence Policy Board.- 1997-2001.

(iv) Assistant Secretary of Defence. - 1993 -1996.

(v) International Security Advisory Board to Secretary of State. - 2006-2008.

(vi) Co-Chairman – Senate Foreign Relation Committee's Policy Advisory Group.

(vii) Involved in negotiating Agreements on Nuclear NPT, CTBT. STARTII, ABM and CFE.

(e) Mr. Sean J Stackley : Assistant Secretary Navy (Research, Development and Acquisition) ASN (RD&T). He is also designated as the Naval Acquisition Executive. -July 2008.

He represents the Department of Navy to USD (AT&L) and to Congress on all matters relating to acquisition policy and programme. He was commissioned as an Engineer Officer in the Navy. And has had vast experience in the field of ship acquisition. His academic and career profile is as follows:

(i) US Naval Academy Graduate - BE.

(ii) MIT PG - ME.

(iii) Naval Surface Warfare Officer – Engineering duties involved in ship design, construction, maintenance, logistics and acquisition policy.

(iv) Production officer for DDG51 and Canadian FFH330. Principle role in design, construction, test and delivery of three first of class of ships.

(v) Programme manager – Navy's LPD17 programme. 2001– 2005.

(vi) Professional staff Senate Armed Forces Committee.

(f) Vice Admiral W Mark Skinner. Principle Military Deputy to ASN(RD&A). 2010.

(i) Degree in Financial Management from Naval PG School.

(ii) PEO – for Tactical aircraft programme.

(iii) CDR - Naval Air Warfare Centre – Weapon Division.

(iv) Assistant Commander – Test and Evaluation. Naval Air System Command.

(v) Chief Test Pilot and CDR of Naval Force aircraft Test Squadron.

(vi) PM – for CNO special project.

(g) Ms Allision Stiller. Deputy ASN (RD&A). 2004 till to date.

She is a highly qualified Engineer with vast hands -on experience in providing engineering and logistic support particularly to submarines. Her Academic and career profile is as follows:

(i) Systems Engineering graduate University of Virginia.

(ii) MS in Engineering Management. Virginia Institute of Technology.

(iii) Senior Executive Fellows Programme. Howard University. JFK School.

(iv) Supporting *Trident* s/m engineering and logistics.

(v) Head of Mechanical Engineering Branch – *Sea Wolf* combat system. 1982-1992.

(vi) Acquisition Manager (s/m). 1992-1994.

(vii) Rotational assignment between ASN, OSD etc. 1994-1997.

(viii) Director Naval Construction. 1997-2000.

(ix) Deputy Programme Manager (Amphibious). 2000-2004.

To get a holistic picture of the over-all acquisition matrix – the respective Service Material Command needs to be considered as a composite part thereof. As illustrated in Fig. 1.10 – the Service Material Command has a major overarching role in the field of acquisition, life-time support and sustainment functions. As an illustration- the complex, integrated matrix focused on to the Navy has been captured in Figs. 1.2, 1.9 and 1.10 In the case of the Navy this is provided under the oversight of the ASN (RD&A) as indicated at Fig. 1.11. In this field of operation – these activities form an over-lapping subset between CNO (Material Command) and ASN (RD&A)

POST 9/11 RESTRUCTURING / REFORMS

At the time of 9/XI attack on the twin towers in New York and the Pentagon – the aero-space defence was largely dependent on close interaction between the Federal Aviation Agency (FAA) and the North American Aerospace Defence Command (NORAD). NORAD was a bi-national command established between USA and Canada. FAA is mandated to regulate the safety and security of civil aviation. In case of any aircraft hijacking - the arrangement required the FAA to inform the Pentagon National Military Command Centre (NMCC) and seek for military escort. On OSD approval – NORAD was thereafter required to arrange tailing the aircraft from a distance. In case of necessity, National Command Centre (NCC) was the entity authorised to order any shooting down of a commercial a/c.

The following steps were initiated immediately after 9/XI attack:

(a) A Department of Homeland Security (DHS) was established – bringing together twenty federal agency offices of Intelligence and Analysis.

(b) The Home-Land Security Council (HLSC) was set up within the White House premises along side the NSC.

(c) The Northern Command was established and was charged with the responsibility for land, sea and air defence of USA, Canada and Mexico. It was also given the added responsibility of military assistance to civil power. For this purpose – elements of NORAD and parts of Space Command were also made available.

(d) Three Unified Commands (i.e. Special Operations / Central / Northern Commands) were assigned counter terrorism as an additional mission.

(e) A bipartisan committee – *"the National Commission on Terrorist attack on USA"* (NCTA) was appointed.

(f) In 2003 – the *Terrorist Threat Integration Centre* (TTIC) was established at CIA HQs. This was staffed by various Agencies reporting to *Director of Central Intelligence* (DCI).

At the time of the 9/XI - the Intelligence community comprised:

(a) **CIA :** The Central Intelligence Agency.

(b) **NSA :** National Security Agency – responsible for signal collection and analysis.

(c) **NGA :** National Geospatial Agency – responsible for imagery collection and analysis.

(d) **NRO :** National Reconnaissance Office – responsible for developing, acquiring - launching of space systems for intelligence collection.

(e) **DIA :** Defence Intelligence Agency of the Department of Defence.

(f) Defence Intelligence entities of the Army, Navy, Air force and the Marines.

(g) **INR :** Bureau of Intelligence Research of the Department of State.

(h) Office of Terrorism and Finance Intelligence of Department of the Treasury.

(i) Office of Intelligence and Counter-terrorism and Counter Intelligence a Division of the FBI of the Department of Justice.

(j) Office of the Intelligence of the Department of Energy.

(k) IAIP : Directorate of Information Analysis and Infrastructure Projection of Homeland Security.

(l) Coast Guard Intelligence of Department of Homeland Security.

The bipartisan *National Commission on the Terrorist Attack on US* (NCTA) published its report in 2004, followed by adoption of the Terrorism Prevention and Intelligence Reform Act 2004.

In 2005 - post Iraq action – another commission rendered its report on intelligence capabilities of US regarding weapons of mass destruction (WMD). Highlights of NCTA's findings and recommendations are listed below:

(a) Lack of inter agency coordination, jointness and sharing of information.

(b) Earlier, intelligence collection was organised around sources – i.e. signals, espionage and imagery etc. While analysis was conducted by Agency. Such an arrangement worked during the cold war period – since, the only target was USSR.

(c) Under the commission's dispensation – new centres were required to adopt the principle of jointness and bring together, analysts, information collectors and operation specialist around problems or issues rather than being structured to reflect collection sources or existing Agencies.

(d) The Commission recommendations favoured adoption of the military practice - separating the *User Process Owner* from the *Service Provider Process Owner.*

(e) Put together all analytical talents residing in CIA, FBI, DIA and make it into a conglomerate.

(f) Emulate the US military in separating the *organising, training and equipping* function from *the operational deployment* functions. Thereby separating responsibilities and assign role for:

   (i) Building Intelligence Forces (as *Service Providers*) to CIA, FBI, DIA and NSA.

   (ii) Intelligence operation deployment to NIC - as a *Unified / Functional Command).*

(g) Under the earlier dispensation – the DCI was responsible for group performance but was not given the wherewithal to see it through. To overcome the shortcoming of authority and enable effective coordination – the commission recommended the following:

   (i) Replace the DCI with National Intelligence Director (NID) focussing his task to:

   - Oversee National Intelligence Centres across the board.
   - Manage national intelligence programmes and oversee the Agencies that contribute to it.
   - Act as the Principal Intelligence Advisor to the President.

   (ii) Additionally, NID was charged with the responsibility of:

   - Submitting unified intelligent budget – in accordance with the priority set by NSC.
   - Approve and submit for nomination to President, names of – heads of CIA, DIA, FBI, NSA, NGA, NRO, II and PD etc.

(h) Defence Department's intelligence programmes – Joint Military Intelligence Programme (JMIP) and Tactical Intelligence and Related Activities (TIARA) to remain part of the Defence Department's responsibility.

(i) The Commission further recommended that the CIA give up its responsibility for directing and executing Para-military operations to the military. They found that the Afghanistan precedent of joint CIA-military teams -

worked well. On the basis of it – they suggested that CIA's capabilities and personnel should be integrated into military directed teams – giving both the CIA and military's Special Operation Forces a role.

(j) Create National Counter-terrorism Centre (NCTC) in place of TTIC. It's role to include:

  (i) *Lead* strategic analyst – pooling all intelligence resources about trans-national terrorist organisations with global reach.

  (ii) Develop net assessments and provide warning – drawing on total national effort / resources of CIA, FBI and HLS.

  (iii) Task - coliection requirements both inside and outside USA.

  (iv) Principle knowledge bank on Islamic Terrorism – drawing on analytical talents residing in CIA (Counter Terrorism Centre) and DIA [Joint Intelligence Task Force – Combating Terrorism (JITF-CT)].

  (v) Perform joint planning functions. Assign operation responsibilities to lead agencies i.e. State, FBI, Defence and its Combatant Commands, Home-land Security etc.

  (vi) NCTC is not required to direct actual execution of these operations. But is required to track its implementation.

  (vii) NCTC is also not a policy making body. The operations and plans are to follow directions of the President and the NSC.

(k) To strengthen NCTC's authority in performing its functions involving Agencies across the board - the following measures need to be taken:

  (i) The NCTC head to be appointed by the President and confirmed by the Senate. When required, he would also testify to the Congress – same as the other statutory Presidential office.

  (ii) He is to be appointed in the rank equivalent to Deputy Head of a Cabinet Department.

(iii) NID is his immediate superior. And indirectly reports to the President.

(iv) His concurrence is essential for the choice of personnel to lead operating entities of Departments and Agencies focused on counter-terrorism.

(v) He along with the Director OMB is to develop - the President's Counter-terrorism budget.

(vi) His line authority would be defined by Law or Executive order.

(l) The eventual merger of the HLSC with the NSC was also recommended.

The above recommendations have been incorporated in the functional flow chart illustrated at Fig. 1.12.

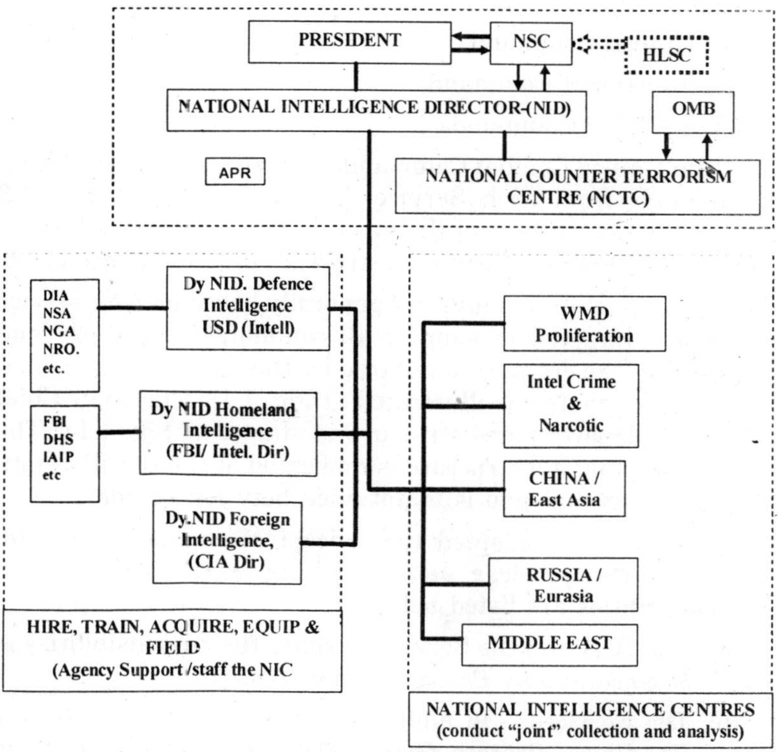

Fig. 1.12. US National Intelligence Director.

US JOINT / UNIFIED / FUNCTIONAL / SPECIFIED COMMANDS

Discussion on the US defence structure would be incomplete without some elaboration of the working of Joint / Unified / Functional / Specified Commands. This is central to the entire issue. Every other institution is expected to provide support service – to enable successful execution of the tasks assigned by the President / NCA to the Combat Commanders. Recent experiences after joint operations in Iraq, Kosovo and Afghanistan have emphasised the need for a single organisation / authority responsible for theatre logistics. Various options have been tried out in the field. The Service *stove piped* arrangements of cold war era has proved to be inadequate and found especially ineffective for rapid response to situations.

The US Combat Forces have been divided into three types of operational commands:

(a) Unified Command.

(b) Functional Command.

(c) Specified Commands.

The Unified Combat Commands are serviced by Component Commands from each Service. The flow chart at Fig. 1.3 illustrates the working of the naval model. This is a sub-set of the overall DOD organisational structure illustrated at Fig. 1.6.

Functional Commands are generally based on *lead* service concept – targeted to support all commands effectively and efficiently. The organisational tree for the Unified / Functional Combat Commands is illustrated at Fig. 1.13. The Joint Chief of Staff's departmental structure is shown at Fig. 1.14. The same departmental structure is replicated at the CCDR's staff. A continuous dialogue is maintained between the two.

US have also adopted the concept of *process ownership*. Some of the *process owners* along with their linked responsibilities are listed below:

(a) The DLA and the Services – share the responsibilities of *Defence Supply Process Owner (DSPO).*

(b) The Services – in addition, act as the *Defence System Readiness Process Owner (DSRPO).* The DSRPO is responsible for maintaining system life cycle readiness

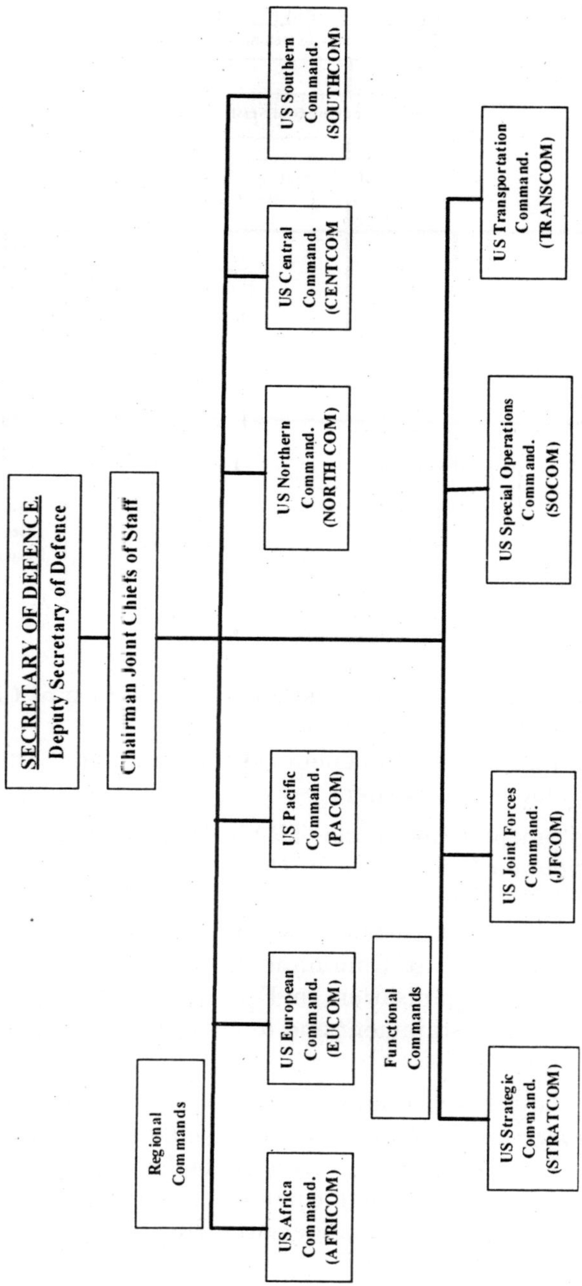

Fig. 1.13. US Unified Combat Command Organisational Tree.

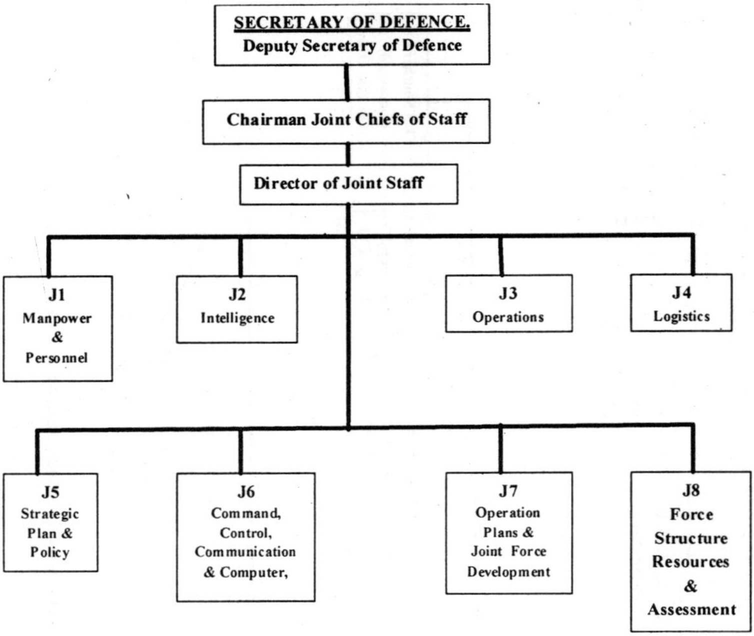

Fig. 1.14. Departmental Organisational Tree US Joint Chiefs of Staff.

of the respective Components in the Command. This has been elaborated earlier.

(c) The Transport Command (TRANSCOM) – is the *Defence Distribution Process Owner (DDPO).* The DDPO combines the role the Air Mobility Command (AMC), the Surface Deployment and Distribution Command (SDDC) and the Military Sea Lift Command (MSLC). It is also the supporting organisation to DLA and the Services for movement, sustainment and to JFCOM for movement of Forces.

(d) The Joint Force Command (JFCOM) – serves as the *Joint Deployment Process Owner (JDPO)* and conventional Force Provider. He is involved in deployment operations – to provide trained and combat ready joint force assets to the Combat Commanders (CCDR), as they require them. Through the service components he is the ultimate customer of the Joint Logistic System. The Joint Force Commander (JFC) has full authority over the logistic resources within his area of responsibility (AOR). He performs the following functions:

(i) Joint Force Trainer.

(ii) Integrator.

(iii) Primary Joint Force Provider.

(iv) Joint Deployment Process Owner.

(v) Supported by DDPO – is focused on perfect capability fulfilment.

(e) The United State Air Force (USAF) – is designated as the Executive Agent for support function to the National Military Command Centre (NMCC) at the Pentagon. They are required to provide logistics, budgeting, facilities and support.

(f) The Joint Logistics Environment (JLE) – comprise USJFCOM, USTRANSCOM and DLA.

(g) The Defence Logistics Agency (DLA) manages, integrates and synchronises suppliers and supply chains to meet the requirements of the Armed Forces. It has liaison officers attached to every Combat Command staff to assist with planning, exercises and current operations.

(h) The CCDR's J4 staff - is the CCDR's principal staff organisation, responsible for integrating logistic planning and execution in support of Joint Operations. J4's responsibility breakdown, in the classic case, are:

(i) Supporting the Operation Staff (J3) – in the planning and execution requirements and base support installation planning and sustainment.

(ii) Ensuring adequate logistics expertise is an integral part of planning process.

(iii) Representation in the Operation Strategic Planning Staff's (J5) planning process. This is critical to ensure early integration of logistics to Operational Plans (OPLANs). Use of war games, simulation and table exercises enable joint logisticians to work directly with OPS planners as they seek to conduct assessments and identify risks.

(iv) Assigning the primary responsibility to work with the operational planning cell of J3 to develop ongoing OPS and other execution orders.

(v) Establishing Joint Operation Logistics Centre (JLOC) to monitor and control execution of logistics in support of ongoing operations. JLOC is an integral part of the CCDR's operation planning cell. JLOC is staffed by J4 staff.

(vi) Through USTRANSCOM's Deployment and Distribution Centre (DDOC) and in collaboration with JDDOC – linking strategic deployment and distribution process to operational and tactical functions in support of the war-fighter. The JDDOC is an integral organisation to the CCDR's staff. Normally – works under the direction of J4 and is collocated with the JLOC during operations.

SPECIAL OPERATIONS COMMAND (SOCOM)

The STRATCOM, JFCOM and TRANSCOM as a unified command concept, has been readily accepted as a rational solution. Some, however, have difficulty in accepting the idea of a unified Special Force Command and prefer operation of the *Special Forces* as a component of the respective Service. US, on the contrary, have found, after vast experience, that the concept is sound and invaluable.

Fig. 1.13 shows SOCOM as a part of the Unified Functional Command structure. Fig. 1.15 illustrates the over all Command structure for the Special Operation Command.

US experience has conclusively established – the need for segregating the SOCOM from the mainstream Service components. To fulfil its functions effectively and efficiently the Special Forces (SF) have to develop a unique work culture and ethos commensurate with its role, function and type of deployment. The second world war concept, of embedded *commando*-trained units still have a role in action but can not effectively take on the varied unique assigned role of the SOCOM.

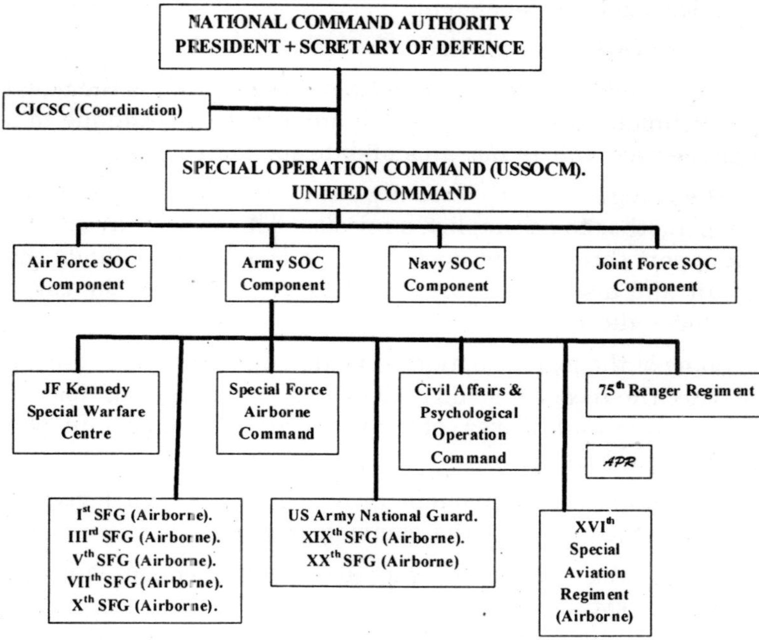

Fig. 1.15. US Special Operations Command.

Due to fundamental difference in functions to be performed and means used – the culture, ethos and training are totally different and incompatible with conventional mainstream service ethos. Each component arm of the SOCOM is also highly focused on their respective specialisation / environment. They are also required to operate in close cooperation with CIA agents etc. Best results can only be achieved by deploying them selectively, on tasks for which each component is trained and appropriately equipped. For most effective utilisation – it is best, to keep the main-stream Armed Force personnel away from the SF personnel. This is vital to avoid dilution / compromise of their respective highly specialised capabilities.

JOINT LOGISTICS

Logistics capabilities can be subdivided into following three categories:

(a) Service independent.

(b) Service Interdependent.

(c) Service Interoperable.

Typical example of *service independent* category is the naval replenishment action at sea. Such an operation is unique to a single service and is not a candidate for joint logistics.

The category S*ervice Interdependent* – implies dependence on one another to accomplish a mission. This is best illustrated by air- port through-put operation e.g. the Air force lands the aircraft and discharges cargo and the Army stages the cargo and clears the port.

Some of the logistic options considered and tried out during and since the recent US and allied forces action in Iraq, Kosovo, Afghanistan and Korea etc. are briefly discussed in the succeeding paragraphs:

(a) Each service component provided for its own logistics. Currently, this is the common practice.

(b) A *lead* service option has also been tried out but not found satisfactory.

(c) An appointed Executive Agent (EA) providing logistics support to all services. The EA is appointed by the Secretary of Defence. This option has also not delivered the goods to the satisfaction of all.

(d) An expanded / enlarged J4 staff coordinating joint logistics. This option has been found to result in diversion of J4's effort and diminish its ability to concentrate on long range logistics planning.

(e) The Joint Theatre Logistics Command (JTLC) coordinated logistics option has been reported favourably. These can be summarised as follows:

   (i) Reduces redundancies as compared to each service component providing its own logistics.

   (ii) Gives CCDR a single organisation to integrate, prioritize and synchronize joint theatre logistics.

   (iii) Provides C^2 architecture that can rapidly expand to large scale contingency.

   (iv) Allows CCDR to focus on other operational issues.

(v) JTLC operates as a joint functional command reporting directly to CCDR.

(vi) JTLC to be on par with other service component commands.

(vii) Total asset visibility is central to the ability of JTLC.

The JTLC is built around three primary building blocks:

(a) Deployment and Distribution Operation Centre (DDOC)'s mission is to support CCDR – by linking strategic deployment and distribution process to operational requirement.

(b) *TSC forward* –is the forward based portion of the Theatre Sustainment Command (TSC). It includes HQs of deployable command post and theatre opening and distribution staff detachment.

(c) Joint logistics plugs are specifically designed to fill capability short falls.

Other JTLC characteristics are:

(a) JTLC must be able to deploy a joint logistics C^2 capability anywhere within the theatre – simultaneously providing rear-area logistics C^2.

(b) JTLC element deployed in support of Joint Task Forces (JTF) is referred to as Joint Force Support Component Command (JFSCC).

(c) JTLC is built around functional centres: Deployment and Distribution Operation Centre (DDOC), Joint Petroleum Office, Medical Logistics Centre, Monition Management Centre, Blood Programme Office, Joint Repair and Maintenance Teams. It also performs joint theatre opening and reception functions, operates Joint Contracting Centre, Joint Engineering Centre, Patient Movement, Mortuary affairs Operation and air drop support teams.

To elaborate on the process involved in the JTLC option – a typical cycle of operation is briefly traced below:

(a) On receipt of a warning order – the JTLC coordinates with CCDR's J3 and J4 staff to develop a deployment concept.

(b) Using the visibility, it already has, over service stocks and readiness – the JTLC prepares readiness assessment and recommends the cross levelling needed to outfit deployment units.

(c) JTLC coordinates with TRANSCOM, JFCOM and DLA so that they have full understanding of CCDR's requirements and *directs* the *fort to port* effort.

(d) If CCDR establishes a Joint Theatre Force (JTF) – then a portion of JTLC forms a Joint Force Support Component Command (JFSCC). The JTF Cdr may also choose to attach some service logistics forces to the JFSCC.

(e) The JFSCC:

  (i) Coordinates theatre opening with TRANSCOM Joint Task Force Port Opening (JTF PO) assets or Tanker Airlift Control Element etc.

  (ii) Develops theatre distribution plan and support plan.

  (iii) Also establishes a joint contingency contract cell and a joint engineering office.

(f) Once the theatre is open – JFSCC supports the joint reception, staging and onward movement process.

(g) The JFSCC coordinates directly with the Director of Mobility Forces – the Air Force designated authority for all air mobility issues in the AOR.

(h) The Director of Mobility Force and the Air Mobility Division remain in the Joint Force Air Component Command.

(i) The JFSCC synchronises end to end inter and intra theatre distribution operation and coordinates with the rear-area JTLC.

(j) Finally, when the mission is complete – the JFSCC coordinates and directs the *foxhole-to-port* movement.

LOGISTICS BRANCH

In May 2006 – the COAS approved creation of a Logistics Corp, Logistics Branch and Logistics Officer's Corp. The Army Combined Arms Support Command (ASCOM) took the lead to implement the scheme. The Logistics Corp comprises all personnel in the three functional logistics branches. i.e. Quarter Master (QM), Ordnance and Transportation. The enlisted personnel including warrant officers would continue as members of their respective functional branches and simultaneously be a member of the Logistics Corp. The logistics commissioned officers were required to begin their career in one of the historical functional branches and would be inducted into the Logistics Branch as a Captain. At fourth and fifth year of service – they would develop into multifunctional logisticians – capable of planning, integrating and executing sustainment operations. At the same time – they would be expected to continue maintaining proficiency in one secondary area of expertise. By 2008 over 60% of all logistic captain's positions were coded multifunctional.

US STRATEGIC GUIDANCE DOCUMENT

In January 2012 - the US President promulgated the US Strategic Guidance Document. This is President Obama's Defence Review Statement for the twenty-first century - a blue print for 2020. It lays down the US National Security Strategy. It shows a clear shift after Iraq and Afghanistan war effort. A shift away from Europe and a clear rebalance towards the Asia Pacific Region.

In respect of India the US has for the first time clearly spelt out the direction in which it proposes to take the relationship to. It states that "US is also investing in a long term strategic partnership with India - to support its ability to serve as a regional economic anchor and provider of security in the broader Indian Ocean Region.

The primary mission for US National Security Strategy has been specified under following heads:

(a) Counter Terrorism and Irregular Warfare.

(b) Deter and Defeat Aggression.

(c) Project Power Despite Anti access / Area Denial Challenges.

(d) Counter Weapon of Mass Destruction.

(e) Operate Effectively in Cyberspace and Space.

(f) Maintain a safe, secure and effective Nuclear Deterrent.
(g) Defend homeland and provide support to civil authority.
(h) Provide stabilising presence.
(i) Conduct stability and Counterinsurgency operations.
(j) Conduct humanitarian disaster relief and other operations.

INTERSERVICE RIVALRY AND TURF WARS

Modern military history clearly testifies to the fact that no country has been able to avoid inter-service rivalry and turf war syndrome. In all democratic countries – the political leadership has had to intervene from time to time and channelize such disruptive forces towards productive national interests.

USA is no exception. In the case of USA – several such instances have led to distorted development patterns, depending on the ability of the parties involved in lobbying. One such glaring example, is the issue of - which service, should be the *sole* keeper of strategic nuclear delivery capability.

In 1945, USAF before it became an independent Service, was the only unit which had the means to deliver the atom bomb to Hiroshima and Nagasaki. Since then, the USAF managed to exploit this accident of history – to manipulate and distort what could have been the normal course of development – to the detriment of the nation. USAF captured this strategic space and denied access to the other services for a long time.

In 1949 – this culminated in the cancellation of the 'super-carrier' project in favour of the B36 strategic bomber for the USAF and led to the famous 'revolt of the Admirals'. Both the CNO and the SECNAV lost their jobs for honestly expressing their dissent with the Secretary of Defence.

In March 1950, USAF managed to extend this domain further and get the exclusive responsibility of long range and Tactical missiles. This was a major set back – responsible for the logical development of ballistic missiles. To protect their 'turf'- till 1954, the USAF continued their stance of sheer neglect and indifference towards ballistic missiles. They blocked all funds for R&D on development of ballistic missile technology – on the grounds of non feasibility of any such project. At the same time, the USAF managed to veto the proposals of other services developing any such capability.

In the 1960s – once the Ballistic Missile Nuclear Submarine (SSBN) achieved submerged launch of Submarine Launched Ballistic Missile (SLBM) – the USAF monopoly was ultimately broken. Even then, the USAF did all that they could to bring the SSBNs under their control.

During the 1970s – fearing a threat to their dominance – especially since this was not central to USAF role and missions – they also discouraged the development of cruise missiles. This was a serious setback to both the ballistic missile and cruise missiles programmes. The resulting handicap was overcome much later at greater cost.

Bibliography

1. Col. Bradley Smith. – "Mandate to revolutionise Military Logistics" Air and Space Power Journal. Summer 2007.
2. Col. Karen E Ledoux. – "LOGCAO102: An Operational Planner's Guide". – Army Logistician. Jul/Aug 2005.
3. Col. Mike G Mullin Army Logistician. Sept / Oct 2005.
4. Daniel Howard. "Innovative ship acquisition approach for USN". National Maritime Foundation Seminar. 21 Nov 2007.
5. DODI50000.01 and 50000.02 OF 08 Dec 2008 – US DOD Instructions on Acquisition Management.
6. Dr Milan Vego. "Modern Naval Logistics" – Naval Force 1/2010
7. en.wikipedia.org/wiki/Weapon_System_ Acquisition_ Reform_ Act_ of_2009.
8. File//:\usnavy.org.structure1.htm.
9. file://A:\usnavyorgstructure1.htm
10. GAO – Report of US Government Accountability Office to Sub committee on Readiness Committee on Armed Forces, House Representative – on Defence Logistics – Better Management and oversight. September 2005.
11. GM Dillin. "Defence Policy Making a comparative Analysis.
12. Graham Allison. – "Rethinking America's security – beyond cold war to New World Order". 1992.

13. http.//www.chifo.navy.mil/navpolib/policy/vision/vis98/vis_b.html.
14. http://en.wikipedia.org/wiki/Defence Logistics Agency.
15. http://www.acquisition.navy.mil/home/organisation/peos_drpms/peo_ships
16. http://www.chinfo.navy.mil/navpalib/vision/vis98/vis-b.html
17. http://www.dau.mil> Office of ASN(RD&A).
18. http://www.defenselink.mil/odam/omp/pub3/GuideBook/pdf/DOD.PDF
19. http://www.defenselink.mil/odam/omp/pubs/GuideBook/Pdf/DoD.PDF.
20. http://www.dtic.mil/whs/directives/corres/pdf/500002p.pdf
21. http://www.nasea-navy.mil/teamships
22. IDSA "International Seminar on Defence Acquisition" 12 to 14 July 2011.
    (a) Lt. Gen. Alian Costes. French Armament Deprtment.
    (b) Maj. Gen.Daniel Argenson. French Armament Department.
    (c) Mr. Duncan Lang. Office of USD (AT&L).
    (d) Mr. Terrrence Elemendord. Director of Finance. Boeing Defence, Space and Security.
    (e) Prof. Gred Becham. US Defence Acquisition University.
23. J. Ronald Fox. "US Defence Management Challenges – Weapon Acquisition" 1988.
24. John F Schank, Gilesk K Smith, John Binkler, Brien Alkire, Michael Boito, Gordon T Tee, Raj Raman, John Ablard – "Acquisition competition strategy options DD(X) – the USN's 21st century Destroyer". 2003.
25. John Schank and Santa Monica. – "USN's 21 century destroyer". 2006.
26. Joint Publication JP4-01.8 – "Joint Tactics, Techniques and Procedure (JTTP) for Joint Reception, Staging, Onward Movement and Integration" (JRSOI)
27. Kristin. F. Lynch, John G Drew, David George, Robert S Tripp, Charles Robert Roll Jr, James A Leftwich "The Air Force COS Logistics Review – Improving Wing Level Logistics". 2000.
28. Lt. Gen. CV Chrtianson. – "Joint Logistics – shaping our future". Army Logistician. July / Aug 2006.
29. Lt Gen. Pahwa "Commans and Control of US Nuclear Forces" Chapter.3 2002.

30. Maj. David R Gibson – "8 step process for improving Logistics activity" Army Logistician. Sept / Oct 2005.
31. Maj. Vickie D Stenfor. – "Logistics Officers Corp – Growing Logistics Pentatheletes for 21st century". – Army Logistician. Sept / Act 2006.
32. Major. Michael E Scarlett Jr – "Role of UMOs and TC – AIMS operator in deployment". Army Logistician. Jul/Aug 2006.
33. Mark Mc Tague and Roger Honck. – Developing a concept for Joint Distribution." – Army Logistician. Jul / Aug 2005.
34. Mark W Akins and George L Topics – "Transformation of Joint Operational – level Logistics". - JFQ. IV Qr. 2007.
35. Military Balance 2008.
36. Naval Force Special addition 2005 :
    (a) "Distant Support: a virtual ship-mate".
    (b) "Executing the Total Force Strategy".
    (c) "Human System Performance Assessment Capability".
    (d) "Human system integration – Developing a skills basis force to support a capability based Navy".
    (e) "Naval Sea Systems Command: Agile, aligned and action oriented"
    (f) "Organisational Structure : putting realignment to work".
    (g) "PEO (Carrier)".
    (h) "PEO (Integrated Warfare System)".
    (i) "PEO (S/M)".
    (j) "Programme Executive Officer (Ships)".
    (k) "Technical Authority – this must improve things we do"
37. Randy S Kendrick – "Joint Logistics for EOCOM AOR" Army Logistician. Nov / Dec 2005.
38. Randy S. Kendrick – "Joint Logistics for the EUCAOR – Part II". Army Logistician. Jan. / Feb. 2006.
39. Robert L. Pfaltzgraft. – National Security Policy – the decision making process". 1984.
40. Robert McKay and Kathy Florence. _ "Transformation in Defence Logistics in Army Logistics" – Military Review. Sept / Oct 2000.
41. Sam C Sarkesian. and Robert E Connor Jr. "US military profession into 21st century". 1999.
42. Sandra I Erwin. "Pentagon Reviewing Proposal to create – Logistics Command". May 2003.

43. US DOD Instructions on Acquisition Management. DODI – 50000.01 and 50000.02.- Dec. 2008.
44. US Federal Acquisition Regulation.
45. US Joint Publication – 4-0 and 3-0. "Joint Logistics"–18 July 2008.
46. US Joint Publication – JP 0-2. UNAAF titled "Unified Action Armed Forces".
47. US Joint Publication (JP) 3-35. – "Joint Deployment and Redeployment Operation" – 7 Sept 1999.
48. US Report – National Commission on Terrorist attack – 11 Sept 2001.
49. USJCS Instruction – CJCSI 3202.01 – "Deployment process improvement.
50. www.givtrack.us/congress/bill.xpd?bill=s111-454.
51. www.nasea.navy.mil/organisation/NASEA_ORGCHART_0ct2010.pdf.

2

Insight Into Evolution of UK HDM System

From India's point of view – the study of the British model is an important one. Not only because of historical reasons but also because of the National Security Council [NSC(I)] directive of 2000, requiring special attention to be paid to the evolution of the HDM in UK. In this chapter – the evolution is examined chronologically – ever since India's independence. Greater emphasis has been laid on the recent restructuring exercises.

HISTORICAL PERSPECTIVE

In UK, during the period 1946 to 1964, the following five Department of State were involved in Defence: the Admiralty, the War office, Air ministry, the Ministry of Aviation and the Ministry of Defence (MoD). In 1964 – the Admiralty, the War office, the Air Ministry and (MoD) were merged. In 1971 the defence function of the Aviation Ministry was also absorbed into the MoD.

The evolutionary restructuring of the MoD in the last three decades along with all its linked ramifications have been captured in the illustrations that follow:

(a) Fig. 2.16. - Post Hastletine Review – 1986.

(b) Fig. 2.17. - MoD Organisational Structure – 1998. (SDR)

(c) Fig. 2.18 - Top Level Budget Structure.

(d) Fig. 2.19. - Chief of Defence Material (DE&S) Functional Organisation Chart. 2007

(e) Fig. 2.20. – MOD Functional Chart. 2008.

(f) Fig. 2.21. – CDS / PUS integrated organisational structure.

(g) Fig. 2.22. – Functional Procurement Flow Chart.

(h) Fig. 2.23. – Typical configuration of Overall UK Supply Chain.

(i) Fig. 2.24. - Macro Level Land Force Supply Chain Model.

POST HASTLETINE REVIEW – 1986

In 1986, Michael Hastletine, the Secretary of State for Defence (SOD), debated and discussed his reforms through a series of informal discussions with selected officials including the Chief of Defence Staff (CDS) and Chiefs of Services (COSs). After finalising the plans he gave the CDS and the Service Chiefs three days to implement his restructuring plan. The basic functional chart is represented at Fig. 2.16. As shown, the Defence Council, the highest defence decision making body, was chaired by the Secretary of State and attended, among others by the Chief of Defence Staff (CDS), Permanent Under-Secretary (PUS) and the Chiefs of Staff. National defence policy was formulated by the Defence and Overseas Policy Sub-Committee of the Cabinet. All its decisions were finally required to be ratified by the Cabinet. The three services were under their respective Service Boards – each headed by a Junior Minister. The executive committee of each service was chaired by the respective Chief and attended by all his Principle Staff Officers (PSO). All the PSOs also attend the respective Board meetings chaired by their minister. For maintaining continuity and coordination between the Services – Vice Chief of Defence Staff (VCDS) was required to attend all Board meetings of the individual service also. This was the model, in place, in UK – when the Kargil Committee was charged with the responsibility of preparing their recommendations on restructuring of India's HDM frame-work. Presumably, therefore, as directed by the NSC (India) - the Committee would have given due weightage to the fundamentals of the Hastletine solution.

POLITICAL DIMENSIONS

To understand the working mechanism, in place, in UK, at the time – there is a need to peep into the then political

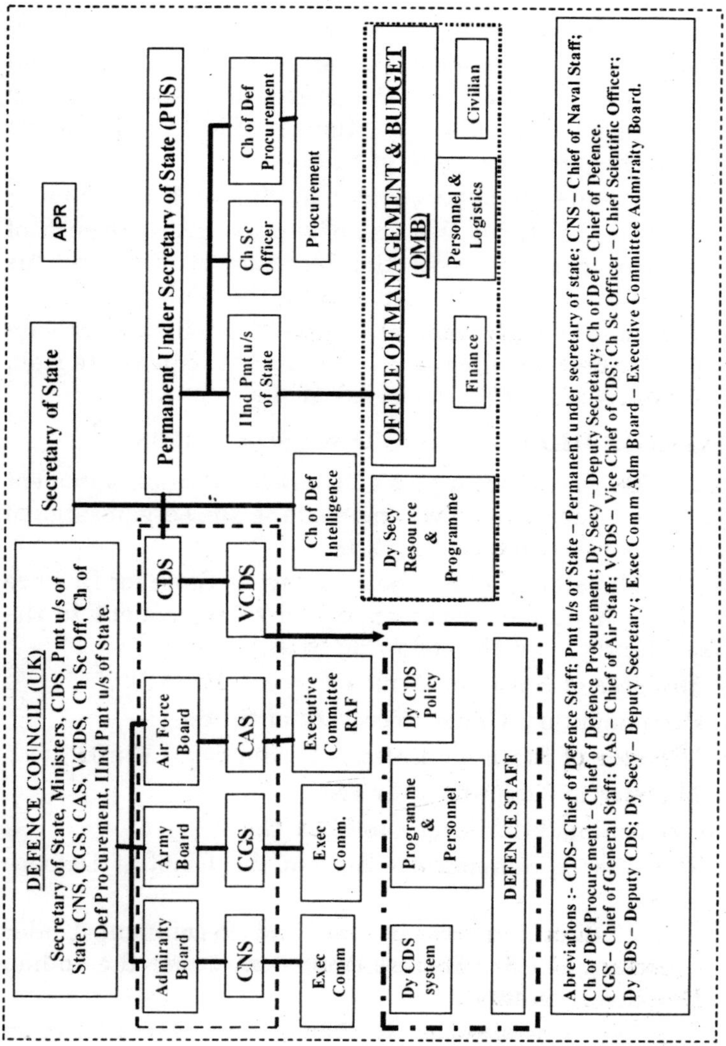

Fig. 2.16. Post Hastletine Review.

dynamics also. These fundamental elements are in force even today and can be enunciated in a nut shell as below.

(a) WESTMINISTER – is the seat of Parliament. The relationship between the Cabinet and Ministry of Defence (MOD) is conducted through the Cabinet Office – which is responsible for:
   - Linking of top echelons of MOD to Defence and Overseas Policy Sub-Committee of Cabinet, Prime Minister (PM), Foreign Minister (FM), Chancellor of Exchequer, Secretary of State.
   - Decisions are subsequently ratified by the cabinet.

(b) WHITE HALL - is the seat of the Executive Branch of the Government – with the Secretary of State and his four Junior Ministers supervising the MoD.

(c) They additionally, mediate between public and private faces of defence discourse – interact between White Hall, Westminster, office desk and Media.

STRATEGIC DEFENCE REVIEW (SDR) - 1998

SDR 1998 was meant to give - UK's Defence vision statement for the 21st century. From that emerged the MoD organisational structure as presented at Fig. 2.17.

At the Ministerial level - the Secretary of State for Defence (SOD) [who in Indian parlance, would be equivalent to the Raksha Mantry] had the following to assist him :

(a) Minister of State for Armed Forces. (MinAF).

(b) Parliamentary Under Secretary of State.

(c) Minister of State for Defence Production. (MinDP).

(d) Minister of Veterans. (MinVA)

At the non-ministerial level - to head the :

(a) The service component - he had the Chief of Defence Staff.

(b) The civilian component - he had Permanent Under Secretary (PUS) (nearest equivalent being the Indian Defence Secretary).

The PUS was retained as the *Principal Civilian* adviser on defence. He was primarily responsible for policy, finance and administration in the Department. He was Ministry of Defence's (MOD)'s accounting officer. He was *personally* responsible to

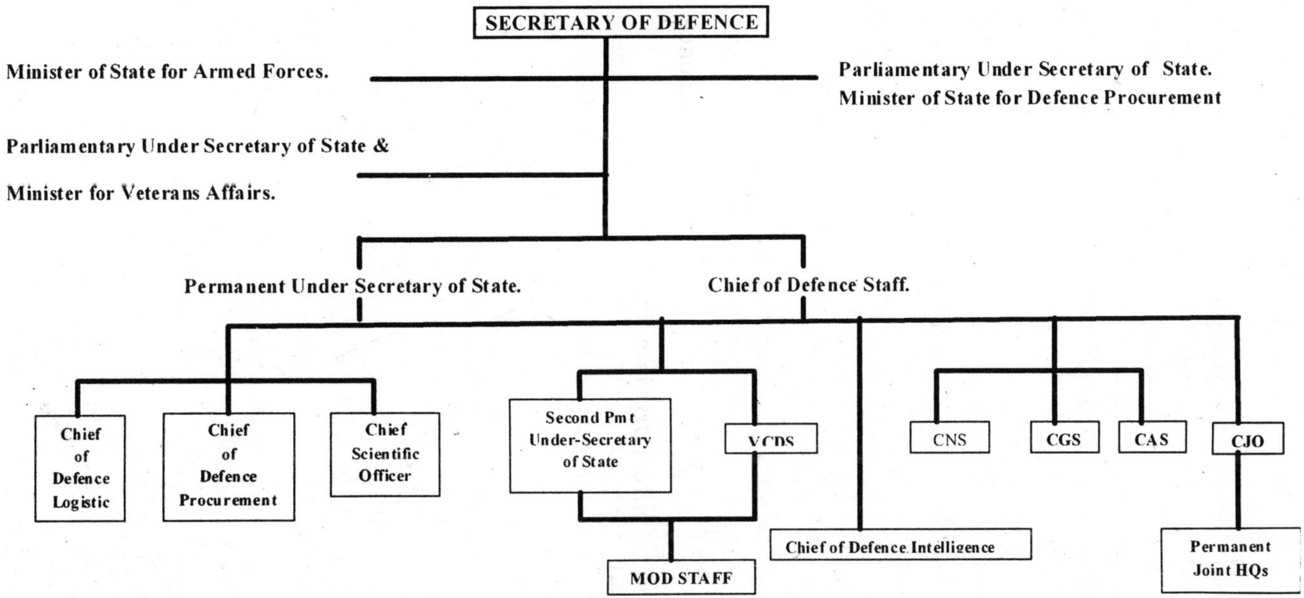

<u>Abbreviations used:</u> CNS – Chief of Naval Staff; CGS – Chief of General Staff; CAS- Chief of Air Staff; CJO – Chief of Joint Operations; VCDS – Vice Chief of Defence Staff; MOD – Ministry of Defence.

Fig. 2.17. UK MOD Organisational Structure.

Parliament for the expenditure of public money voted for defence purposes.

Similarly, the CDS was the professional head of the Armed Forces and the *Principal Military Adviser* to the Secretary of State and the Government. The chain of command for planning and conduct of military operations flows from the Cabinet and Secretary of State to the CDS and from him to the Operational Commanders.

The Defence Council retained its status as the highest decision making body on Defence. It comprised the SOD along with his four ministerial colleagues listed above and the following officials: CDS, PUS, Navy Chief (CNS), Army Chief (CGS), Air Chief (CAS), Vice Chief of Defence Staff (VCDS), Second PUS, Chief of Procurement, Chief of Defence Logistics (CDL) and the CSA (Chief Scientific Adviser).

The statutory powers given by the Defence (Transfer of Function) Act 1964 - provides the Defence Council (DC) the legal authority for conduct and administration of Defence.

The Defence Board (DB) is a non-ministerial Committee co-chaired by the PUS and CDS. The DB has the collective responsibility for the management of all activities of the MoD and the armed forces with the exception for planning and conduct of military operations.

The Service Boards (SB) under the Defence Council (DC) are responsible for the management of the respective Service. Each of the SBs is chaired by the Secretary of Defence (SOD) and comprises of the Deputy Minister concerned along with the respective COS and his PSOs. Each SB has an executive Committee chaired by the respective COS.

The following operational concepts were also adopted for execution in the SDR (1998):

(a) Chief of Joint Operation (CJO).

(b) Joint Helicopter Command – conjoining the helicopter assets of the three services. Specialised assets such as, those of the Navy's –dedicated to Aircraft Early Warning (AEW) and Anti-Submarine Warfare Aircraft (ASW) tasks were excluded.

Chief of Joint Operations	Commander in Chief Fleet	Commander in Chief Strike	Commander in Chief Land	**OPERATIONS**
APR	Chief of Naval Personnel	Personnel and Training Command	Adjutant General	**PERSONNEL**
Defence Procurement Agency	Defence Logistics Organisation	Defence Estate	Science Innovation and Technology	**Central**

Fig. 2.18. UK Top Level Budget Structure.

(c) Similarly, all Harrier aircraft assets of the three services were grouped together into Joint Force 2000. The RAF harriers were also planned to operate from the RN aircraft carriers. This concept was also to be followed with the Joint combat aircraft on the anvil.

(d) Conjoin the existing Defence Transport and Movements Executive, the Air Movement Executive and the Joint Transport and Movements staff into a single Defence Transport and Movement Organisation with responsibility for land, sea and air movement.

Defence activity was managed through *Top Level Budget* (TLB) holders as tabulated at Fig. 2.18. PUS was charged with the responsibility of granting each TLB holder extensive delegated powers over personnel, infrastructure and budget. Each TLB had a contract with MoD Head Office known as a *Service Delivery Agreement.*

With a few exceptions – Commander Joint Operations (CJO) was responsible for running all military operations from the Permanent Joint HQs. (PJHQ). Military assets were assigned to the CJO for the duration of the Operations only.

Commander in Chief (CinC) Fleet was responsible for delivery of warships and trained crew to CJO, at agreed readiness states. The CinC Fleet TLB merged with Chief of Naval Personnel / Home TLB in 2006.

CinC Land and Strike Command (STC), likewise, were responsible for their part of ship to CJO. In addition, STC was required to maintain aircraft and aircrew for Quick Reaction Alert to defend the UK airspace and conduct search and rescue operations.

Chief of Naval Personnel / C in C Naval Home (CNH) Command were responsible for providing raw material of trained naval personnel to C in C Fleet. Bringing individuals into coherent ships crew and working-up as the fleet remained the responsibility of the C in C Fleet.

REVOLUTION IN MILITARY LOGISTICS (RML) 2007-08

Post break-up of USSR and dismantling of the Warsaw Pact – the global security scenario changed drastically. The experience in dealing with Iraq / Kosovo / Afghanistan / Iran and the threat from Global Terrorism post 9/11 – again led to

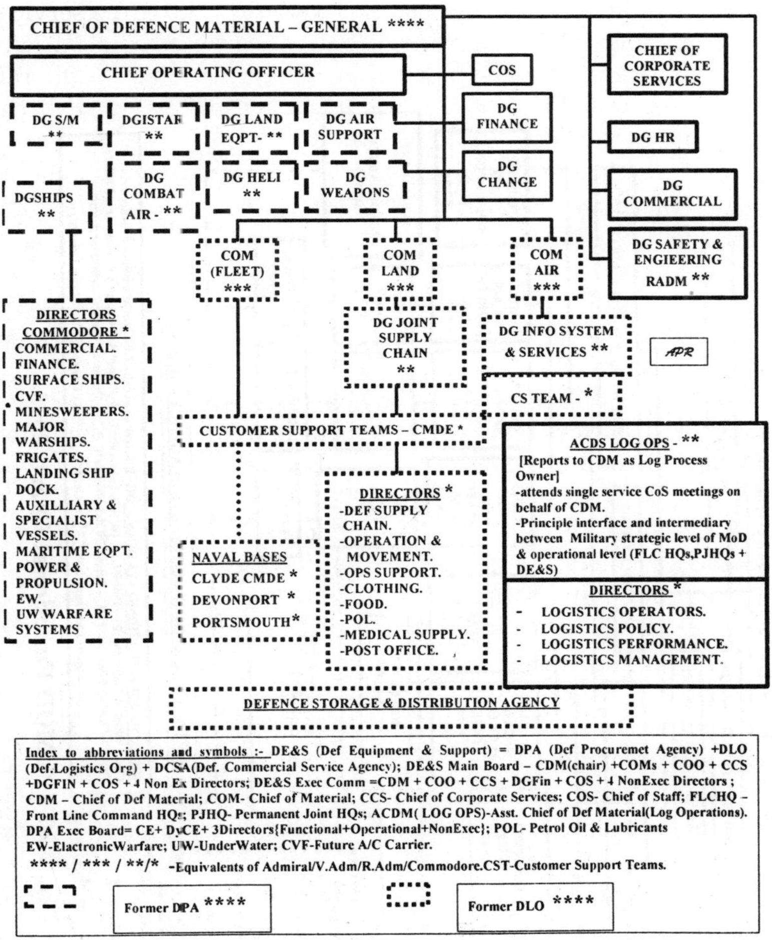

Fig. 2.19. UK Chief of Defence Material (DE AND S).

the total overhaul of UK's HDM structure. These factors gave additional impetus to RML. That eventually, led to the creation of Chief of Defence Material (CDM). The linked organisational reorientation is represented at Figs. 2.19 and 2.20.

In the Logistics arena, during the last fifty years, the British Defence Management system has undergone a series of changes, in the following sequence:-

(a) Introduction of computerised logistics management.

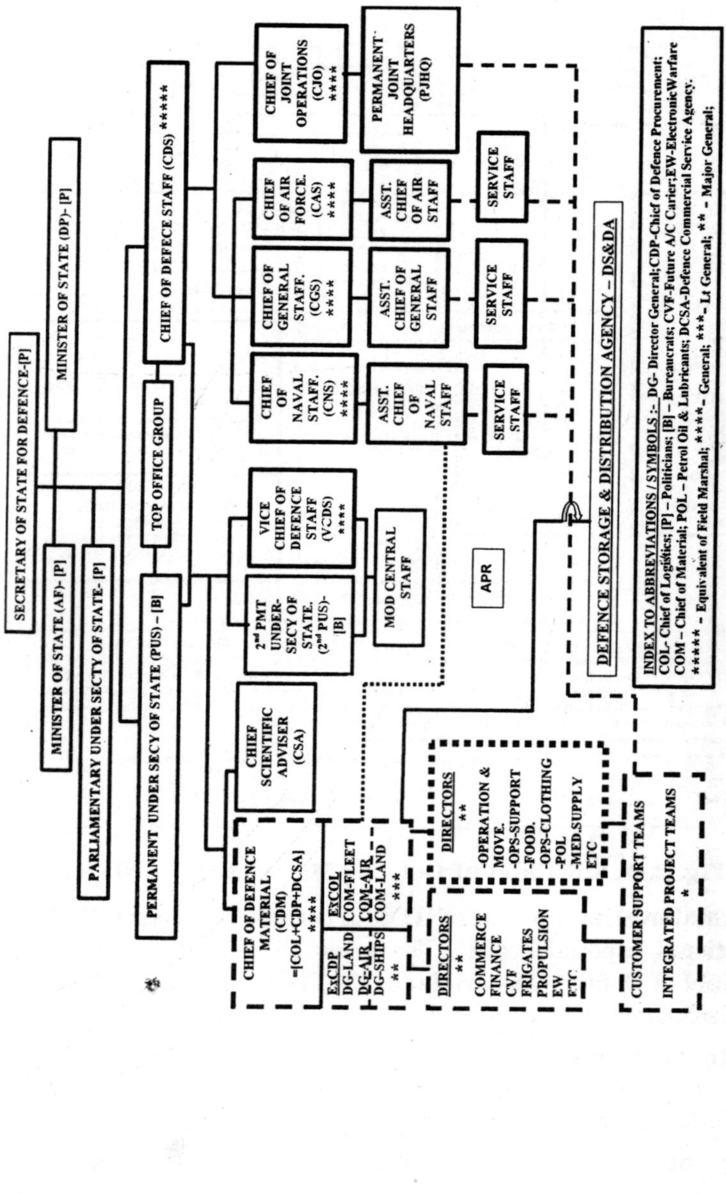

Fig. 2.20. UK MOD Functional Chart. 2008.

(b) Integration of all intra-service activities on conventional logistics.

(c) Corporatisation of repair infrastructure – till then, an in-house service.

(d) Privatisation of repair infrastructure followed by outsourcing of other support infrastructure.

(e) Integration of all inter-service logistics, under broad heads of Defence Logistics Organisation (DLO) and Defence Procurement Agency (DPA).

(f) Finally, merger of DPA + DLO + Defence Commercial Service Agency (DCSA) into Defence Equipment and Support Agency (DE&SA) – with the Chief of Defence Material (CDM) in charge, as a four star General / equivalent. The present incumbent, in 2011, is a civilian professional.

(g) Creation of Logistics Cadre by merging the MGO, QMG and the Transport Branches of the Army.

DEFENCE LOGISTICS BOARD (DLB)

The DLO Board is charged with the responsibility of providing strategic direction to the DLO. It comprised:

(a) Chief of Defence Logistics (CDL) – General.

(b) Deputy CDL – Senior Civil Servant (SCS).

(c) Director General Logistics (Fleet) – Rear Admiral (R. Adm).

(d) DGL (Land) – Major General (Maj Gen).

(e) DGL (Strike) – Air Vice Marshal (AVM).

(f) DGL (Supply Chain) – Maj. Gen.

(g) DGL (Nuclear) – R. Adm.

(h) DGL (Procurement) – SCS.

(i) DG Def Log Transformation – AVM.

(j) DGL (Resources). – SCS.

(k) Technical Director. – R Adm.

(l) Assistant Chief of Defence Staff (Operation Logistics) – AVM.

(m) DG Acquisition (People) – SCS.

(n) Chief of Defence Communication Service. – R Adm.

The functional chart of CDM is illustrated at Fig. 2.19.

It would be observed that the organisation has two major Divisions:

(a) One dealing with capital acquisition. This division was subdivided on functional basis into DG Ships, submarine, combat a/c, land equipment etc. The next level is illustrated, using DG Ships as an example – with each Director responsible for a class of ship.

(b) The second division - deals with support infrastructure – with three Chief of Material (COMs) in the rank of a three star generals heading their respective service support division.

As stated earlier, in April 2007 – the DLO merged with the DPA to form Defence Equipment and Support (DE&S) Agency. This combine is headed by the CDM – in the rank of a four star Flag officer. At the first echelon the erstwhile DLO wing now comprises of COM (Fleet), (Land) and (Air). Each of these limbs is headed by a three star flag officer. The Naval Wing's primary task is to provide total support to the ships, submarines, RFAs and supporting crafts – from induction into service, till final disposal to a scrap yard. This entails providing help in maintenance, upgradation, modernisation and engineering support, in the form of onboard repairs and defect rectification work on all naval assets. To enable fulfil these functions – partnership contracts were worked out with the three existing dock-yard operators i.e. Devonport Management Ltd., Fleet Support Ltd. at Portsmouth and Babcock Naval Services at Clyde.

The Naval Base Commander was charged with the responsibility of determining the work package for delivery by the respective Commercial partner. The Naval bases serve as a hotel cum garage and provide total water-front service – including shore supply, barrack accommodation, feeding, medical, spiritual care, administrative and security services. Running of the port and managing all ship movement also forms part of his ship.

Similarly, it would be seen that the Chief of Material [COM] (Land) has a Director General (DG) responsible for the Joint Supply Chain. Under him - he has the Customer Support Teams (CST), at the Brigadier level. The CSTs in turn have functional departments, as shown, headed by Directors responsible for:

(a) Defence Supply Chain.

(b) Operation and Movement.

(c) Medical Supplies etc.

The Defence Storage and Distribution Agency (DE&S) is an integrated facility / organisation – under the CDM.

The Assistant Chief of Defence Staff [ACDS] (Operational Logistics), as the Logistics Process Owner – attends all single service COS meetings on behalf of the CDM. He is the principle interface and intermediary between military strategic levels of MOD and the theatre / field at operational / tactical levels i.e. through the Front Line Command (FLC) HQs, Permanent Joint HQs (PJHQs) and DE&S etc.

The Executive Body of the DE&S is made up of the CDM (Chairman), COM's, Chief Operations Officer (COO), Chief of Corporate Services (CCS), DG Finance (DGFIN), COSs and four non-executive members.

The overall MoD (UK) set-up, with the CDM subset incorporated therein, is illustrated at Fig. 2.20.

It would be observed here, that the CDM is a four star general / equivalent - same as the Chiefs of Naval / General/ Air staff.

In the Indian context, if adopted – this would essentially mean delegation to the CDM (I), the responsibility and empowerment of the following existing authorities: -

(a) Master General of Ordinance (MGO) + Quartermaster General (QMG) + Engineer in Chief (E in C) + Part of Adjutant General (AG).

(b) Air Officer in Charge Maintenance (AOM).

(c) Chief of Material (COM) + Controller of Warship

Production and Acquisition of the Navy + Director General of Naval Design (DGND).

(d) Special Secretary / DG Acquisition – MoD.

(e) Department of Defence Production (DDP) of MoD.

STATUS AT THE SDR IN 2011

In 2011 – the CDM set-up, functionally remains the same, as at Fig. 2.19. Except that the DGs are now responsible to the COO. And the COMs report directly to the CDM - with dotted line horizontal linkage to the Chiefs of respective Service.

Institutional horizontal linkages are provided at multi-levels – inclusive at the Customer Support Team (CST) and Integrated Project Team (IPT) levels.

Following reorientation, at the ministerial level has also been implemented. The division of responsibility at the minister level, is now as follows:

(a) Minister of State for Armed Forces.

(b) Minister for Defence Equipment, Support and Technology.

(c) Minister for Defence Personnel, Welfare and Veterans.

(d) Minister for International Security Strategy.

(e) Under Secretary of State and the Lords Spokesman on Defence

The integrated working concept is further elaborated at Fig. 2.21. The *top office group* is shared between CDS and the PUS. Similarly, the *combined office* is shared between the VCDS and Second PUS. These offices follow an integrated concept and are manned by a mixture of civilian and military personnel.

An institutionalised systematic and interactive process between the *User Process Owner* and the *Service Provider Process Owner* is illustrated in the functional chart at Fig. 2.22. It illustrates the process involved, in converting the strategic / capability requirements into hardware procurement and continued provisioning of logistics and life time support to the user till its final disposal stage. The institutions involved and their inter-linkages have been elaborated. This needs to be seen along with the linked illustrations at Figs. 2.19, 2.20

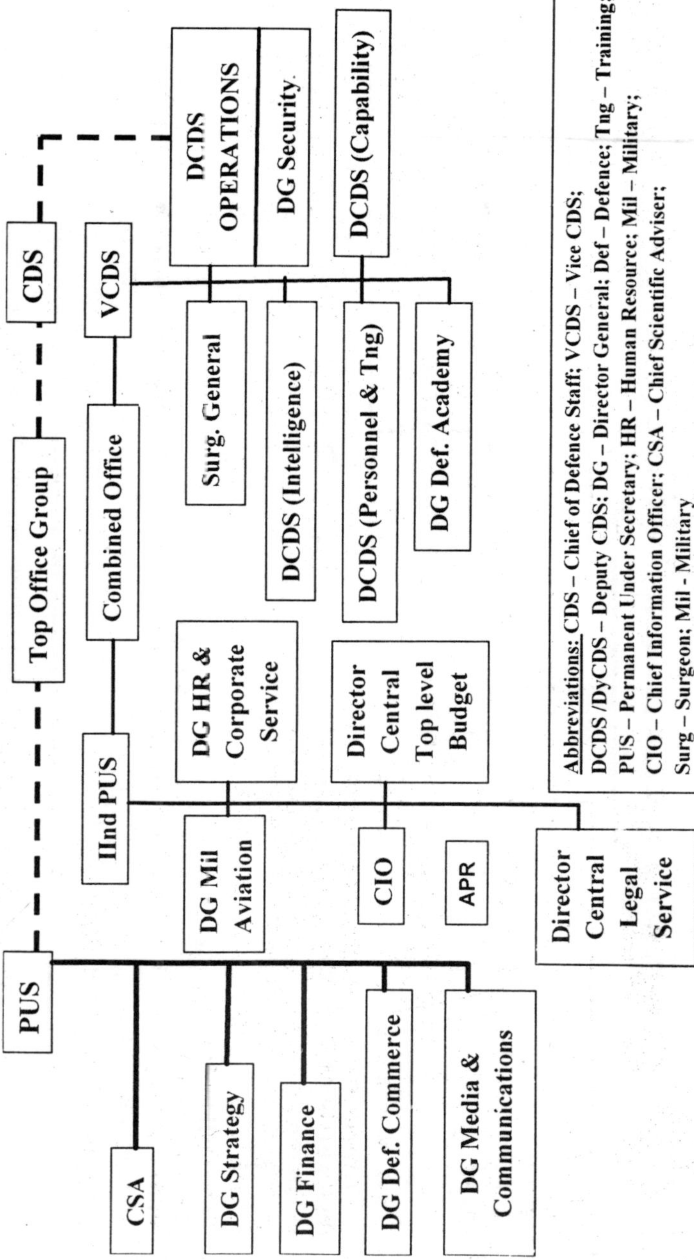

Abbreviations: CDS – Chief of Defence Staff; VCDS – Vice CDS; DCDS /DyCDS – Deputy CDS; DG – Director General; Def – Defence; Tng – Training; PUS – Permanent Under Secretary; HR – Human Resource; Mil – Military; CIO – Chief Information Officer; CSA – Chief Scientific Adviser; Surg – Surgeon; Mil - Military

Fig. 2.21. UK CDS / PUS Integrated Organisational Structure.

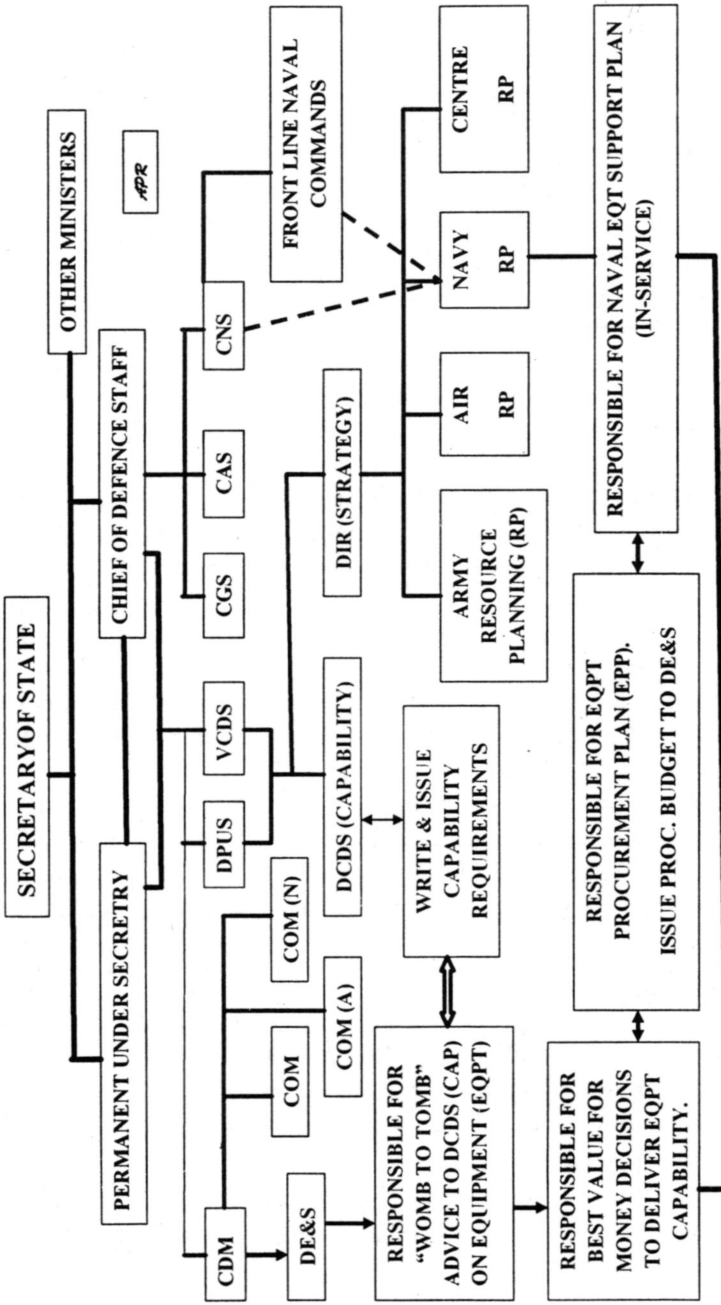

Fig. 2.22.UK Functional Procurement Flow Chart.

and 2.21.

Since the SDR 2011 and the formation of the new Conservative / Liberal Party coalition government - further review has been undertaken of the Defence Organisation Structure. The process is still going on. The relevant highlights are as follows:

(a) A civilian – Dr Bernard Crag has taken over as the CDM from General Sir Kevin O'Donoghue.

(b) The acquisition system prior to 2010 as illustrated at Figs. 2.19 and 2.20 has been rationalised and grouped together as Service specific composite entity under respective single Service COMs. The Capital Acquisition Division and the Support Infrastructure Divisions have been merged.

(c) The COO's post has been declared redundant. And relevant portion of his charge has been distributed amongst the single service COMs.

(d) Each single service COM has been given total responsibility for respective projects under the *womb to tomb concept.* This starts at the concept design stage and leads to development, production, commissioning and continues with logistics and lifetime support provisioning till its final disposal.

(e) A new civilian COM has been created. Directors *Information Systems Services, ISTAR and Helicopters* report to COM (Joint Enabler).

(f) The COMs continue to be directly responsible to the CDM.

(g) The above – in no way compromises or dilutes the overbearing principle of jointness. Institutionalised cross-linkages at all level take care of that.

Fig. 2.23 illustrates a flow chart in respect of the logistic chain, at the macro level – from Industry to the Central Depots and further on to the deployed forces.

Fig. 2.24 illustrates the functional process involved at the next stage in the joint supply chain process – with specific case of the Land Forces.

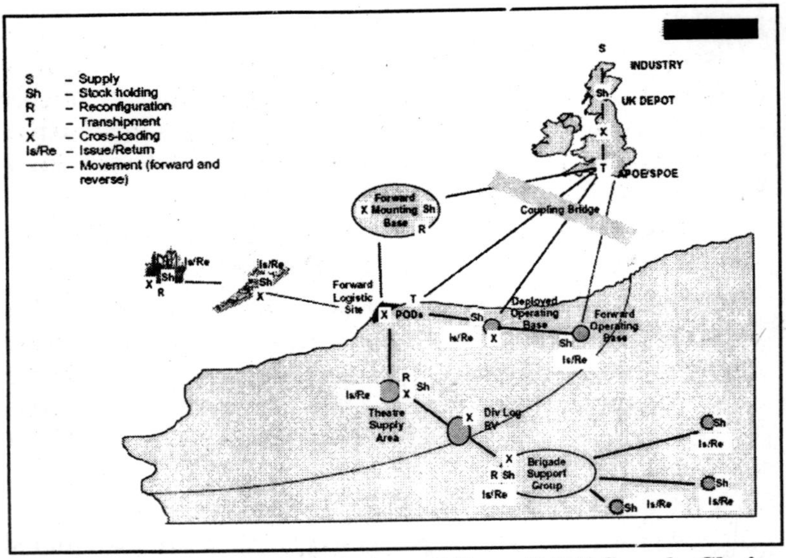

Fig. 2.23. Typical Configeration of Overall UK Supply Chain.

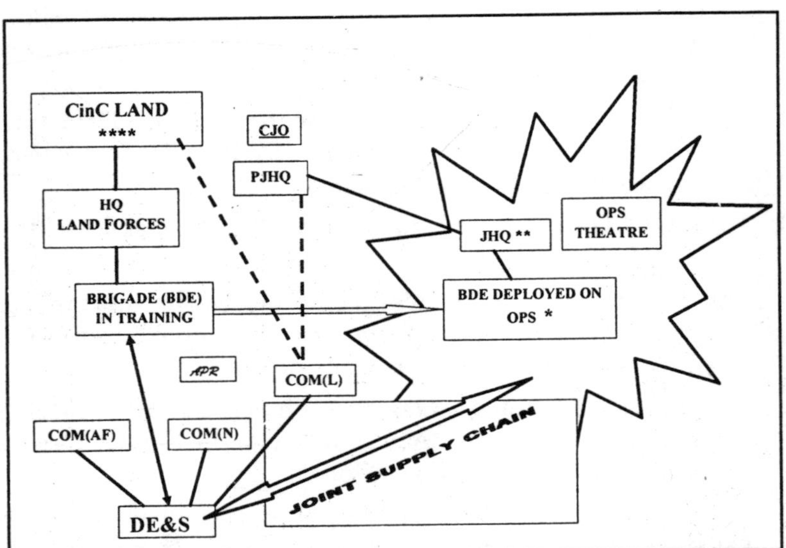

Fig. 2.24. Macro Level UK Land Force Supply Chain Model.

HRD FACT SHEET - DE&S

In the Indian context - while considering the above discourse, the following essential facts need to be seriously factored in:

(a) The professional profile of the key civilian incumbent of senior appointments are as follows:

(i) Permanent Under-Secretary of Defence (PUS).

- Ms. Ursula Brennan – took over from Sir. Bill Jeffrey in November 2010.
- Belongs to the 1975 batch of civil servants.
- IInd PUS from October 2008. Deeply involved in the MOD restructuring exercise.

(ii) IInd PUS - since 2011

- Mr. Jon Day. CBE – has had a long and distinguished career of over 32 years in the Defence field.
- DG Security Policy - 2008 – 2011.
- DG OPS and PLANING 2007 – 2008.
- Command Secretary Fleet. 2004 – 2007.
- Seconded to NATO. 2001 – 2003.
- Chief of Joint Intelligence Committee Assessment Staff – Cabinet Office. 2000 – 2001.
- Director Defence Policy 1997 – 1999.
- Deputy Command Secretary Land. 1995 – 1997.
- Seconded to NATO. 1992 – 1995.

(iii) Former Chief of Defence Material.

- General Sir Kevin O'Donoghue (Retd).
- Royal Engineers. 1968.
- Troop Commander. 75 Engineer Regiment. 1971 – 1973.
- British Army of the Rhine. 1973 – 1976.
- RMA Sandhurst. Company Instructor.
- MA to CGS.
- FRG Support 7 Armoured Brigade.

- Directing Staff. Army Staff College.
- CO 25 Engineer Regiment – deployed in Falkland Island.
- Commander Corps Royal Engineer 1.
- Chief Engineer Allied Command Europe and Commander Hameln Garrison.
- COS. HQs QMG.
- Assistant Chief of General Staff.
- Deputy Chief of Defence Staff. 2002 – 2004.
- Chief of Logistics. 2005 – 2007.
- The first Chief of Defence Material. 2007 – 2011.

(iv) Chief of Defence Material.

- Mr Bernard Gray – took over from General Sir Kevin O'Donnoghue in January 2011.
- Over twenty years association with Defence.
- Author of "Report on Acquisition" prepared for SOD John Hutton in 2009.
- Special adviser to SOD - 1997 – 1999.

(b) At a cursory glance one may be swayed by the statistics of a 75:25 divide between the civilian and military personnel involved in the DE&S function.

(c) A serious look at the illustrations at Fig. 2.19 will however show that at senior levels the uniformed personnel form the overwhelming majority. This is only pragmatic.

(d) Rationally, as was originally contemplated, the top assignment of the CDM should normally remain as a four star Flag Officer. The professional credential, as shown above of the founder CDM speaks for itself. He vacated his chair on retirement in January 2011.

(e) The present case is considered an aberration due to the perceived exceptional expertise of the individual in steering the restructuring phase of DE&S. It is believed that his long and close personal relationship with SODs has also played a part in his selection.

(f) In the Indian context, two very important and significant points to note, as food for thought, are:

(i) The CDM was a four star General of the same rank as the Navy, Army and the Air Force Chiefs.

(ii) The CDM, COMs and COLs till to date – with the exception of one, all have been from the support services. Where as in the Indian Army – ever since independence - even the MGO has never been from the support services.

(g) Rationally speaking – the UK model would ideally be, in the long term, the desirable and pragmatic way forward for India.

OTHER GLOBAL PLAYERS

In this context, functionally, the US, French and the British systems are similar to each other. All of them have created a dedicated logistics cadre. The US and British Armies have opted for inducting officers at the junior levels from the QM and MGO's Branches into the logistics branch. But they have been allowed to retain their parent branch status and specialisation – to enable them continuity, promotional prospects, retain skills and emotional / regimental bonding in their original branch.

The French and the Germans have an Armament Branch separate from the Combat Arms. The point to note here is that in all these countries, the promotion prospects in the Combat Arms and the Support Services are comparable. Institutionally, at the functional working level – the two work together in close consort and coordination, as if a single entity.

From the outset, USSR and China have had a dedicated logistics branch to support the military. In pre break-up USSR – the Russian military had a dedicated Marshal of SU as Deputy Minister of Defence and responsible for the logistics of the entire Armed Forces. He was also the coordinating authority at the national level with the Planning Commission (GOSPLAN) and other Ministries. This would be further elaborated in the next two chapters.

Indian military is perhaps the only modern Armed Forces in the world, which has the distinction of not believing in a joint logistics organisation even at the intra-service level.

Bibliography

1. "Defence Logistic Support Chain Manual" (UK) - JSP886. Vol. 1. Parts 1 and 4.
2. "Defence Procurement Agency". Naval Force Special Issue. 2005.
3. "The DLO world class support for a world class Navy". Naval Force. Special Issue. 2005.
4. "The strategic Defence Review—1998" London. The Stationary Office.
5. "UK's Defence Logistics Transformation Programme—Learning lessons from Iraq."
6. "Logistics Support—Development in logistics Branch and Operational Support". Naval Force Special Issue 2005.
7. <DESSEC-internet@mod.ok>
8. <en.wikipedia.org/wiki/Ministry_of_Defence_(United Kingdom)> accessed 20Apr. 2011.at 2040hrs.
9. <http://en.wikioedra.org/wiko/DefenceLogisticsOrganisation>.
10. <http://en.wikipedia.org/wiki/Defence Logistics Organisation>.
11. <http://www.dan.mil/pubs/dam/05_06_2005/dow_mjos/.pdf>.
12. <http://www.matflowpmo.dii.r.mil.uk>.
13. <www.livingstonpartners.co.uk/file_uploads/defence_security_booklet_3.pdf>.
14. <www.mod.uk/DefenceInternat/AboutDefence/Organisation/KeyFactsAboutDefence/DefenceOrg>
15. <www.mod.uk/DefenceInternet/MicroSite/DES/OurPublications/DeandsOrganisation C hart.html>
16. <www.mod.uk/DefenceInternet?LargeImageTemplate.aspx?img=/NR/rdonlyres/4FD3BC>.
17. <www.mod.uk/NR/edoulyres/8220542/7F9C4-4802-875C-BEEC2BA22888D/0 /201110225.DES.Org.Ct> accessed 20 APR 3011—1745.
18. <www.mod.uk/NR/rdonlyres/08FC4FC5-0416-4834-8CF3-232307BB467/0 /2011023_mod_min> accessed 20 Apr.2011.
19. www.mod.uk/NR/rdonlyres/82205420-F9C4-4802-875C-BEE2BA22888D/0/DESOrg.Chart_oct2010
20. www.mod.uk/nr/rdonlyres/IC0516CC-7FDC-4D45-890D-087752025C/A710/201011105 accessed 20 Apr. 2011. 2100hrs.
21. <www.moduk/NR/rdoulyres/8220542/07-F9C4-4802-875c-Bee2BA22888D/0 /201110225DESOrg.ct>.

22. www.mod.uk/NR/rdonlyres/82205420-F9C4-4802-875c-BEE2BA22888D/0/0910DES_Org_Chart.pdf - accessed 01Aug2011.l

23. GM Dillon. "Defence Policy Making—a comprehensive analysis.".

24. IDSA – International Seminar on Defence Acquisition. 12 to 14 July. 2011.

    (a) Gen. Sir Kevin O'Donoghue (Retd). Former COL and CDM. UK.

    (b) Lt. GEN. (ARMAMENT). Alain Costes. DGA. Fronce.

    (c) Maj. Gen. (Armement) Daniel Argerson. DGA. France.

    (d) Mr. Vivek Rae. DG (Acquisition). MoD. GOI.

    (e) Mr. SN Misra. PCDA (Navy). Mod. GOI.

    (f) Mr. VK Misra. Former Secretary Defence (Finance).

    (g) Mr. Ranjan Kumar Ghose. JS. Acquisition Manager. MoD. GOI.

    (h) Dr. Kogila Balakrishnan. Under Secretary. MOD. Malasia.

25. Informal discussion with - Admiral Sir Mark Stanhope. First Sea Lord UK _04 Feb 2011.

26. Informal discussion with - Lt. Col. Charlie Wareer. RA. MA UKHC. New Delhi—03 March 2011.

27. Informal discussion with - Mr .Vincent Devine UK. 23 Feb 2011.

28. Informal discussion with - Mr Peter Luff. Minister for DES&T. UK - 08 Feb. 2011.

29. Informal discussions with - Group Captain Ian Draper RAF. NA and AA. UKHC. New Delhi.

30. M Chichester and L Wilkinson. "British Defence Blue print for reforms" - 1982.

31. M.Sabharwal "Joint operation in modern warfare" Air Power Journal. Vol. 3. No. 1 Spring 2006. p. 30.

32. MChrichester and J. Wilkinson "British Defence a blue-print for reforms". 1987.

33. Maj. Gen. Tony Raper UK Army. "Operation TELIC—part of UK contribution to operation Iraq Freedom".

34. Para 2(a) of NSC Directive No.C-180/1/200-NSC(CS). 17 May 2000.

    "Since accountability to Parliament constitutes the basic feature of GoI, the Task Force, while making recommendations will examine the evolution and changes in this respect that have taken place in other parliamentary democracies. In particular, the UK model should be studied closely".

35. R.Adm.A.P.Revi "Revolution in military logistics". India Defence Review. Vol. 23 (#0. July 2008).
36. Rear Admiral (Rtd) A.P. Revi in "Revolution in military logistics—relevance to India". Journal of Indian Ocean Studies. Vol. 14 (3). July 2008.
37. R. Adm. A.P. Revi (Rtd.) "RML – relevance to India". NDC. MPhil Thesis: Madras University.
38. UK Defence White-paper (Cm6041). Dec 2003) . <http//:www.mod.uk/publication/whitepaper 2003/index.html>.
39. UK MOD to Parliament "Government Expenditure Plan 2005-2006, 2007—2008". Cm6532 (2005).
40. U.K. MoD. June 2009 – "How Defence Works – Defence Frame Work".

3

Russian Federation Perestroika

Most of us in India are reasonably familiar with the working of a democratic government – whether it is Westminster type Parliamentary Democracy or Presidential form. However, most of us have a very sketchy idea of the working of a Communist single party autocratic government. Hence, before looking at the Higher Defence Management (HDM) under such a dispensation - there is a need to grasp at least the fundamental structure / institutions that make the whole wheel turn and their inter-relationship in respect to National Security matters, in particular. With that objective in mind - introduction to the primary institutions that were involved in USSR and their inter-relationship is briefly enunciated in the succeeding paragraphs. Over and above that, in the present context – such an understanding is also important for the following reasons:

(a) The Chinese structure is a derivative from the Soviet system. Since information in respect of China is even skewed than that of Soviet Union (SU) – insight into the Soviet system would give a better understanding of China's.

(b) After the break up of Union of Soviet Socialist Republic (USSR) and Warsaw Pact alliance - the Russian Federation (RF) has been trying to evolve into a Presidential form of democracy. There are many lessons to be learnt by India – in the process of restructuring of their Armed Forces.

THE SOVIET MODEL

The Soviet Union's (SU) constitution provided for a single party Communist government. The Communist Party of the Soviet Union (CPSU) was the only authorised political party. In reality, membership of the CPSU worked out to about 10% of the eligible population only. The Party was empowered to formulate national policies. The various elements of the hierarchy are discussed briefly in the following paragraphs.

THE CONGRESS

The Congress in theory was considered the supreme party body – which was required to meet every five years for about a couple of weeks. Some of its main responsibilities were to:

(a) Formulate important domestic and external affair policies for the next five years.

(b) Ratify the five year economic plans and requirements of defence industry.

(c) Accept the General Secretary's report.

(d) Details of policy formulation were left to the Permanent Secretariat and the Politburo.

CENTRAL COMMITTEE

Some of the salient features of the Central Committee are listed below:

(a) The candidates were appointed by the Congress from among their 300 odd members.

(b) Around 7% of them were usually high ranking military officers.

(c) Generally, there were around hundred and seventy odd non-voting Candidate Members – of which over 12% held senior military positions – including Defence Minister (DM), Chief of General Staff (CGS), Chiefs of Staff (C of S)s and Theatre Commanders etc.

(d) They met at least twice a year.

(e) They were empowered to decide on changes in the Politburo membership and Party Secretary.

(f) To become a law – all decisions of the Central Committee needed to be ratified by the Supreme Soviet.

THE SECRETARIAT

The Secretariat of the Central Committee comprised about twelve Secretaries. Each was in charge of a Department of the Central Committee with specific areas of responsibilities.

By convention the General Secretary of the CPSU was normally considered to be *the Soviet Leader* and not the Chairman of the Presidium of the Council of Ministers (i.e. The PM) nor the Chairman of the Presidium of the Supreme Soviet (i.e. The Head of State).

THE POLITBURO

The Politburo was the nerve centre of decision making in all major areas of domestic and external affair policies. It comprised about Twenty Five members and met once a week.

THE SUPREME SOVIET

The Supreme Soviet was considered to be the highest body of state authority. It was a bicameral body each with seven hundred and fifty members-which consisted of:

(a) The Soviet of Union.

(b) The Soviet of Nationalities.

There was a thirty nine member standing committee of the Supreme Soviet. The Presidium was elected at a Joint Session. The Chairman of the Presidium was considered the *Head of State*. Brezhnev, Andropov and Cherenkov combined this position with the *General Secretary of CPSU.* This body was charged with the responsibility of ratifying treaties, proclaiming *state of war* and appointing / dismissal of High Command officers.

COUNCIL OF MINISTERS

This was the highest executive and administrative body of the state. These Ministers were appointed by and accountable to the Supreme Soviet. The Defence Minister was always a member.

DEFENCE COUNCIL

It owes its origin to Lenin's Council of Labour and Defence (STO) which continued through to 1937. In 1941, Stalin created the war time State Committee for Defence (GKO) – which

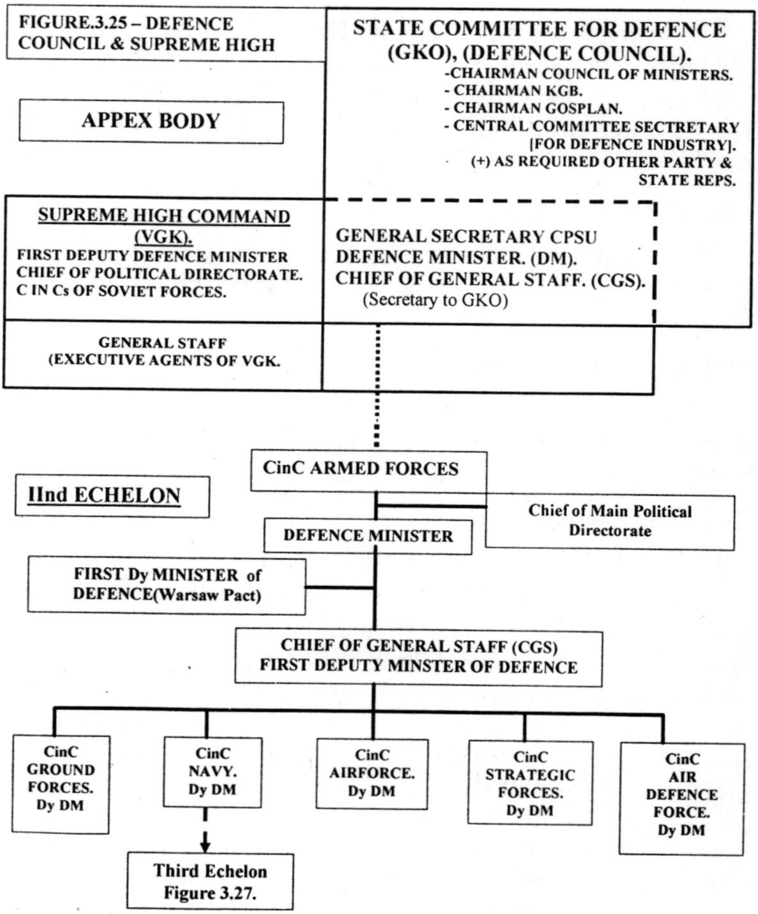

Fig. 3.26. Soviet Armed Forces Organisation Tree – Second Echelon.

lasted through the Second World War (WW.II) till 1945. In 1972, the new Soviet Constitution designated the GKO as a state institution as opposed to a party institution. In 1982, the Chief of General Staff (CGS) was given the position of secretary to GKO. As stated earlier, GKO was a subset of the Politburo, chaired by the Gen Secretary of CPSU. This was also referred to, at some stage, as the Defence Council. The Council was appointed by the Supreme Soviet. Brezhnev, Andropov, Cherenkov and Garbachov were all Chairman of the Council. The DM, CGS, Chairman Council of Ministers (PM) / the State Planning Commission (GOSPLAN) and Central Committee Secretary responsible for Defence Industries were the usual members of GKO. The CGS was the secretary to the council. It also formed the war cabinet.

THE SUPREME HIGH COMMAND (VGK)

Under the GKO was the Supreme High Command – the highest organisation of strategic leadership. As shown at Fig. 3.25 – this was a subset of GKO. The GKO controlled the military commands through the General Staff. Organisationally, the soviet forces generally conformed to a unified command structure under the General Staff. According to the Soviet concept, at the strategic level, the globe was divided into - thirteen geographical Theatre of Military Operations (TVD). The commander TVD was directly responsible to the GS.

GENERAL STAFF (GS)

The Chief of GS (CGS) was the head of the unified military establishment and the Chiefs of the five Services (CoSs). The GS exercised operational control over the armed forces and was charged with the responsibility of translating strategy, doctrine and policy into action. To perform these functions the CGS was provided with a competent professional military staff. The GS comprised following functional Directorates:

(a) Operation – GOU.

(b) Intelligence – GRU.

(c) Mobilisation / Organisation.

(d) Communication.

(e) Topography.

(f) Cryptography.

(g) ABC warfare.

(h) Military Science – responsible for formulation of military doctrine etc.

(i) Foreign Assistance.

(j) Warsaw Pact.

In the 1980s Marshal Ogarkov, as the CGS, introduced the concept of centralised strategic level control with decentralised battle management. Theatre commands formed the link between the GS and field formations. As will be shown later, after the break-up of USSR - the role of CGS in the new RF was progressively discounted.

EVOLUTION OF MILTARY STRATEGY

In the Soviet construct – the Grand Strategy and the National Security Concept was evolved at the Politburo and on that basis the State Committee for Defence (GKO) formulated the Military Doctrine and Foreign Policy Concept. There after, the GS was delegated the authority to formulate the Military Strategy. This is functionally illustrated at Figs.3.25 and 3.29.

THE MILITARY HIERARCHY

As brought out earlier - all policy decisions were made at the Politburo. The apex body represented by GKO in Fig. 3.25 was charged with the responsibility of taking those decisions forward. The Supreme High Command (VGK), a subset of the GKO, was required to translate those into action through the integrated GS. The second echelon organisational tree is illustrated at Fig. 3.26. For illustration purposes the Soviet Naval High Command at the third echelon level is represented at Fig. 3.27. The *Glavkom* (Navy) exercised operational control through the Chief of Main Naval Staff and the First Deputy Commander in Chief (C in C). Technical and administrative control was exercised through the six functional Deputy C in Cs as shown. The organisational tree at the operational level of the Soviet Fleet is presented at Fig. 3.28. Naval Forces were under direct jurisdiction of the *Glavkom*.

Matters connected with combat training, material and technical supplies for the Fleet were entirely within the

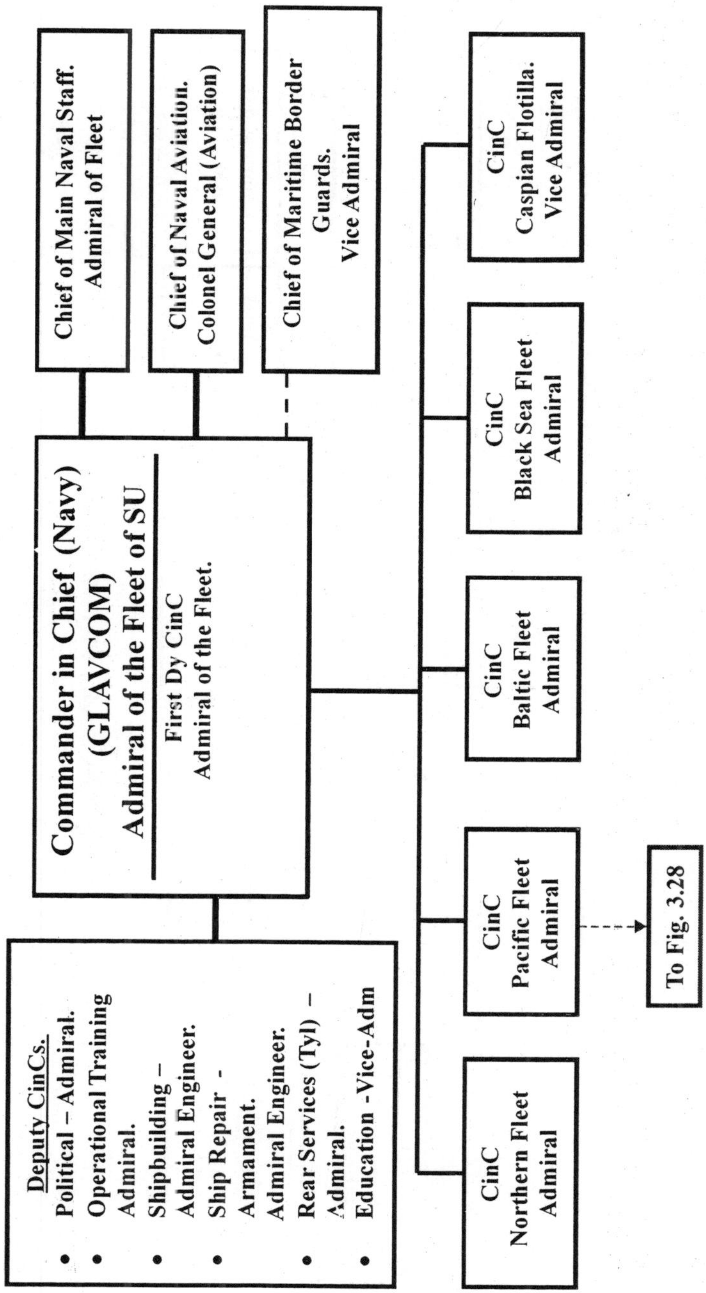

Fig. 3.27. Soviet Naval High Command (Pre 1989) – Third Echelon.

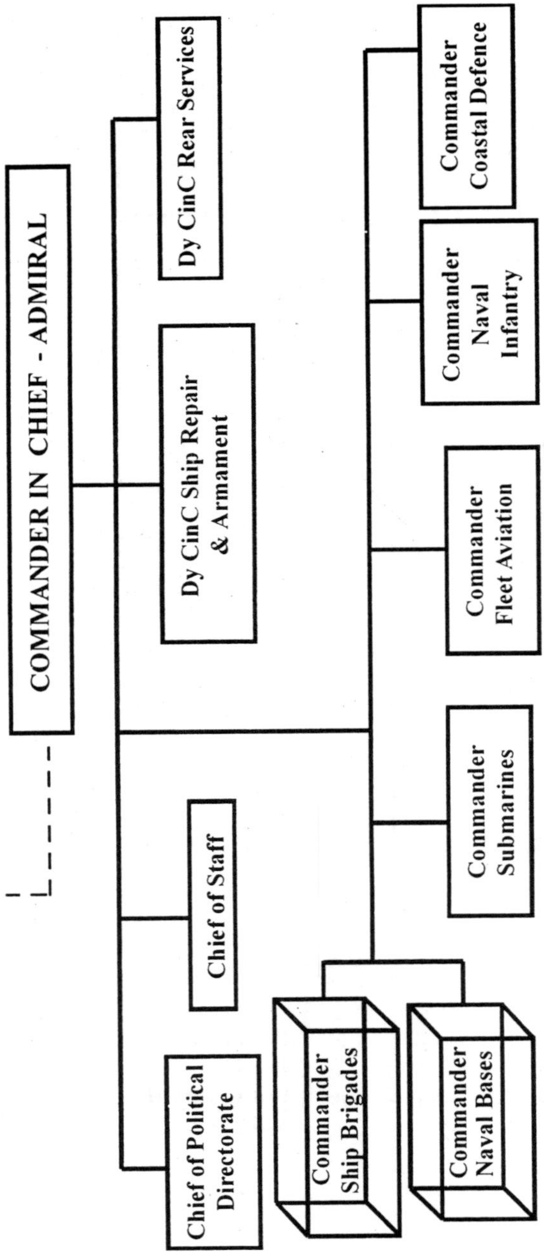

Fig. 3.28. Soviet Fleet Organisation.

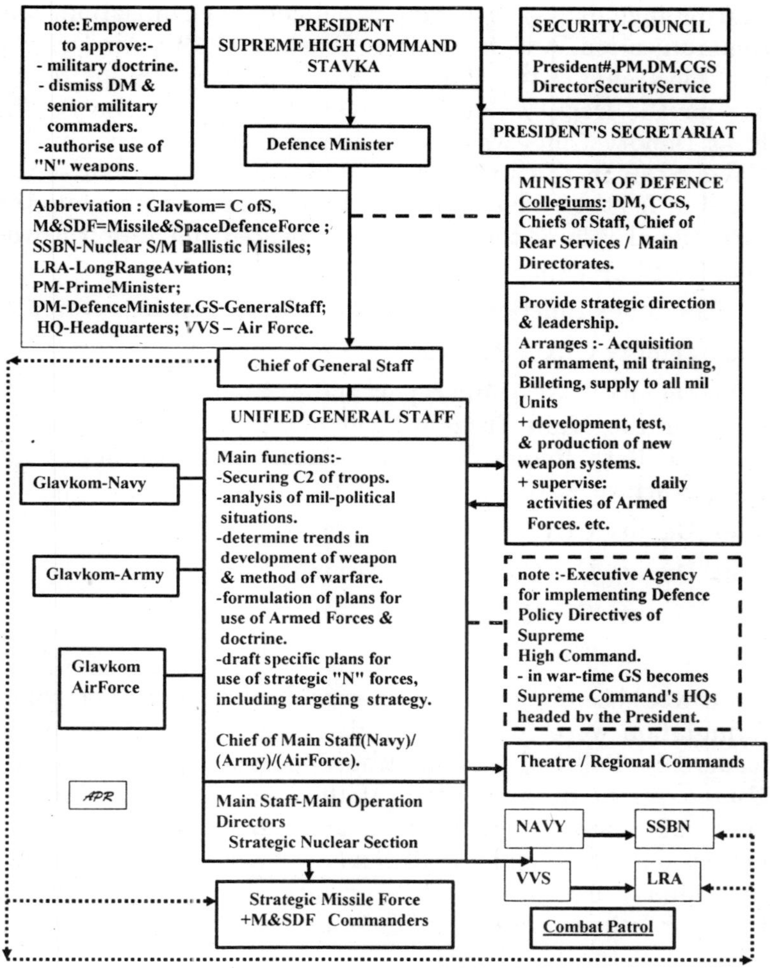

Fig. 3.29. RF Higher Defence Management Flow Chart.

jurisdiction of the Fleet Commander.

The Chief of Main Naval Staff (CMNS) under the *Glavkom* was responsible for planning of naval operation and determination of long term naval development plans. His charter included – operation, intelligence, mobilisation, and communication, Anti Submarine Warfare (ASW), Air Defence and Electronic (EW). CMNS's charter is very similar to the one for the Deputy Chief of Naval Staff (Indian Navy). The First Deputy CinC was the equivalent of the Vice Chief of Naval Staff in the Indian Navy (IN) and was authorised to stand-in for the Glavkom in his absence. To accommodate the exceptional role of the Navy - a dedicated full Admiral was found a place as a special *Aide* to the CGS.

The other functional Deputy CinCs to *Glavkom* were:

(a) Deputy CINC Political.

(b) Deputy CINC (Ship repair and Armament) – responsible for the Main Technical Directorates, Naval Missiles / Artillery, Radio- Technical Services and Anti-Submarine Warfare (ASW).

(c) Deputy CINC – Ship building.

(d) Deputy CINC (Combat Training).

(e) Deputy CINC (Rear Services).

(f) CinCs Fleet.

It would be observed here that political direction and policy formulation were fully and firmly in the hands of the party leadership. Political presence was all pervasive - including the *Commissar* at the unit level. At the same time, the military was well represented and in a position of influence, at all professional National institutions – where security related decisions were being taken or advice rendered. During Brezhnev's long innings – Marshal Ustinov, the DM, was a member of the Politburo.

MILITARY DISTRICT

For purposes of efficient administration, the SU was divided into several military districts (MD). Their primary role was:

(a) Training.

(b) Mobilisation.

(c) Agents for coordination and implementation of civil defence measures.

For purposes of military operations - the continental land mass of SU was divided into three main geographic *theatres*: Western, Southern and Far Eastern. These were further subdivided, for operational-command and strategic-planning purposes, into several continental and maritime theatres (TVDs).

INTEGRATED LOGISTICS

Integrated logistics was deeply embedded into the system from the very beginning. *'Tyl'* was the common acronym associated with the Rear Service of the Soviet Armed Forces (NTVS). Its Chief of Rear Services was designated as a Deputy Defence Minister. He was located at the Ministry of Defence (MoD) HQs and was responsible to administer fuel, food, clothing, military supplies / material and veterinary services to the entire military establishment.

All aspects of movement of military supplies were managed by the Rear Service. They were also responsible for coordinating the activities of the Deputy Commanders for Rear Services with the respective Service, Military Districts, and Group of Forces and at the tactical levels too. There was a NTVS counterpart at each subordinate echelon down to the regiment. The Deputy Commander (*TYL*) besides being the Chief of Rear Services locally - was directly subordinate to his Unit / Formation Cdr and carried out the policies and guidelines of Rear Service representatives at higher levels.

EVOLUTION OF THE ARMED FORCE ORGANISATION STRUCTURE

The evolution of the Soviet / RF Armed force Structure was primarily dictated by:

(a) Being a large continental entity.

(b) Historical military experience from the time of Tsar's Imperial Army to WW II, through cold war, break up of SU / Warsaw Pact alliance and recent exposure at

Chechnya / Afghanistan occupation and to US allied force action in Bosnia, Iraq, and Afghanistan etc.

SOVIET UNION

Prior to the breakup of SU – the Soviet Armed Forces comprised the following five services:

(a) Strategic Rocket Forces - (RSVN) / (SRF)

(b) Ground Forces – (SV).

(c) Navy – (VMF).

(d) Air Force – (VVS).

(e) Air Defence Force – VPVO).

The aviation assets were distributed among the following:

(a) The Navy.

(b) Air Force.

(c) Strategic Aviation / Long Range Aviation – (DA).

(d) Anti-air Defence – (VPVO).

(e) Air Transportation Force - (VTA).

(f) Tactical Aviation – (FA).

(g) Ground Force Support Aviation (mainly helicopters) – (ASV).

The Naval aviation was an integral part of the Navy. DA and VTA could be called upon to augment the Navy in meeting its strategic roles. The Air Force on the other hand has had a chequered life. During WWI the command and control of the Air Force (AF) was in the hands of the AF Commander. Just prior to WWII and till 1942 control of the Air Power was handed over to the Ground Force Commander. Subsequently the control was returned to the AF Cdr. In the 1980s the issue raised its head again and FA and ASV were made subordinate to the MDs. To and fro movements took place several times. Post 1998 – a complete restructuring exercise was attempted. What emerged is illustrated functionally at Fig. 3.30. The FA and ASV were put under operational command of the MDs. The administrative and technical control remained with the VVS Chief. This would be discussed in greater detail later.

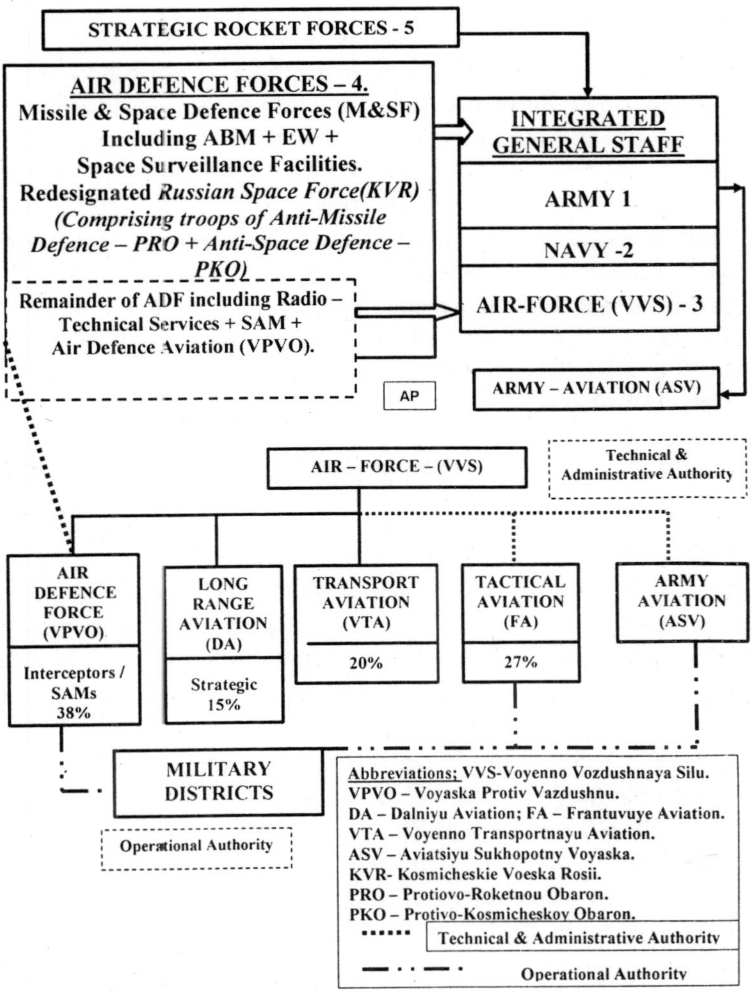

Fig. 3.30. RF Military Reforms 1999.

HISTORICAL PERSPECTIVE

After the demise of President Leonid Ilich Brezhnev - the top leadership changed in quick succession till Gorbachov came to power. Gorbachov introduced *perestroika* and *glasnost* within the Soviet Union architecture. In 1991 he also issued a decree creating a new *Service – Strategic Deterrence Force (SSS)* – by putting all the strategic assets under one head. As will be brought out later - within one month, USSR disintegrated and the whole concept became defunct.

This followed a period of existential and material crisis. The country went through a traumatic change which led to the failed attempt of a *coup d'état* and prolonged period of uncertainty / instability as illustrated by the calendar of events that followed. The August 1991 *Putsch* was engineered by the Chairman of KGB, Vladimir Krychkov and supported by the *gang of eight* which included the CPSU heavy weights such as the Valentine Pavlov (PM), Dimitry Yazov (DM), Boris Pugo (Home Minister), Gennady Yanyev Vice President (VP) etc. The whole rebellion was perpetuated / conceived as a protest against Garbachov's. new *Union Treaty, Communist Party reforms* and *restructuring of the Armed Forces* – which they considered would lead to Balkanisation of USSR and dilution of the party's hold over the state. Military stalwarts like Marshal Akhrameyev the CGS, got caught in the cross fire and committed suicide.

In Jan 1992 – after the failed *putsch*– Yeltsin took over the reigns of power. In Mar 1992 he signed the *law on security* which led to the revival of Russian Federation Security Council (SCRF) in its new incarnation. The formulation of Grand Strategy again became part of its charter.

On 02 Nov 1993 – Yeltsin signed the *Military Doctrine* which emerged out of the *National Security Concept* as formulated by the CGS. This called for a change in thrust - over the use of nuclear forces and *no first use* was withdrawn from the nuclear vocabulary. The 1993 Constitution granted the President far reaching powers in the field of security. It was the President and not the government who was now in charge of foreign and security policy and the armed forces and troops with the other eleven government departments.

POST PERESTROIKA RUSSIAN FEDERATION (RF) HDM

The frame-work of the RF HDM organisation functional chart is illustrated at Fig.3.31. At the apex level, the President was designated as the Supreme High Command. He was assisted by the Security Council (RFSC) and his Presidential Secretariat. He was empowered by the constitution to:

(a) Approve military doctrine.

(b) Dismiss DM and senior military commanders.

(c) Authorize use of 'N' weapon.

The MoD, GS, Ministry of External Affairs (MID) and the eleven so called *Power Ministries* were responsible for implementing the decisions meted out by the President. The Power Ministries comprised of:

(a) Federal Border Guard Services.

(b) Federal Services of Railway Troops.

(c) Federal Protection Service.

(d) Main Directorate of Special Programme.

(e) Ministry of Emergencies with civil defence commitments.

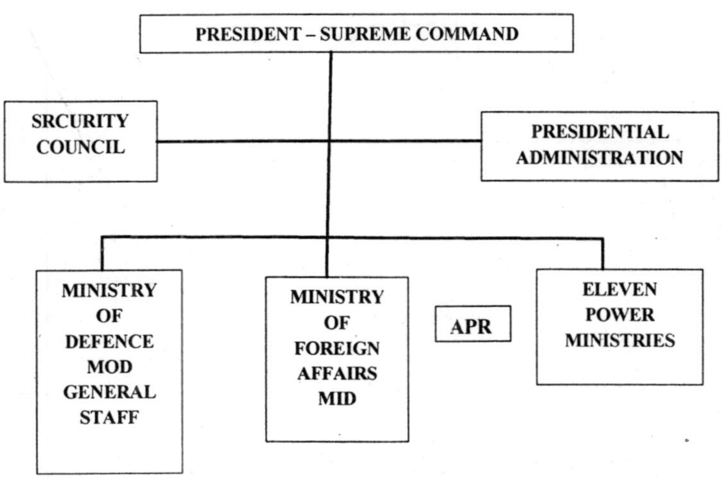

Fig. 3.31. RF Organs of National Security.

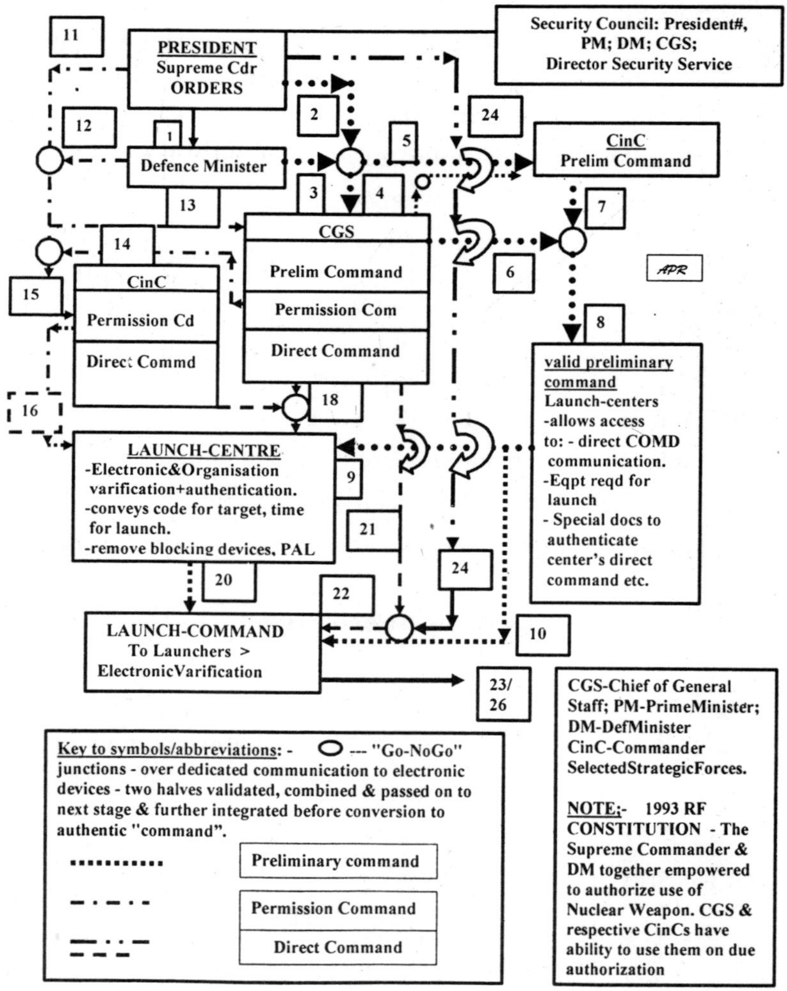

Fig. 3.32. USSR Nuclear Command Cycle.

(f) Ministry of Internal Affairs. (MVD).

(g) Federal Communication Services.

(h) Foreign Intelligence Services. (SVR).

(i) Federal Services for Special construction.

(j) State Commission on Technology.

Members of the Security Council (SCRF) / erstwhile (GKO) were not military professionals except for the CGS who was the secretary. The President's chain of military command continued to be exercised through the DM and the CGS.

The DM was the head of the MoD. The MoD continued to comprise mainly of uniformed personnel. Functionally, the illustrations at Figs. 3.25 and 3.29 were still valid. The MOD Collegiums consisted of its top officials and the service chiefs. Their main concern was with administration and providing policy planning guidance, strategic direction and leadership to the GS and the armed forces.

Operational matters were the responsibility of the GS. The GS controlled all the services through the respective Service Chiefs and the Chiefs of Main Staff. The operational command of the strategic forces was exercised by the CGS. Main Staff of the Operation Directors - managed the nitty-gritty issues. Use of nuclear weapons could only be authorised by the Supreme High Command. The SSBNs were administered, on his behalf, by the Naval Chief. It would be seen later that President Putin diluted this situation further after he positioned a civilian DM in Feb 2007.

RF NUCLEAR COMMAND CYCLE

The nuclear command cycle as it existed during the soviet regime is illustrated in the functional chart at Fig. 3.32. Normally, on the advice of the Security Council (RFSC) – the Supreme Command would authorize the use of nuclear weapon. These orders were normally required to be issued through the DM and CGS via the launch centre to the launch stations. The *command* was expected to be routed through several secure nodes and only after verification / authentication and validation by a second authority in the chain, would that order have been allowed to proceed to the next stage. Normally, it went through three stages before being operationalised:

(a) Preliminary;

(b) Permission;

(c) Direct commands

These are illustrated at Fig. 3.32. Depending on a specific contingency - there is provision for the Supreme Command to by-pass the DM and /or the CGS.

CHACHEN WAR AND ITS CONSEQUENCES

The first Chechen conflict stretched from end 1994 to Aug 1996. At the time, major tussle ensued within the military - both due to the dire state of the country's finances and the increased demands made on the GF to cope with the festering insurgency / separatist movements across the country e.g. Chechnya etc, The situation was further exasperated due to the military not being given the wherewithal necessary to fulfil the task assigned to it. To meet these commitments, within the financial constraints and having taken into account the changed global threat perception - one side was all for cutting down the size of SRF. The year 1996 also saw the Presidential election and the return of Yeltsin to power. The period also saw the sacking of Grachev and instalment of Yuri Lebed as the DM. The Challenging transformation imposed after the collapse of Soviet Union is discussed in the following paragraphs.

YELTSIN's PRESIDENTIAL DECREE OF 1997

Taking Garbachov's basic scheme forward – Yeltsin's July 1997, Presidential Decree called for a long-term phased structural reform. It demanded a phased merger / restructuring of the existing five Service structure to a four Service one and finally by 2005 to a three Service structure. At the interim phase, it called for the break-up of the ADF and attachment of Missile and Space Defence Force (M&SDF) including Anti Ballistics Missile (ABM), Electronic Warfare (EW) and Space surveillance facilities to the RSVN (SRF). Rest of the ADF – including radio technical services, SAM and Air Defence Aviation was required to be transferred to the Air Force.

Though, at the time, such a transfer was considered logical and rational – subsequently, the Strategic Rocket Force (RSVN) was found not able to cope, adequately, with managing *space* related missions, previously with the Military Space Force. They also faced considerable difficulty in managing the complex info-management structure that formed the core of the EW and Space surveillance system. Consequently, it will be seen later that, in 2000 these elements were formed into a separate Branch of the Armed Forces – reporting to the GS. And in 2002 - the prestigious RSVN (SRF) was also required to be stripped of its prime position and relegated to a Branch of the Armed Forces reporting to the GS. This is functionally superimposed on Fig. 3.30. How this played out in reality is spelt out in the succeeding paragraphs.

The process of implementing the above long pending Armed Forces reforms led to further discontentment among the military hierarchy. This was followed, in quick succession, by the dismissal of Igor Rodinov, Victor Samsanov and Batumin for poor implementation of the reform process. In their place, Igor Sergeyev (the former Chief of SRF from 1993 to 1997) and Anatoly Kvashin were appointed as the DM and CGS respectively.

The DM, Sergeyev managed to convince Yeltsin that nuclear weapon (NW) was the ultimate solution to Russia's woes. Accordingly, the Dec 1997 National Security Concept (NCP.1997) - accepted enhanced value of sub-strategic NW and withdrew its pledge to *nuclear no first use.* This was mainly perceived to compensate for the deficiencies in the conventional forces – particularly in the Far-East opposite China (PRC). At the same time, he systematically went about downgrading the Ground Force (GF). Further, to curtail any GF resistance to his restructuring programme – he appointed his candidates to key GS positions.

In August 1999 – Vladimir Putin the Director of Federal Security Services and Secretary to SCRF became the PM. The economic melt down in 1998 and the opposition to NATO's intervention in Kosovo followed by the Second round in Chechnya - again derailed the restructuring process. On 31 Dec. 1999 – Yeltsin resigned and Putin took over the reigns as the acting President. He was formally elected the President in Mar 2000. In quick succession a new Military Doctrine and

Foreign Policy Concept were given Presidential assent.

The Military Doctrine 2000 was the culmination of countless attempts / revisions since the formation of the RF. This formally shifted the focus from global threat perspective to threats emanating from within the country and elaborated on the distinction between:

(a) Ethnic / religious armed conflict within RF.

(b) Local Wars.

(c) Regional wars.

(d) Global wars.

In the case of the last two situations - extended the options to include:

(a) First use of NW in response to conventional attack.

(b) Allowed use of NW against other *Weapons of Mass Destruction* (WMD) attacks also.

(c) Extended the scope of RF security to international stability and peace etc.

Essentially, the military organisation remained the same functionally as illustrated at Fig. 3.29 - with minor adjustments. It would be observed that depending on the incumbent President – the constituents of both the Security Council and the MoD Collegiums have been changing.

In Putin's regime - the SC comprised twelve permanent members {PM, 2xDy PMs, MEA, DM, HM, Chief of President's Administration, Chief of / Domestic Intelligence [FSB] and Foreign Intelligence [SVR], Speaker of both Houses and Secretary of Council [CGS]}. Over and above that, there were twelve non voting members also. The MOD Collegiums comprise of eight members – 2x First Deputy Defence Ministers + 5x Deputy Defence Ministers (3x Service Chiefs +2) with the DM in the chair.

As opposed to his DM - the CGS, Anatoly Kvashin's analysis was considered more realistic and arrived at the conclusion that it was not the United States (US) and North Atlantic Treaty Organisation (NATO) that were the main threat to Russia but the internal conflicts in Chechnya etc. In July 2000 – this led to CGS's radical proposal to further down-grade SRF and emphasised on the GF along with closer ties with Europe and NATO. This was strongly opposed by Sergeyev the DM and MEA (MID). The situation became irreconcilable. To send a clear message that he meant business – Putin dismissed six Generals allied to the DM for obstructing the restructuring process.

In January 2001 Putin approved the Military restructuring plan taking it upto 2005. This envisaged SRF being converted to a combat Arm of the Armed Forces by 2002 and incorporated into the Air Force by 2006. He further promulgated that any one who made public comments against the plan would face instant dismissal. Finally in Mar 2001, Igor Sergeyev was also relieved and Ivanov Sergei a Federal Intelligence Agency (FSB) General took over as the DM. He was the first non military man ever appointed as the DM - customarily occupied by a career soldier.

In June 2004 a bill was passed by the Parliament – reforming the Politico Military Defence Structure which:

(a) Designated the President as the Supreme Commander and gave the DM the powers to exercise operational control.

(b) And required the CGS to implement the decisions of the DM as directed by the President. Earlier the CGS exercised operational authority over the military.

During the period 2010 to 2015 – it envisaged the Military Districts to be transformed into Joint Regional / Strategic Commands.

In February 2007 – Anatoly Serdyukov was appointed as the first civilian DM in history - putting the final *nail on the coffin,* to also symbolically project supremacy of the civil / political control over the military.

Further, in the changed global scenario and radically changed nuclear equation between the Nuclear Weapon States (NWS), the following emerged:

(a) Under the 24 May 2002 Strategic Offensive Reduction Treaty (SORT) which came into force on 01 June 2003 – US and RF agreed to cut their operationally deployed strategic war heads to 1700 – 2200 over a ten year period.

(b) The improved relationship between USA and RF was pushing them towards - Mutually Assured Security from their earlier MAD posture of the cold war years.

(c) As a result of economic / financial constraints and Russia's incapability to match USA or stay ahead of China in the nuclear race - called for a change in approach demanding that the naval contribution to the Russian triad would need to be increased up to 50% of the total nuclear delivery systems.

(d) SORT was replaced by the *new START treaty* on 08 April 2010. This is legally binding, verifiable and restricts the deployed strategic nuclear warheads to 1500 and strategic delivery systems (including ICBMs, SLBMs and Strategic Bombers) to 700. The treaty came into force on 05 February 2011 and is effective up to 05 February 2021.

According to Presidential decree No 836 of 25 May 2008 (and as amended periodically up to No 718 of 07 June 2011) – the RFSC under Medvedev comprised the following permanent members: PM, Federal Security Service Director, State Dumas Speaker, Foreign Minister (FM), Federation Council Speaker, Head of Presidential Administration, Interior Minister, Security Council Permanent Secretary, DM, Foreign Intelligence Service Director and former FSB Director Nikolai Patrushen.

In the RFSC the CGS is one of seventeen additional members included subsequently.

Significant reforms were also announced in late 2008 by DM Serdyukov. Major second phase restructuring that began in 2009 called for following:

(a) Reduction in Armed forces strength from 1.2 million to 1.0 million.

(b) Cut in Military Units by:

  (i) 90% in Ground Force.

  (ii) 48% in the Air Force.

  (iii) 49% in the Navy.

  (iv) 30% in Strategic Missile Forces.

(c) Reduction in over all officer cadre strength by 61%.

(d) Concerted effort to professionalise the military by progressively converting from conscription to a volunteer force. In 2008 almost 4.8 lakhs were conscripted into the Army.

(e) The conscription period had to be reduced to one year from two years earlier.

The Russian military is now divided into following branches:

(a) Ground Forces.

(b) Air Force.

(c) Navy.

In addition there are now three independent arms of Service – all reporting directly to the centre:

(a) Strategic Missile Force.

(b) Military Space Force.

(c) Russian Airborne Troops.

The 14 July 2010 Presidential decree – transformed, the existing six MDs into the following four Strategic Operation Commands (SOC). Turning these Commands into full fledged entities will take some time. All sections of the military, including the Navy, Air Force and the Air Defence units in the region will be required to operate like integral *components* of the Command. An attempt was being made to move towards the US Unified Command model. For this to be effective in the existing global scenario - will require a mind-set change from the ground force centric approach earlier:

(a) Central Strategic Command with HQs at Yekaterinburg.

(b) Southern Strategic Command with HQs at Rostov –Na-Donu.

(c) Eastern Strategic Command with HQs at Khabarovsk.

(d) Western Strategic Command with HQs at St Petersburg.

As per report of the Russian Institute of Contemporary Development (INSOR) 2011 – in 2005, 30% of the Russian Armed Forces were contract servicemen. Their recommendation was that by 2018 the armed Forces should aim to transit into an all volunteer force.

Bibliography

1. Anne C Aldis and Roger N McDermott "Russian Military Reforms - 1992 – 2002". 2003.
2. en.wikipedia.org/wki/Armed_Forces_of_the _Russian_Federation
3. http://www.bu.edu/phpbinnews-cms/news/?dept=732&id=56306
4. http://www.cia.gov/library/publication/the-world-factbook/geos/rs.html
5. http://www.zampawiki.com/?t=Ministry_of_Defence_(Russia)
6. http://www.zampawiki.com/?t=Russia_Space_Force_(VKSI)
7. Lt. Gen Pahwa "Command and Control Indian Nuclear Forces". 2002.
8. Marcel De Hass "Russian Security and Air Power – 1992 – 2002" 2004.
9. Mark Galeoth " Force Projection – the future of Russian Military Reforms" Janes Intelligence Review. February 2010.
10. Miller and Trennin "The Russian Military". 2004.
11. Paul J Murphy "Naval Power in Soviet Policy".
12. Pavel Podvig "Russian Strategic Nuclear Forces". 2001.
13. Robert L Pfaltzgraft "National Security Policy". 1984.
14. www.fas.org/nuke/guide/russia/doctrine.concept.in
15. www.scrf.gov.ru/Document/Decree/2000/07-10html - "Foreign Policy Concept ratified 28 June 2000.
16. www.scrf.gov.ru/Document/Decree/2000/706-1-html - "Military Doctrine Ratified" 21 Apr 2000.
17. www.scrf.gov.ru/Documents/decree/2000/24-10html - "National Security Concept ratified" 10Jan2000.
18. http//www.scrf.gov.ru/persons/section/6/ - Composition of RFSC – Presidential decree No836 of 25 May 2008 as amended by No. 718 of 07 June 2011.

4

Transformation of China's People's Liberation Army

INTRODUCTION

While pondering over the extent / pace of restructuring that India ought to adopt - India needs to pause and consider the revolutionary changes that the other nations have been compelled to subject themselves to and under much more severe conditions. Earlier Chapters have already considered - the United States of America (US), United Kingdom (UK) and Russian Federation (RF) scenario. Now there is a need to look at People's Republic of China (PRC) also.

Looking at China is not an easy proposition. As far as the politico-military organisational structure is concerned – it is for all practical purposes a mirror image of what existed in Union of Soviet Socialist Republic (USSR), at a point of time. Being a closed and opaque society – access to information to outsiders is difficult. To make any realistic assessment – one is mostly dependent on information released by the state. Separating facts from fiction is not a simple exercise. Information is often conveyed to its targeted audience selectively and in their own characteristic manner.

In the circumstances, after reviewing the available literature on the subject – an attempt is made here, to make as realistic an assessment as possible. PLA's evolution and its restructuring efforts need to be considered in the back-drop of evolving and ongoing changes in the overall political / social / economic environment in China.

HISTORICAL PERSPECTIVE

People's Liberation Army (PLA) was launched primarily with a peasant / rural base – run under a communist political / social revolutionary banner. It started as a peasant's revolutionary army. It took up arms with the aim to bring in a communist government through a revolution, against the so called feudal Chiang Kai Sheik's Kuomintang (KMT) government.

Perforce the bulk of the PLA, at that stage, comprised uneducated peasants and rural population. Primary motivation was the communist ideology indoctrination. Russian revolution was their icon and the Soviet systems were embraced enthusiastically. As will be shown later – the PLA has had to cope with more than their share of restructuring to keep pace with its ever changing environment.

Historically, PLA traces its origin to the 1920s. The PLA came to being as the Chinese Communist Party's (CCP) military arm and remained so until the PRC was established in 1949 – after KMT was vanquished and expelled from the mainland. However, only in 1954 - the PRC's first Constitution formally promulgated that *"the Chairman of the PRC"* would command the nation's Armed Forces. In 1959, however, Mao Zedong reversed this position and asserted his personal authority over the PLA through the party Central Military Commission (CMC). This was later formalised in the Constitution – post, the *Cultural Revolution (CR)* in the late 1970s.

The fifth National People's Congress (NPC) session in November 1982 - established a new PRC-CMC. But they did not abolish the Party CMC. To differentiate between the two - the State CMC is sometimes referred to as National Military Council (NMC). Eventually, a compromise solution was evolved retaining the same members in both the CMC and the NMC. Also, Deng Xiaoping was made the chairman of both the Commissions. In effect, this situation continues till date.

The evolution of the PLA from its inception could, for convenience, be divided into three broad phases:

(*a*) *Revolutionary* Phase.

(*b*) *Politisation* Phase.

(c) *Professionalisation* Phase.

The PLA's evolution needs also to be viewed, along with the generational changes on the political front. The personalities involved, along with the characteristics of the period are listed below for a better understanding of the process:

(a) First Generation –is associated with the *long-march* and linked to *people's war group* and Mao Zedong.

(b) Second Generation –is associated with the anti–Japanese war, *local war group* and Deng Xiaoping period. Most first and second Generation leaders started their careers, with some exposure to western countries and later USSR.

(c) Third Generation – is associated with the Socialist Transformation and Jiang Zemin. By this generation – the leaders had lost their *"made in USSR"* label. The war over demarcation of the boundary across *Usuri* River finally broke the long standing relationship. After May 1989 Tiananmen Square incident - the military was put under Jiang Zemin. In May 1998 the PLA was directed to pull out, from commercial holdings. Revisions were initiated in National Defence Strategy. The 1993 strategy of fighting a regional war under *high technological conditions,* gave way to conditions of *informationalisation. And in* 2002 / 03 – *to Revolution in Military Affairs (RMA)* – leading to a composite dual mission *of mechanisation and information-based military.*

(d) Fourth Generation – The present generation represented by Hu Jin Tao and Wen Jiabao, stands for *the RMA school of thought.* They have the indigenous stamp firmly imprinted on them. Hu Jin Tao was instrumental in appointing the all civilian Politburo Standing Committee and led the *party guided military* reforms. The military was gradually weaned out, of the top party decision making bodies examples are the Politburo, the Standing Committee and the NPC.

Break-up of USSR, the Warsaw Pact and termination of the cold war period has eventually brought back PRC and RF together.

(e) Fifth Generation - is likely to take over the reigns in 2013

(f) Sixth Generation - is expected to come to power, after the 20th NPC in 2020.

REVOLUTIONARY PHASE: 1927 – 1949

The Revolutionary period could be characterised by the following:

(a) Initially, strict political control over military was exercised through the institution of the *commissar,* at every layer.

(b) To begin with – most commissars were non military. By 1930s – more and more commissars rose to the position from the army.

(c) Though, theoretically, the *Commander (Cdr) and the Commissars* were considered equivalent in status – the Cdr, on the ground, had a clear edge over the commissar – particularly at the operational level. The Commissar's responsibility was focused on political / legal affairs, morale, propaganda and liaison with civil authorities.

(d) The institutional formulation also favoured the Cdr – due to the power of numbers, of his fraternity, in the Party Committees taking decisions.

(e) Also, in due course - the reforms under way, gave better promotion prospect to the military. As a result, most PLA officers preferred a Cdr's post to a job in the political department.

(f) Long March – 1934 – 1935.

(g) Yanan Period 1935 – 1948.

(h) So called *War of liberation* – July 1946 to Jun 1950.

POLITISATION PHASE: 1949 – 1978

The *Politisation* phase is identified with following developments :

(a) In 1955, PLA had just started getting over the effects of the Korean War.

(b) PLA got extensively involved in both policy making and power struggle at all levels.

(c) PLA effectively became the only functional institution in PRC - as Mao deliberately destroyed the bureaucracy, in both administration and party mechanism.

(d) Cultural Revolution: 1966 – 1969.

(e) During 1966–76 - PLA got deeply involved in commercial activities and took over many enterprises. They became proficient at local entrepreneurship. Soon profiteering, racketeering, corruption and bribery became rampant. This became part of their daily life – jeopardising professionalism and morale of the Forces.

(f) In 1975-76 – Deng Xiaoping was once again rehabilitated and became the Supreme Commander. He tried to *defactionalize*, restructure, modernize and professionalise the PLA. Unfortunately, with the demise of Zao-En-Lai in Jan 1976 – his efforts were brought to a close. Deng was accused of being involved in the *Gang of Four* counter revolution riots and sent to political exile once again.

PROFESSIONALISATION PHASE

Professionalisation is an ongoing phase. The outcome of 1979 Vietnam War was there, for every one to see. PLA set out to teach Vietnam a lesson but landed up with a bloody nose instead. They had to pay the price for allowing diversion of their attention to economic activities rather than focusing on professional training and preparing for their primary task. PLA emerged with its credentials in shreds.

Before the lessons learnt could be sincerely implemented – PLA was once again dragged into party politics. Quelling of the *Tiananmen Square* demonstration and dealing with its aftermath within the PLA took precedence. This was yet again a traumatic period for the PLA. Which was soon followed by attempts to again depoliticise the PLA, under a new CMC chairman Jiang Zemin, with a fresh mandate.

By April 1998 – PLA was totally cut-off from commercial activities. Command and control system was completely overhauled - leading to a Unified PLA General Armament Department (GAD) alongside the General Staff Department (GSD) / General Political and Logistics Departments (GPD) and (GLD). The years 2002 / 2003 also saw the PLA transiting through – *mechanisation* and *informationalisation* based Military, to *Revolution in Military Affairs* (RMA).

This period was also marked with serious social / constitutional upheavals – finally leading the way to a Chinese style, free market economy. Progressively, it brought about, in its wake :

(a) Recognition of self employment - as a supplement to the state economy.

(b) Gradual social changes - bringing about transfer of people's commune responsibility to the house holds.

(c) Acceptability of private management of state enterprises. This further led to loosening of the state control over manpower and resources.

(d) Strict implementation of the *one child family norm* - brought about a total demographic change in the social fabric. The house-hold structure took the form of 4:2:1 (four grand parents, two parents and one child). This in turn brought about a marked change in the family out look – particularly, in rural surroundings – where the social *safety net* was least effective. As a result, there was serious resistance in complying with the conscription programme. And the source of maximum conscription started drying up.

(e) Market forces linked to economic reforms – created larger demand for human resources and offered better prospects in civil occupations.

(f) Exodus of rural population to urban centres - seeking for lucrative jobs.

(g) Considerable portion of youth eligible for conscription - escaping the net.

(h) The respective Regions that had the responsibility to provide the allotted conscription quota, becoming a victim to this dilemma. The scope for corruption became immense. Fudging of age, qualification, state of health etc led to considerable dilution in quality of intake.

To off-set the above disadvantages – the establishment had to resort to following means:

(a) To reduce burden on elderly parents, with only one child – the period of conscription for the Army was reduced from 3/4 years to 2 years.

(b) Offering the following, as an incentive to prospective officer candidates. This was to become effective only after completion of conscription period :

(i) Sponsor scholarships to college.

(ii) Choice preference for subjects in college.

(iii) Absorption in civil sector.

(c) To meet the upgraded requirement of officers – after 1984 - the induction of officers from the ranks was discontinued.

(d) As part of the restructuring – along with large-scale demobilisation – the proportion of NCO recruitment was vastly increased.

In spite of all the incentives – the response from University graduates to join the PLA remains disappointing.

This phase is also characterised by a marked shift in the political arena – from personalised leadership to an institutionalised / collective leadership. The transition from the third to the fourth and then on to the on-going fifth generation - seems to indicate a systematic, gradual and deliberate effort in deemphasising any political role for the military. The emerging factional groups in the arena are introducing a new dimension to the game. The three important factions likely to effect the evolving civil-military dynamics are:

(a) The Communist Youth League (CYL).

(b) The Gang of Prince-lings (Off springs of service officials and ministers having a strong constitution in the military). (GPL)

(c) The military itself.

In the above context, an interesting statistical data, relevant to the current period, is listed below. This could serve as an indicator of what to expect in the future. And needs to be closely monitored:

Central Committee (CC) of NPC

(a) Over twenty percent of the CC of NPC belongs to the CYL.

Standing Committee (SC) of NPC

(b) All members of the SC of NPC are graduates.

(c) Almost eighty percent of the SC members are engineers.

(d) There is no military representation in the SC.

Politburo Members (PB)

(e) Over thirty percent of the PB members belong to the CYL.

(f) Almost half of the PB members are newly elected.

(g) The PB only has two military members.

Central / National Military Commission (CMC) / (NMC)

(h) The CMC comprise of :

- (i) The PRC President / CINC Armed Forces / as the Chairman of the CMC.
- (ii) Two PB members i.e. Vice Chairman: Generals Guo Boxing and Xu Cai Hao.
- (iii) The Defence Minister – a member of the State Council.
- (iv) PLA Chief of General Staff (CGS).
- (v) Directors of GPD, GLD and GAD.
- (vi) Three Commanders of PLAN, PLAAF and Second Artillery.
- (vii) Xi Jinping – the PRC Vice President and likely leader of fifth generation leadership.

TRANSFORMATION OF PLA - SLOGANS / BANNERS and GROUND REALITY

Ever since the formation of PRC – national unification and territorial integrity remains the corner-stone of China's strategic calculus. The military build up / restructuring efforts to achieve that goal naturally had to be commensurate with the economic, technological and human resource available, during the respective phases. Some of the important milestones traversed during the restructuring process, are listed chronologically, in the following paragraphs.

By late 1970s – Deng Xiaoping had come to recognize the fact that the PLA's debacle at Vietnamese hand, was brought about by the total unpreparedness and severe lack of professional training in the PLA cadre. As discussed earlier, the primary reason for the dire state of the PLA was attributed to the *politicisation phase*. At that stage of China's history - Deng set the goal towards *peace and development.* Accordingly, he changed the priority for resource allocation too. Some of the highlights of his reformation moves are as follows:

(a) His *four modernisation schemes* put the military at the bottom of the list – below industry, agriculture and science and technology.

(b) To cut out the flab - a deep cut in the PLA strength by one million was announced.

(c) Shifted the emphasis of *motorisation* to *mechanisation* for the PLA.

(d) Offered an extension of service option to the conscripts, before retirement.

(e) With the object of bringing about qualitative enhancement in the officer cadre - the option for direct promotion from the rank was withdrawn.

As time went by – with the increase in prosperity and continuing economic growth – it became possible for China to change tack and divert more and more of its resources, progressively, towards modernising the military capabilities to meet its territorial ambitions. What was on the backburner earlier was systematically brought forward with determination.

The 2002 Defence White Paper (DWP) high-lighted the following important land mark achievements in the field of Human Resource Development (HRD) indices:

(a) A marked improvement in the technical / educational level of the PLA officers.

(b) There was extensive generational turnover in the PLA leadership.

(c) In the period 1985 to 2003, China claims to have

demobilised a record number of 1.7 million personnel from the PLA.

In DWP 2004 – particular emphasis was laid on '*RMA with Chinese Characteristics*' as the guiding principle of Defence reforms. At that time, a serious debate was raging - as to whether China should try accomplishing *mechanisation* and *digitisation*, as articulated by Jiang Zemin or follow Hu Jintao's idea of leapfrogging straight to *informationalisation* phase.

In 2005 – Russia / China military cooperation entered a new phase. For the first time - transfer of doctrine / tactics and such software became a part of the deal. Submarines (S/Ms) from both countries participated in blockade, anti-ship and ASW exercises, as part of the '*Peace Mission 2005*' combined exercises. This was the first time that the PLAN s/ms exercised with a modern professional Navy.

The DWP 2007 indicated the following time-frame for their three stage PLA modernisation strategy:

(a) By 2010 – accomplish mechanisation.

(b) By 2020 – be well on the way to *informationalisation*.

(c) By2050 —complete *modernisation* of the military-incorporating *informationalisation* to its full extent.

In context of China's integrity and security - the DWP 2008, for the first time, formally included – social instability in the Tibetan and Xinjiang region in their calculus of threat perceptions. Till then their focus was on Taiwan.

Iraq / Afghanistan / Kosovo wars had a deep impression on China. In the wars - the US and its allied forces clearly demonstrated their information technology (IT) prowess. Simultaneous attacks with long range precision strikes, in a multi-dimensional scenario had become a reality.

PLA was still in the process of transiting from *foot-soldiering* to *motorisation / mechanisation* phases. It was realised that this technology divide, was far too wide, to be able to be bridged, in any reasonable period. In spite of, adequate financial resources becoming available - considerable difficulty was being experienced, in acquiring cutting edge capabilities. This was accentuated by the very restrictive international embargo, put in place - in response, to the Tiananmen Square crack-down.

Russian Federation (RF) was the only source, readily willing to respond. It was realised that indigenous development, was indeed the most desirable option – but involved a long drawn process.

The DWP 2010 released in March 2011, takes the perestroika a step further – emphasising, on transformation in the following areas:

(a) Integral Army Aviation.

(b) Integrated and multifunctional support force with rapid response capability.

(c) Composite combat and support basis – linking strategic, operational and tactical levels.

(d) Create, enhanced psychological service by 2014 to provide, at least:

  (i) One therapist per regiment.

  (ii) Three psychological assistants for each company level institution.

To overcome the serious handicaps brought out earlier – China was driven to adopt a two pronged innovative strategy. This was over and above the on-going immediate hardware up gradation programme, with Russian assistance. That was being pursued in parallel, with vigour:

(a) Informationalisation with Chinese character.

(b) Assassin's mace programme.

Informationalisation with Chinese character – meant China abandoning the costly and time consuming western model of sequential modernisation, in favour of *leapfrogging* into *informationalisation* directly. Perfecting the *mechanisation* process, could wait. The thrust was directed to selectively, prioritise and focus on Information Technology (IT) and develop specific pockets of excellence. And go about, perfecting conventional force capabilities in due course.

The terminology *"Assassin's Mace' / "Shashanjian"* has emerged after a famous Chinese folklore – akin to the *sling-shot* fable associated with *David and Goliath.* This strategy was evolved to counter the overwhelming superiority that the

US enjoyed. The emphasis of the *Assassin's Mace programme* was to:

(a) Identify and target the critical vulnerable areas of the adversary C4ISR (Command, Control, Communication, Computer, Intelligence, Surveillance and Reconnaissance) systems.

(b) Achieve selective Electro-magnetic (EM) combat superiority.

(c) Focus on building Anti-Satellite (ASAT) and Anti-Ballistic Missile (ABM) capabilities.

(d) Develop information warfare tools and viruses to attack and immobilise enemy networks etc.

(e) Develop stealth combat aircraft J20 and quietly prioritise the unmanned underwater vehicle (UVV) projects.

ORGANISATIONAL STRUCTURE REFORMS - PRESENT STATUS

Functionally, the PRC's politico-military organisational structure is basically, a derivative of the Soviet system. For historical reasons, the institutions are labelled differently. And, as in the Soviet system - the Communist Party organs permeate right down to the unit level.

The National Peoples Congress (NPC) is the highest decision making body and is the ultimate authority, on state policy. It has a term of five years and is convened annually. It comprises the Central Committee (CC) chaired by the General Secretary. The CC is elected by the NPC for a five year term. The Politburo (PB), its Standing Committee (SC) and the General Secretary are all elected, at the plenary session of the CC. The SC is also elected, for a term of five years and is convened, every alternate month. When the CC is not in session – the SC and the PB exercise its powers. The Secretariat looks after the day to day bureaucratic functions of the government. The PRC President is normally the General Secretary of the CCP and the head of the Secretariat. The SC also included Deputies elected from the Armed Forces. At the moment, this practice has been discontinued.

The Central Military Commission (CMC) is the Supreme High Command. All its members are appointed by the NPC and are party members. The Chairman is the state President and the CinC of the Armed Forces. Normally, he has also been the General Secretary of CCP. The membership is not very rigid nor is it constitutionally specific. It has varied from time to time – on the basis of the inclination of the leadership and prevalent environmental conditions. Today, the CMC comprises of :

(a) Two PB members.

(b) The Defence Minister (who is a councillor in the State Council, under the Premier).

(c) The PLA Chief of General Staff (CGS).

(d) Members of the General Political / Logistic / Armament Departments (GPD, GLD AND GAD).

(e) The three Commanders of the Armed Forces (i.e. Navy, Air force and Second Artillery).

(f) The up and coming, fifth generation leader Xi Jinping (the current Vice President of PRC) -who was inducted in 2010.

The State Council is a government apparatus as opposed to a *party* body – under which the Ministry of National Defence (MND) and the State National Defence Mobilisation Commission operates. This arrangement is at present undergoing a process of transformation. Progressively, more authority is being delegated to the State Council.

Events since the mid1980s, also, give an impression of a slow but deliberate attempt to transform the *party-military* relationship to a *party-state-military* relationship. The military also seems to be trying to assert its corporate autonomy from the *party* without in any way impinging on its party loyalty. In any case, all colonels and above are necessarily members of the CP. This is reinforced by the National Defence Law 1997 – which only talks about, subordination of the *military* to the *state* and no where does it mention - any *Party* control. This gives the impression of intent - to significantly shift the *civil-military* relationship.

One will have to wait and see how this eventually plays-out, in reality. This, however, can not be expected to fall into the classic western style of an *apolitical-professional-military-*

civil relationship. All it seems to imply is that the *baton* is in the process of being passed-on from the *party* to the *state* institutions. The military will continue to be required to be loyal to the party. In this context, at one level, the party is considered synonymous with the state. This dichotomy continues to exist. The dual relationship is at present sustained by the NMC and CMC coexisting in parallel and having the same constituent members – including the General Secretary and the Supreme Commander continuing to be the Chairman of both the organisation.

The General Armament Department (GAD) was created in an effort to replicate the French *Delegation generale pour I'armement.* It is still in its formative years and is an organisation in transit. In the Indian context, the GAD is meant to eventually, perform the combined equivalent function of the Secretary of Defence Production, Defence Research and Development Organisation and the Special Secretary Acquisition.

The Politico-Military Functional Organisational Tree is illustrated at Fig.4.33. It will be seen that at the fourth echelon – there is the General Staff Department (GSD), General Political Department (GPD), General Logistics Department (GLD) and General Armament Department (GAD). The Peoples Liberation Army (PLA), PLAN (Navy), PLAAF (Air Force), the Second Artillery and People's Armed Police (PAP) are all at the fifth echelon. Important deviations to note here are: the inclusion of the People's Armed Police and the direct command link of the CMC with the Second Artillery through the GSD. The PAP has a dual link with the State Council also. The next echelon comprise the seven Military Regions (MR) followed by Military Districts (MD) and Sub-Districts etc.

The GSD is the largest and the most important of the four main departments. It has a highly centralised set up – with a mini Head Quarters (HQ) element permeating down to the sub-district levels. The GSD has the following main departments. Most of the main departments are mirrored and replicated down the line:

(a) First Department – Operations.

(b) Second Department- Intelligence.

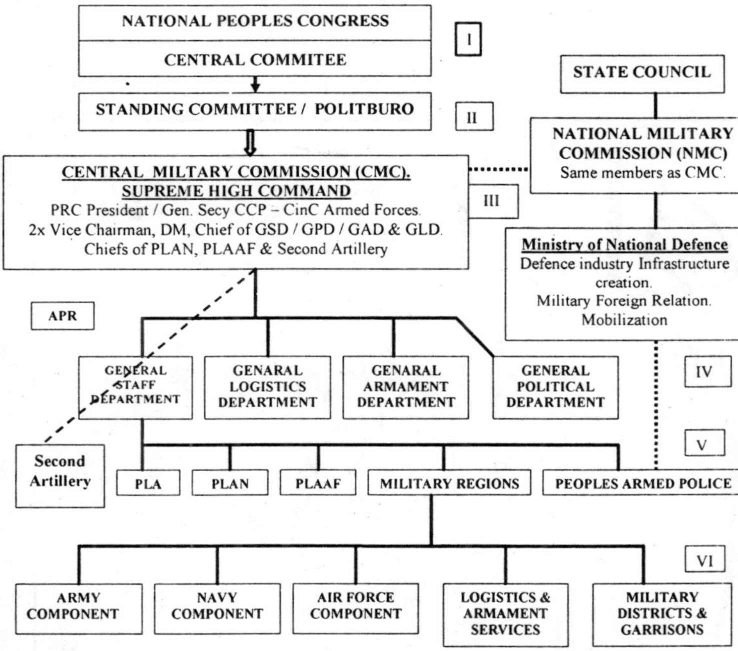

Abbreviations used:
PLA – People's Liberation Army; PLAN – PLA Navy; PLAAF – PLA Air force.
GHQ – General Headquarters; PRC – Peoples Republic of China;
CCP – Chinese Communist Party; DM – Defence Minister; CinC – Commander in Chief.
GSD – General Staff Department; GLD – General Logistics Department;
GPD – General Political Department; GAD – General Armament Department.
PAP – People's Armed Police:

Fig. 4.33. Functional Command Structure of Chinese Armed Forces.

(c) Third Department- Communication.

(d) Fourth Department- ECM and Radar.

(e) Fifth Department- Manpower, Organisation and Planning.

(f) Sixth Department- Training.

(g) Seventh Department- Service Arms – Artillery, Armour and Engineers etc.

(h) Eighth Department- Army Aviation.

(i) Ninth Department- Foreign Affairs.

(j) Tenth Department- Mobilisation.

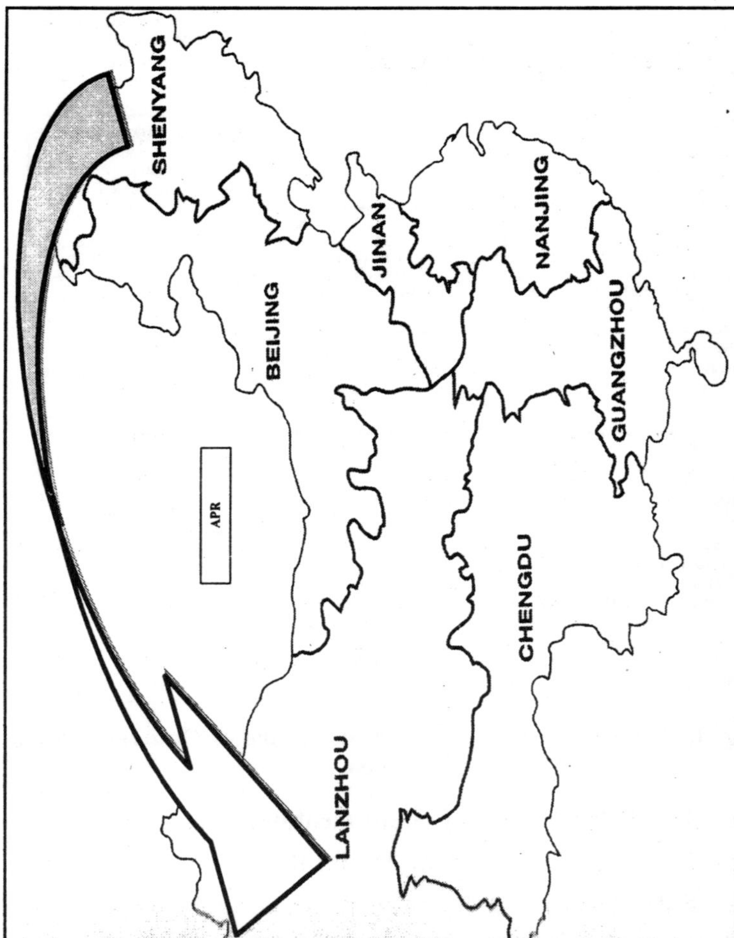

Fig. 4.34. prc Military Districts and *Kuauyue* Regional Mobility Exercise 2009.

The continental China has been divided into seven Military Regions (MR)s and further divided into Military Districts (MD)s. For orientation purposes - Fig. 4.34 illustrates lay-out of the seven regions. The Army, Air force, Logistics and Armament Department, and where applicable, the regional Naval units are subordinate to the Regional Commander. All the four are represented at Regional Head Quarters (RHQ) by their respective Component Commanders – who are overseen by the MR Chief of Staff. Invariably, the Regional Commander belongs to the Ground forces and he is assisted by a Political Commissar. The Military District Commander among his other duties is required to oversee the logistic depots, bases and armament repair / maintenance depots in his district. The Garrison has the duties of guarding military facilities and carry out military policing (MP) functions in his region. This arrangement is presently under review.

The PRC did not inherit the five service system from the Soviets. They were basically a three service system - till the emergence of the Second Artillery in late 1988. Though the Second Artillery is a strategic force, directly controlled by the CMC – it has not been given the status of a *Service* but is considered a *Branch* of the Military. Being a continental entity and for historical reasons – the military has been Ground Force (GF) centric. Unlike the Soviet military's decentralisation plan introduced by Marshal Ogarkov in the 1980s - the PLA continues in a highly centralised mode. The military modernisation drive was initially focused on *mechanisation* leading to more, lean, mean, mobile, technologically advanced forces. For reasons explained earlier - every effort is being made now to upgrade the skills with emphasis on attaining asymmetric superiority over the adversary. Intensive drive has been initiated to recruit graduates as officers directly from the universities. In human resource, their main weakness lies with the Non-Commissioned Officer (NCO) cadre and their inability to get conscripts of the required technical calibre. A realistic assessment of their *'human system performance capabilities'* is of paramount importance to India. Historically their capability / performance as a soldier on the battle-field is well recorded – whether it was during their National Revolution against the KMT, the war in Korea or against India in 1962 and similarly the failed attempt to humiliate / teach a lesson to Vietnam. The outcome, subsequent to the attempted introduction of RMA into the game is an ongoing process and its end result is yet to be ascertained.

PLA NAVY (PLAN)

The PLAN has evolved their naval strategy on the basis of Soviet experience / practice and adopted the Soviet style "Bastion Strategy" to its environment / circumstances. For maritime defence purposes, particularly in the Soviet Far-East (FE) – the Soviet Navy had divided their domain into following rough zones:

(a) Innermost area for sea control.
(b) Middle zone for sea denial regime.
(c) Further- most zone – region for Long Range (LR) reconnaissance and submarine interdiction.

During the cold war period - the Soviet Navy knew that, in the immediate future they could not be expected to take on the US carrier battle groups head-on, with carrier groups of its own. Hence, they concentrated their energies towards building submarine (s/m) interdiction and long range stand-off strike capabilities. Their response was in the form of *Slava, Sovromenny, Akula, Delta IV, Tu22M* etc. The carrier, at that stage, would only have been a liability and extremely vulnerable to USN's far superior carrier task forces. Accordingly, the carrier project was processed at a low priority. It is another matter that by the time they graduated to *Kuznitsov* / nuclear powered *Ulyanovsk* and were getting ready to launch into the higher league - that the Soviet Union (SU) itself collapsed.

PRC's long term goal is to become a global super-power. To attain that objective – they realize that China needs regional and global peace, tranquillity and unimpaired freedom to grow. For assessing their progress towards that goal, they have formulated / coined a new realistic and over-arching yardstick in the form of CNP. The Comprehensive National Power (CNP) is the summation of military, economic, scientific, technological and social development index that manifests itself in the ability to govern also. To meet their above national objectives they have devised a short / medium / long term plan. Presently the thrust of all military modernisation is directed towards that end. This has given birth to following concepts – akin to that followed by Soviet Union (SU) under similar constraints:

(a) *"Assassin's Mace" / "Shashanjian"* strategy.

(b) First, Second and Third island chains – to meet their threat perceptions in South/East China Sea, Sea of Japan, Philippeen Sea and the East Pacific Ocean regions.

(c) SSBN bastion at Hainan.

(d) String of Pearls strategy – to meet the long term goal in the Indian Ocean Region (IOR) – in respect of an assured SLC protection, to fulfil their energy needs and over-seas commercial interest.

(e) Development of Anti Satellite (ASAT) / Anti Ballistic Missile (ABM) capability.

(f) Development of J20 stealth combat a/c. An American citizen has been convicted for passing on stealth aircraft design data to China. The extent of Russian contribution towards this project is also very speculative. A realistic evaluation must wait for some time.

(g) Quietly prioritise the development of Unmanned Underwater Vehicle (UVV).

China's hectic pace of hardware modernisation – particularly in respect of the Navy, Air-Force and the Second Artillery is very visible. It is well dovetailed into their long term objectives. Acquisition of *Sovremenny* class destroyers, 877 EKM s/ms from Russian Federation (RF), deployment of new Nuclear Powered Attack S/M (SSN) (093), Nuclear Powered Ballistic Missile S/M (SSBN)s (094) along with their S/M Launched Ballistic Missile (SLBM)s, supported by their massive indigenous surface ships and s/m building programme are all indicative of their determination. A large cruiser size warship, similar to the soviet *'Slava'* class is also reported to be building at the Dalyan ship-yard.

In parallel, they are working quietly but aggressively towards building carrier battle groups, to field in the long term. Time, effort and expenses incurred in acquiring Varyag from Ukraine and several other decommissioned carriers and catapult and arrester gear from RF etc are clear indications of their determination and intents. According to an US assessment – China could include an indigenous aircraft carrier (Project

089) in the next five year plan, launched in March 2011. Also, China is planning for a mega nuclear aircraft carrier (Project 085) in the next phase for 2020. This is expected to be similar in design to the aborted soviet *'Ulynosk'* class carrier. In addition, according to an Indian Express report Varyag has now been renamed *Shilang.* And that the first group of naval aviation pilots are undergoing carrier operation training and are due to pass out of the Academy in 2012.

The PLAN is no doubt severely handicapped due to human resource development (HRD) deficiencies discussed earlier and their serious combat inexperience, in the maritime domain. Presumably, before transfer of the sophisticated ships mentioned earlier – the PLAN has received in-depth training and work-up with the Russian Fleet. Also, in 2005, Russian Navy and PLAN defence export regime, entered a new phase. Transfer of doctrine / tactics for the first time became a part of defence cooperation. S/Ms from both the Navies participated in blockade, anti-ship and Anti Submarine Warfare (ASW) exercises as a part of *Peace Mission 2005* joint exercises. This was the first time that PLAN s/ms exercised with modern blue water Navy. Though they have no maritime combat experience – these should give them a leg up. It would be interesting to see how PLAN proposes to transform a conscript Navy to a professional all volunteer force in a period of four years – as directed by DWP of 2010.

Notwithstanding the unveiling of the J20 stealth combat aircraft in January 2011 and the massive indigenous ship and s/m building programme - the present trend of large scale import of cutting edge technology, particularly into the Navy and the Air force seems to indicate that for tactical reasons, there has been a shift in emphasis, from indigenisation to rapid induction of hardware. Parallely, the emphasis has shifted to acquiring asymmetric capabilities both in the hardware and the soft-ware domain.

CONCLUSIONS

There can be little doubt that China's ultimate objective is to become a super-power. For the time being, for global consumption, they are projecting an image of a benign, emerging power, seeking international justice and having no extra-territorial ambitions, out side its traditional boundaries.

Their proclaimed core national objective may be summarised as follows:

(a) Regional peace and tranquillity to enable sustained growth and national prosperity.

(b) Focus on building and consolidating China's Comprehensive National Power.

(c) Maintain territorial integrity of the state, with emphasis on:

(i) Reclamation of Taiwan.

(ii) Keeping at bay, powers perceived to be inimical to their national objectives.

(iii) Containment of dissent and break-away tendencies amongst minority communities – especially in Tibet and Xinjiang etc.

(iv) Keeping Terrorism at bay.

(d) Protect Sea Lane of Communication (SLC) to meet the increased energy needs and commercial interests of its people.

With the above aganda – a summary of PRC's success story in the transformation of PLA is listed in the following paragraphs.

PLA has come a long way from the time they *got a rubbing* at the hands of Vietnam in 1970. Full credit must be given to the political leadership for bringing them out of the abyss. It is no mean achievement to :

(a) Demobilise up to 1.7 million PLA cadre personnel.

(b) Raise the educational level of PLA officers from less than two percent graduates to over ninety percent.

(c) Break PLA out of the grips of commercial activities.

(d) Wean them out of all political institutions of power.

(e) Empower them professionally – by including them in the CMC – the Supreme Command Authority of the State.

(f) Lead the PLA from *foot-slogging* phase to *motorisation, mechanisation* and on to *RMA with informationalisation* and *Chinese characteristics,* as the core objective.

(g) Since this is a long drawn process – as an immediate measure they have adopted the strategy of:

informationalisation with *Chinese characteristics* and adoption of *Assassin's Mace* strategy.

Some of the other high-lights of the PLA *perestroika* attempts are summarised in the succeeding paragraphs.

Hardware acquisition programmes have been in the forefront of PLA's modernisation attempt. In high technology areas, PLA is largely dependent on Russia. In recent times, the thrust of hardware modernisation has been directed towards the Navy, Air Force and the Second Artillery – in that order of priority. It is well dovetailed into their long term national objectives.

In conformity with the *informationalisation* and Joint Operation compulsions - a concerted effort is also under way to modernise the archaic Logistics and Equipment Support Services. Further, to cope with the insurgency / terrorism / separatist movements in such regions as Tibet and Xingjian etc. – the capability for Military Operations other than War (MOOTW) has been considerably enhanced. The orientation of the Regional Commands and its establishment is also undergoing a mind-set change, to prepare for trans-regional operational possibilities. It is reported that in 2009 – a mobilisation exercise involving movement of two divisional size formations from North East MR (Shenyang MR) to South Western MR (Lanzhou MR) on to Ladhak border was conducted. This indicates how seriously they are working on developing their inter-regional capabilities. Fig. 4.34 illustrates the magnitude of mobilisation required. China – Pakistan joint exercise off India's western border is a clear demonstration of China preparing for out of area contingencies in that area.

Highly demanding and challenging organisational *perestroika* is also, an ongoing process. In spite of strong resistance on the social front – the build-up of the human resource (HRD) up gradation schemes, particularly, in the officer and NCO cadre are in full swing. The outcome will be based on the political equations that will emerge with the fifth / sixth generation leadership transition. This aspect has been further elaborated earlier.

There is considerable scope for readjustment / reorientation in the MR front too. This is being brought about by the enhanced global aspirations, leading to greater demands arising, for out of area responsibilities and the need for joint operations across the seas – initially focused on the Taiwan objective. Expeditionary ambition, emerging across the horizon, is also very much on the cards. The transition so far has been quite painful and full of challenges. Their approach has been very selective and pragmatic – with the objective of achieving quick returns.

Also, enforcement of retirement on basis of lowered age ceilings has been yet another serious endeavour in that direction.

The military is presently well represented in the CMC – the Supreme High Command. PLA officials are now also part of many reputed think tanks e.g. Academy of Military Sciences (AMS), Shangai Institute of International Strategic Studies (SIIS) and the National Defence University (NDU) etc. These institutions are increasingly being used in the culture of *institutional decision making* – encouraged by the present political leadership. These clearly indicate, the intention of the present leadership, to wean the military away from involvement in the political institutions and at the same time – empower them to fully participate in corporate professional decision making in military affairs

Attempts at curtailment of the flab in the PLA - seems quite dramatic and striking. The huge demobilisation effort is no doubt very impressive. The scale is mind boggling. And has been implemented with grit and determination. None of these have been popular measures – meeting with strong opposition, in every quarter, at every stage. In fact, the drive has been basically motivated by the dire necessity to trim the flab and induce long overdue modernisation, mechanisation and inculcate efficiency in the large unwieldy and archaic PLA Force.

A large proportion of the claimed demobilisation has, however, been affected by mass transfer from PLA to:

(a) Peoples Armed Police (PAP) to enhance law enforcement capabilities across the country.
(b) Undeveloped remote regions of the country as construction workers.
(c) Infrastructure projects across the country and abroad.

The military modernisation drive was initially focused on

mechanisation leading to more, lean, mean, mobile, technologically advanced forces. Intensive drive has been initiated to recruit graduates as officers directly from the universities. In HR terms - their main weakness lies with the Non-Commissioned Officer (NCO) cadre and their inability to get conscripts of the technical calibre required. A realistic assessment of their *'human system performance capabilities'* is of paramount importance to India. The outcome subsequent to the attempted introduction of RMA into the game is an ongoing process. Its end result are yet to be ascertained. PLA has now been directed to professionalise by 2015 and do away with conscription. This is, no doubt, an extremely ambitious aim.

As an immediate solution to their predicament – China seems to have decided to leap-frog onto the option of *assassin's mace / informationalisation with Chinese character* concept.

The present assessment of PRC's financial / economic / developmental growth trajectory is clear. The jury is still out - on how the domestic inequality situation and ethnic divide will play-out. PLA still remains an *enigma* to the out side world. A closed society and lack of transparency – makes reality check a difficult proposition. The perceived trends have been out lined.

The forecast for PLA in the near and middle terms will largely depend on how the civil-military relationship will emerge with the anticipated change of guards under the fifth / sixth generation political leadership and the influence of the so called CYLs and GPLs.

WAKE-UP CALL FOR INDIA

India should take all of this, as yet another wake-up call. India's own restructuring effort – post approval of the Group of Minister's (GOM)'s recommendations, over a decade ago, would rate, dismal compared to China's revolutionary perestroika presented above. India seems to be quite satisfied with the cosmetic restructuring exercises.

India does not have the will to even implement the:

(a) Chief of Defence (CDS) concept. NOR even

(b) The Pilot project of Theatre Command - in the form of Andaman and Nicobar (A&N) Joint Command- which was meant to be, a stepping stone leading to - the nation-wide Theatre Commands concept.

The Navy has upgraded the minimum intake requirement for Executive officers to B.Tech. But no one is talking about linked job content reforms or restructuring cadre to take-on higher professional responsibilities – a call consistently made for over three decades.

Similarly, the Army has introduced 'operation logistics' in their lexicon. But what about intra-service:

(a) Integrated logistics and

(b) Common computerised logistics management system etc.

Bibliography

1. 'Planning modernisation of PLAN' Vayu III 2008 p. 64.
2. "China's Growing Power, Troubled Diplomacy". Military Balance 2005-2006. pp. 306-311.
3. "China's Missile modernisation in Space warfare plan" Asian Security IDSA Strategic Analysis Vol. 32. No. 5. Sept. 2008.
4. "Enigma of the Varyag". Vayu III 2008. p. 71.
5. "Mega size, Mega ambitions – PLAN's emerging shape" p. 32. Defence and Technology – May / June 2007.
6. <www.jamestown.org/programme/chinabrief/single/?tx_ttnews%5Btt_news%5D=347898&cHash=ffd7cc62f6>
7. A Times of India report – 14 Jan. 2011.
8. A.P. Revi – "Revolution in Military Logistics" *India Defence Review*. Vol. 23 (3) September 2008.
9. A.P. Revi "Naval Academy and HRD Challenges ahead" USI Journal. June 2009.
10. Andrew S Erickson "China's future Nuclear s/m Force". Naval Institute Press Annapolis and China Maritime Study Institute.
11. Bo Zhiyie "China's Elite Politics: Political Transition and Power Balance" Contemprory China Vol. 8. World Scientific Press, Shangai. pp. 139-202.
12. Cdr Peter A Dutton "Through a Chinese Line" USN Proceeding Apr 1010. p. 24.
13. Cdr. P Gregory USN. "China in Space – implications for US military Strategy" JFQ Joint Force Quarterly Issue 47. IVth Qr 2007. pp. 96-98.
14. Dan Blumenthal and Christopher Griffin "Understanding strategy: A delicate dance America must learn to comprehend China's culture and tactics" – *Armed Forces Journal*. Apr 2006. p. 24.
15. David M Finkelstein and Kristen Gunness "Civil Military relations in today's China"

16. David Sham Baugh "Modernising China's military – Progress, Problem and Perspective". 1999.
17. David Shambaugh "Civil military relation in China: Party – Army or National Military" Copenhagen Journal of Asian Studies 16 Sept. 2002. <cjas.dk/index.php/ejas/article/view File/3/3>
18. Defence White Paper <eng.mod.gov.cn/Database/whitepaper/2009-07/21/content_4006236.htm>.
19. Denis J. Blaske "Chinese Army today- tradition and transformation for 21st century" – Rotledge Taylor and Francis Group 2006.
20. Dr Giuseppe Anz Philips C Saunders and Erik R Quam "China's Air Force" JFQ issue 47. IVth Qtr 2002.
21. Gurmeet S Kanwal "A concerned India: Chinese submarine base in Hainan" Vayu III 2008, p. 73.
22. Gurpreet S Khurana "China's new s/m base at Hainan" IDSA Strategic Analysis Vol. 32. No. 5. Sept. 2008
23. Gurpreet S Khurana "China's String of Pearls in the Indian Ocean – its security implicatrions" Strategic Analysis. Vol. 32. No.1 (2008). pp. 1-39.
24. http://www.china.org.cn/english/feature/book/194486.htm
25. http://www.china.org.cn/government/whitepaper/node_7060059.htm

IN Ships in Line Abreast Formation

5

Higher Defence Management Option for India

MACRO-LEVEL INDIAN SCENARIO

The objective of reform and restructuring is to put in place a more efficient, effective and economic system – to meet the existing and future requirements of the Armed Forces and National Security. The approach must necessarily be pragmatic result oriented and avoid getting into any academic / subjective/ parochial pit-falls.

Before formulating an *Out of the Box Option* for India – a summary of the main characteristics, of the four HDM models considered in the last four chapters - are recapitulated here, for convenience.

The common thread that runs across the board, globally, emphasises the following:

(a) Clear political control over military (not bureaucratic control).

(b) Management Structure in three functional Divisions: Staff/ Operation / Support functions.

(c) Revolution in Military Affairs (RMA).

(d) Out of Area operations.

(e) Joint Operations.

(f) Theatre Commands.

(g) Integrated / Joint / Unified / Functional Operational Commands.

(h) The Military divided into two distinct cadres: Combatant and Support Services.

(i) Revolution in Military Logistics (RML) – contemporary definition of logistics covers all support / acquisition activities from conceptual design to R&D, proto-type manufacture, testing, serial production, induction into service, life-time product support, modernisation, till final disposal.

(j) Dedicated cadre for logistics.

In the case of USA - having a Presidential form of Government the following are distinctly embedded into the HDM structure:

(a) The Unified Theatre Commanders are, for all practical proposes, directly responsible to the President – through the Secretary of Defence, under the over-sight of the CDS. The President is the Supreme Commander. In that capacity he exercises operational command over the Armed Forces.

(b) He could opt to exercise operational Command through the Secretary of Defence and the Chief of Defence Staff (CDS).

(c) The respective Service Chiefs have no operational authority over the Combatant Commands. They are required to provide the Theatre Commands (Unified Commands) with the where-withal as directed by the JCSC. They only have administrative / technical authority and responsibility over their respective Component Commands.

(d) To emphasise on the importance of jointness between the Services – for promotion to higher rank - serving on joint assignments is considered a criteria appointment for promotion.

(e) The Secretary of Defence is a member of the President's cabinet and is the equivalent of a Defence Minister in other countries.

(f) The functional flow chart of the National Security Council (NSC) is illustrated at Fig. 1.4. NSC is an advisory body to the President. The National Security Advisor heads the Secretariat of the NSC. He has no executive powers nor is he a member of the NSC. He is the principal security adviser to the President.

(g) The military follows the concept of functional ownership. The following are the designated basic functional owners:

 (i) Combat Action Process Owner.

 (ii) Combat Capacity Process Owner.

 (iii) Combat Support Process Owner.

 (iv) Combat Movement Process Owner.

(h) The Office of the Secretary of Defence and the Offices of the respective Service Secretaries are manned by a mixed staff of Service and civilian personnel. As illustrated at Fig. 1.2 most of the civilian Departmental heads in the Department of Defence (DOD) are appointees of the President. They are not civil servants. They are nominated by the President on the basis of the individual's specialised capabilities most suited for the task assigned. He / she is cleared, accepted and duly empowered by the Congress.

(i) The respective Service Materials Commands have a dual role - one as a part of the Service Establishment, the other to provide total support as a *process owner* to the Secretary of Defence (SOD) set-up, as a technical/professional adviser and implementer of all material matters. The Material Command is responsible for seeing through all such issues from the conceptual design stage on *womb to tomb* basis. They are subject to over-sight by the respective President nominated authority embedded in an intricate network as part of the Office of Secretary of Defence (OSD). This is illustrated at Fig. 1.2.

(j) As per US statute:

 (i) All personnel involved with the Acquisition functions (civilian and service) are required to be acquisition compliant – officially certified by the Defence Acquisition University at appropriate levels.

 (ii) Programme Managers are to have a minimum of four years assignment. Exceptional cases require written exemption from the respective Service Chief and Service Secretary.

(iii) The Acquisition cadre has been classified into specialist streams (ACF). As they go up the ladder – they are required to broaden their base by exposure to at least two streams.

(k) The US Army has formed an integrated Logistics Cadre / Command.

(l) The civil servant bureaucrats have an important role to play, particularly in the administrative, commercial and financial functions – in providing continuity. They invariably are permanent fixtures in the DOD.

The British system conforms to the Westminster Parliamentary Democracy model. Significant characteristics of its linked Higher Defence Management System (HDM), as it exists today, are listed below:

(a) The Highest Defence Policy making body is the Defence and Overseas Policy Sub-Committee of the Cabinet – with the PM in the chair and Foreign Minister, Chancellor of Exchequer, Secretary of State and the Secretary of State for Defence as members.

(b) The Defence Council, at the next echelon, chaired by the Secretary of Defence is responsible for taking policy decisions for the department and running the department efficiently. The Council comprises the Ministers of Defence, CDS, Principal Under Secretary (PUS), Chief of Navy (CNS), Chief of Army (CGS), Chief of Air Force (CAS), Vice Chief of Defence Staff (VCDS), Chief of Joint Operations (CJO), Chief of Defence Material (CDM) and Chief Scientific Officer.

(c) The CDS is the *Principal Military Adviser* to the Secretary of Defence and the Government.

(d) The PUS is the *Principal Civilian Adviser* on defence. He is primarily responsible for policy, finance and administration of the Department of Defence. He is Ministry of Defence (MOD)'s *accounting officer* and is *personally* responsible to Parliament for expenditure of public money *voted* for defence purposes.

(e) As illustrated at Fig. 2.20 and 2.21–the top office group is shared between the CDS and PUS. Similarly, the combined office is shared between the VCDS and the Second PUS. Both these offices are manned by civilian and military personnel. This helps in maintaining an integrated approach within the DOD.

(f) The concept of *User Process Owner* and *the Service Provider Owner* has been implemented.

(g) There is a clear division of role between the *combatant* and the *support services. The Chief of Defence Material* is responsible for all hardware requirements – from concept design stage to R&D, production, delivery, product life-time support, modernisation till final disposal. The CDM is a four star service officer of the same rank as the CNS, CGS, CAS, VCDS and CJO. General Sir Kevin O'Donoghue of Royal Engineers was the CDM from 2007 to 2011.

(h) The institutionalised, inter-active process between the *User* and the *Provider* to generate optimum solutions are illustrated at Fig. 2.22. The capital equipment requirements and life-time support solutions are generated through an interactive process between institutions responsible for capability development, strategy, resource planning and DE&S.

(i) Similar to the US system - the CNS, CGS and CAS have been relieved of direct operational responsibilities. They have no operational authority over the forces deployed with the CJO. They remain the technical and administrative authority of the respective Component Commands. They continue to be responsible for personnel induction, training, preparation/ equipping/ arming of the forces adequately, and providing them in designated time and place to the Joint Force Commander, as directed by the CDS.

(j) Primary role of the Armed Forces is *expeditionary* in character, based and geared for *out of area* operation – same as for USA.

FRANCE AND GERMANY

France and Germany also have two different streams in their military – Combatant and Armament. the promotion prospects in both the streams are comparable.

PEOPLES LIBERATION ARMY (PLA)

Now China also has a dedicated General Armament Department alongside the General Staff Department, the General Logistics Department and the General Political Department.

SOVIET UNION AND THE RUSSIAN FEDERATION

During the cold war period, the integrated General Staff model was very effective. In the 1980s – in the process of executing RMA, the CGS Marshal of the Soviet Union. NV.Ogarkov introduced the concept of centralised strategic level control with decentralised battle management. Russia has been in the perestroika mode - ever since the break-up of USSR. The restructuring effort has been remarkable. The political leadership has been relentless. It has been a very painful period. It has cost them dearly. Several Defence Ministers (DM), Chief of General Staffs (CGSs) and over half a dozen Generals -lost their jobs, for perceived obstruction to the ordained restructuring effort. They have still a long way to go. On the surface – they give the impression of trying to go the US way. Their attempt to break-up the traditional integrated General Staff concept is likely to lead to a disaster.

OUT OF BOX OPTION FOR INDIA

One is generally aware of the existing HDM system in operation in India and the developments that have taken place since the restructuring process was initiated some ten odd years ago. Chief of Integrated Defence Staff (CIDS) has done a sterling service in taking forward the jointness concept. In the absence of the CDS - conversion of these concepts into action is seriously handicapped. They have reached the end of the road. Only an *out of the box* solution can break the impasse. The question that arises now is, whether to:

(a) Scrap the present concept, and start afresh and evolve *an out of the box* pragmatic option, taking into account the global experience in this matter.

(b) Allow things to drag on and let it collapse under its own contradictions.

(c) Revert to the old system.

(d) To find ways and means to get around the roadblocks and complete the ongoing process – within the broad framework recommended by the Group of Ministers (GOMs) and approved by Cabinet Committee on Security (CCS) in 2002.

For the immediate term - it is proposed here, to attempt option (d) first. Some may say that, this would be tantamount to *flogging a dead horse*. There is no doubt, that in the long run – option (a) would be the most rational option – taking UK as a pragmatic model. This would also be, in conformity with the NSC directive of 2000.

To recapitulate - relevant portion of the NSC directive is reproduced below for ready reference:

Para 2 (a) to NSC Directive No. C-180/1/2000 – NSCS (CS) directive dtd 17 May 2000.

"Since accountability to Parliament constitutes the basic feature of Government of India, the task force, while making recommendations, will examine the evolution and changes in this respect that have taken place in other parliamentary democracies. In particular, the UK model should be studied closely."

The CCS approved model, taken in totality, is basically considered a sound concept. Although, there are, no doubt, a few serious difficulties to resolve, built in flaws. These could have been corrected had the counter measures been taken in time – with courage and conviction. It must also be admitted that the country has invested heavily, in time, effort and resources – towards building up institutional infrastructure to support that model. This effort should now be channelised to meet the revised concept. If not attended to promptly, firmly and pragmatically now – then the concept is likely to become irrelevant soon.

Chapters one to four clearly shows that India is by no means the first to tread on this journey. And no nation is known to have gone through this exercise without great pains.

Hence, India should not expect to be an exception. We have the advantage of having several models before us and know the pitfalls they have been through. We should not permit our pride to come in the way, and deny ourselves the opportunity to learn from their experience.

INHERENT INADEQUACIES IN INDIAN ENVIRONMENT

Whilst considering an Indian option one must not lose sight of the following overbearing realities of the environment and provide for adequate systemic compensation for these inadequacies:

(a) All global models considered here have had at least two to three generations of conscription imposed on them. This in its wake has given all the political and bureaucratic leadership the benefit of *hands on exposure* in military affairs. In the case of USA – it would be observed that :

- (i) One dozen Generals became Presidents.
- (ii) Thirty one of the forty four Presidents had served in the military in one capacity or another.
- (iii) In 1970 - the Congress had 74% members, who had served in the military. Even today 23% of the members had served in the military before.
- (iv) President Kennedy, who was himself a decorated WWII veteran had only two cabinet ministers who had not served in the military.

(b) In the Indian political context, not only is this element missing but also historically, the defence has been treated as a safe constituency – relatively free from opposition party attacks. As a consequence, more often than otherwise, the billet is used to park heavy weight politicians in transit. Many of them with no inclination to strategic / military thinking and looking for better pastures else where. In such circumstances, heavy dependence on bureaucracy is only natural. The matter gets further compounded – with the generalist bureaucracy equally lacking any military exposure.

(c) The political acumen and leadership ability is not in question here.

(d) On this subject - it may not be out of place here to quote from late Shri K Subrahmanian's (the Doyen of Indian strategic thinkers) interview to an Institute of Defence Studies and Analysis (IDSA) scholar in March 2008 - *"politicians enjoy power without any responsibility, bureaucrats wield power without any accountability and military assumes responsibility without any direction".*

(e) In this context, one needs to revisit the "MOD's rules of Business" also. This owes its origin to the immediate post colonial mind-set of the bureaucrats, who framed it. The fear of a military take over is embedded there in. In spite of, over six decades of unquestionable loyalty and dedicated service to the nation - for their self serving reasons, the bureaucrats still continue to nurture this frame of mind. For the reasons stated above - the political leadership does not have the inclination or will to bring about a change.

In the above context, the *out of the box option* for India is considered in two parts:

(a) Long term option, fully incorporating the RMA and RML developments - with clear demarcation of responsibility between CDS, Defence Secretary, Chief of Defence Material (CDM), Chief of Army Staff (COAS), CNS, CAS and CJO. This also entails adoption of a management structure with three clear functional Divisions: Staff / Operation / Support Divisions.

(b) An interim option – taking the CCS decision of 2002 forward, in two stages. This would incorporate PM Nehru's commitment to Parliament on the issue of Defence Council and the affirmative understanding given to Lord Louis Mountbatten on adoption of the CDS concept by India:

  (i) Immediate upgradation of CIDS to same rank as the three Service Chiefs, similar to the VCDS and Chief of Joint Operations (CJO) in UK. In this capacity he will wear two hats. Division of his responsibilities will be as follows:

- Head of JCSC Secretariat – reporting to CJCSC for all the traditional roles of the secretariat.
- Envisaged joint operation role / function of CDS designate – including full scope development of Andaman and Nicobar Command (A&NC), Strategic Force Command (SFC). Further, extending this to include all joint concepts on the anvil i.e. Space Command, C^3ISR and Logistics etc.
- In view of an institutional resistance to change and failure of the present set-up to deliver, in the last decade, on the tasks set by the CCS - CIDS to report in this capacity to Defence Council (DC).

(ii) An institutionalised review of progress to be undertaken by CJCSC and DC regularly.

(iii) In the mid term context - after the conditionalities (detailed later) have been met and CDS is fully in the saddle – the Theatre Commands are to be put in place. By that time, the A&NC and SFC would have stabilised and fulfilled the purpose of a pilot programme for creating the *Unified Command* ethos. At that stage, the CDS would need to be upgraded to a Field Marshal and the Theatre Commanders to the rank of General. This would be in consistent with global practice – particularly taking into account the size of the Armed Forces. To overcome the serious reservations that the Service Chiefs would have, on parting with operational authority - the CDS would initially take on a modified role, heading an integrated General Staff. Operational control, over the Theatre / Functional Commands would be exercised by the Corporate General Staff with CDS in the chair - keeping the respective Service Chiefs in the loop. Alternatively, the Corporate General Staff could exercise operational control through the CIDS as the Chief of Joint Operations (CJO). The Service Chiefs will continue to exercise administrative and technical control over their respective components deployed with the Theatre / Functional Commands. CDS would remain over all in-charge and the Principle Military Adviser to the Government.

HISTORICAL PERSPECTIVE OF PERESTROIKA

In January 1999, almost thirteen years ago – Shri George Fernandes, the former Raksha Mantri (RM), declared that within three months, he would integrate and restructure the Ministry of Defence (MoD) and Service HQs. RM may have thought then, that he could replicate Hastletine's performance. In 1989, Hastletine only gave his Chiefs of Staff (COSs) in UK, three days to implement his ambitious restructuring programme. Thirteen years down the line, India still does not have a clear road map. It is heartening to observe that a high powered task force led by Shri Naresh Chandra has now been assigned the work to review the progress made in implementing the Cabinet decision on MOD restructuring and hopefully recommend a way forward.

There can be no doubt, that many alternatives must have been formulated and discussed, within the four walls of Joint Chiefs of Staff Committee (JCOSC), Integrated Defence Staff (IDS), Service HQs and among the various Think Tanks. However, there has not been any tangible progress, on this front, for some years. Hence, the attempt here is to present an *"out of the box"* option, which could be taken forward.

MILESTONES COVERED

In this context, review of the current status shows the milestones crossed till date as follows:

(a) Former DM, George Fernandes – declared his intention to integrate and restructure MoD and Service HQs within 3 months. Jan. 1999.

(b) GOMs were constituted. 17 Jan. 2000.

(c) Terms of reference for GOMs/ Task Force was promulgated, emphasising criteria as:

  (i) Accountability to Parliament. 17 May 2001.

  (ii) Examine evolution in other Parliamentary Democracies, especially UK.

(d) Cabinet approval to the GOM's report given. 26 Feb. 2002.

(e) Strategic Force Command (SFC), Andaman and Nicobar Command (A&NC), Defence Intelligence Agency (DIA) and Chief of Integrated Defence Staff (CIDS) – were energised, soon thereafter.

(f) Defence Procurement / Production / R&D Boards and Service Acquisition Wings were energised.

(g) RM's Operational Directive was issued. 2002.

(h) Long Term Perspective Plans (LTPP) Navy was formulated. Sept. 2002.

(i) Defence Procurement Procedure was promulgated and updated regularly. 2002/2004/2006/ 2008 / 2010 etc.

(j) CCS decision to operationalise the "Nuclear Doctrine" taken. Apr. 2003.

(k) LTPP (Army) / (IAF). Jun. 2003.

(l) Integrated LTPP by IDS. Oct. 2003.

(m) Dr Chidambaran's clarification on role of NCA executive Committee – was reported in Pioneer. 06 Feb. 2005.

(n) Report of Parliamentary Standing Committee on Defence (PSCD) – taking Government to task for undue delay in the appointment of CDS, placed on the table of the house. 20 March 2006.

(o) The PSCD of 14th Lok Sabha had also strongly recommended the change in MOD staffing pattern to ensure Armed Forces were "intrinsically involved in national security management and apex decision making process".

(p) Considerable progress has been made in the delegation of financial powers in respect of revenue expenditure to COSs, PSOs and CinCs of Command HQs etc.

(q) High powered task force headed by Shri. Naresh Chandra appointed to review progress made on Cabinet approved restructuring of the MOD and make recommendations for a way forward. Sept. 2011.

It would be observed from above that in the initial four years, there was considerable movement, particularly in the Defence Acquisition Council (DAC) arena. In other areas, things have been more or less stagnant Hence, the Parliamentary Standing Committee on Defence (PSCD) has asked the government for an explanation.

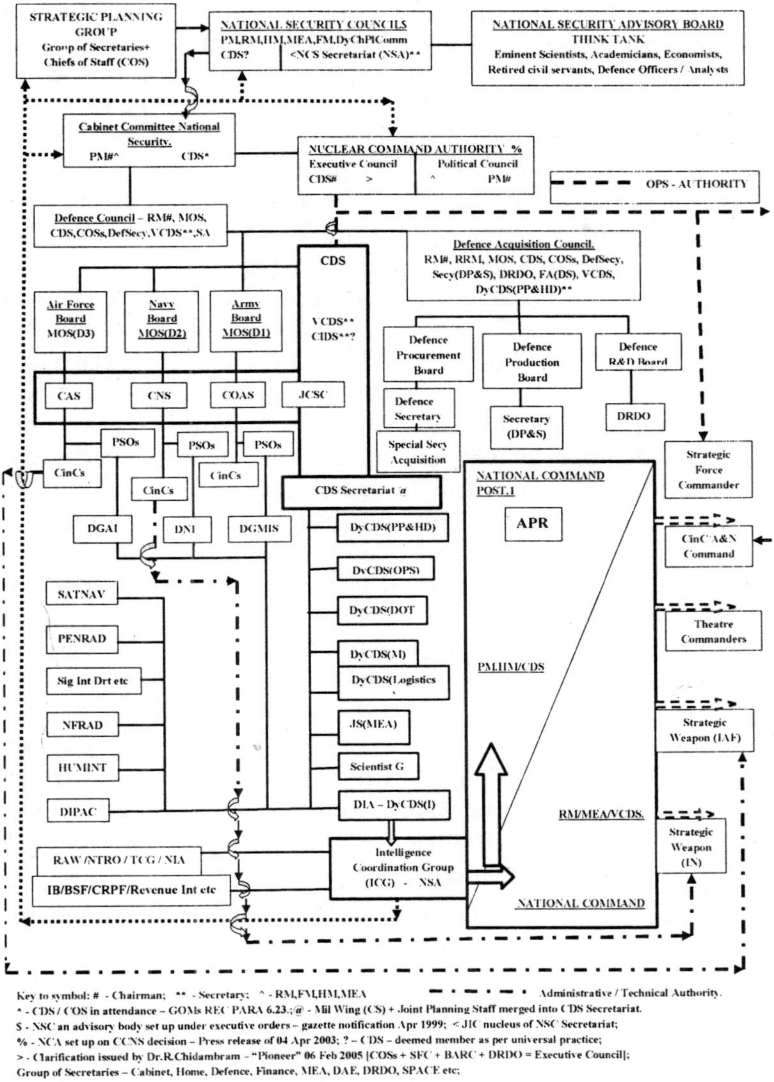

Fig. 5.35. Out of Box Option for HDM (India).

It would be prudent to remind oneself, at this stage, of two historical commitments made by India's late PM Nehru:

(a) *PM Nehru's Commitment to Parliament in 1953 of introducing the UK type Defence Council concept.* That would have put in place a real civilian political control over the military vis-a-vis the existing bureaucratic control over the Military. In India's context, at that point of time, the Defence Council concept was very relevant. It could have led to direct civil political control of the Military as envisaged in the Constitution. Even the Hastletine model which was prevalent in UK at the time of Kargil Review would have been acceptable. As illustrated at Fig. 2.16 – the management structure in UK, at that point of time, comprised the Defence Council chaired by the Secretary of Defence and the Admiralty / Army / Air Force Boards chaired by the respective Junior Ministers. This was the model in vogue in UK – at the time that Kargil Review Committee Task Force was directed by NSC to consider the UK model seriously. In their wisdom - the Task Force picked up most of the ideas embedded in the Hastletine Review model except the concept of Defence Council along with its Service Boards. The fundamental issue of establishing political control over the military was left unaddressed and allowed to fester. The author's version of an out of the box option for India, incorporating the above fundamental requirement was published in December 2006 issue of The Journal of India Ocean Studied Volume 1.14. Number 3. The updated version of the HDM organisation structure is at Figs. 5.35 and 6.46. The historical perspective and the process of evolution of a pragmatic solution are discussed in the succeeding paragraphs.

(b) Lord Louis Mountbatten of Burma's letter to General Chibber dtd 27 Sept 1977 indicating PM Nehru's *inclination towards accepting the concept of CDS.* A copy of the letter is placed at enclosure 1 for ready reference.

At the time of CCS according its approval to the restructuring process - the HDM structure conceptualised was basically sound and workable. Some aberrations that had crept in - needed to be ironed out. With the entrenched parochial positions of the affected parties – an evolutionary solution in this case is considered not practicable now. Globally also, such an approach has not worked out. Indian experience – only confirms the same. The evolutionary expectations have been given a long enough try. Before any serious disaster strikes the country – time has come, to take affirmative action – adopting both a top-down and simultaneously a bottom-up approach.

LONG-TERM OPTION

First, the ultimate aim must be finalised and formalised. The existing UK model as illustrated at Fig. 2.20 is considered a pragmatic and rational solution with some changes to accommodate local conditions. This would also be in line with NSC directive of 2000. And also meet the concerns of the PSCD. Detailed phased, time-bound action plan would need to be formulated and promulgated. Empowered implementing authority clearly identified and put in place – directly responsible and accountable to the Defence Council. Review of progress must be institutionalised under the DC – initially on a monthly basis to give an impetus.

Basically, the above calls for the functional concept within the military to be institutionalised into: Staff / Operation / Support Divisions.

On the subject of the present dual functional responsibility of the COSs – General JN Chaudhury the former COAS, at the time of 1965 war, had the following to say at the USI National Security lecture which he delivered in 1973: "*While this dual responsibility role* (of Staff and Operation) *was just workable when each service was much smaller and less technical, today it puts far too much strain on the individual in times of comparative quiet and an unbearable strain on him during a war. Very often, the two functions can be incompatible - for an honest COS can disagree with himself as an honest C in C*".

INTERIM SHORT AND MEDIUM TERM OPTION

Since the above would be a long term objective – in the interim, the option presented at Fig. 5.35 attempts to break the impasse in the ongoing process and puts it back on the rail. At the same time, the eventual goal must be kept full focus. No action should be initiated that would close the door to the ultimate objective. All action should be part of the building block – eventually leading to the final objective.

Basically, it superimposes the Defence Council (DC) and

Service Board (SB) system, as assured by P.M. Nehru to Parliament in 1953, on the basic CCS approved model. The Institution of DC and SB will not only enable pacifying of the perception of bureaucratic control over the military – but also, open up a range of possible direct political leadership interaction and intervention role at the PSO / APSO levels at the SHQs. Late, K. Subrahmanyam had also pointed to to such a solution in his article on "Higher Direction of Defence and its Organisation".

In conformity with global practice – the proposal further includes the Chief of Defence Staff (CDS) as a member of vital institutions, charged with taking decisions on security concerns. All these are in conformity with the concerns raised by the PSCD. It also inserts an additional Deputy CDS (Logistics) in the CDS Secretariat – charged with the responsibility of giving a serious impetus to RML with emphasis on evolving, on a fast track, a modern computerised logistic system around a common architecture. In this context, taking Army's historical baggage into account - this is considered the single most important, *out of the box* measure necessary to pull the military out of the morass. In the existing system - under Deputy CIDS (OPS) there is already a Joint Operation Logistics Division with a dedicated DDG (OPS-LOGISTICS) focused on an important but miniscule part of the over-all issue. This merely replicates the Army HQ's approach and takes it forward in the limited Joint Operations domain and does not address the fundamental issue holistically. The need and modus operandi for such an extraordinary measure would be elaborated later.

FUNCTIONAL HIGHLIGHTS OF THE STRUCTURE

The core of the HDM structure presented, comprise the National Security Council (NSC) – which is chaired by the PM with some of his cabinet colleagues, Deputy Chairman of the Planning Commission and CDS as members. This needs to be institutionalised under an Act of Parliament.

The NSC is assisted by three institutions: -

(a) NSC Secretariat with NSA as its head and suitable representation from the services and the bureaucracy. Like in the US system – the NSC secretariat, on a case by case basis, prepares a brief outline plan and coordinates development of National Security Policy and puts up proffered options to the NSC. It coordinates and closely follows the progress of NSC recommendations through the CCS. It also monitors the implementation of the CCS decisions and regularly provides a feed back to NSC/ CCS / PMO. The NSA is the National Security Adviser to the PM and the NSC.

(b) The Strategic Planning Group (SPG) – with Group of Secretaries and the COSs as members.

(c) National Security Advisory Board (NSAB) – a rotating think tank with eminent scientists, academicians, economists, retired civil servants / defence officers and analysts etc. as members.

Proposals along with NSC recommendations are put up to the CCS for their approval. The CCS is chaired by the PM with CDS again in attendance. The attendance of CDS at the CCS is further justified due to *the "inherent inadequacies in the Indian environment"*, discussed earlier. *The* CCS decisions are taken forward by the RM / National Command Authority (NCA)/ Defence Council (DC) / Defence Acquisition Council (DAC) as appropriate.

NCA with the PM in the chair is the sole entity empowered to authorize the use of nuclear weapon. The NCA comprises the Political Council and the Executive Council. The Executive council implements the decisions of NCA and is chaired by CDS. The NSA has no constitutional position or legal authority to issue executive operational orders to the Military / Strategic Force Commander (SFC). The COSs, SFC, Defence Research and Development Organisation (DRDO) and Bhabha Atomic Research Centre (BARC) are members of the NCA Executive Council.

It would be seen from Fig. 5.35 that one half of the organisation is already serviced by the *Defence Acquisition Council* (DAC) subset and the linked *Boards* dedicated to Acquisition / Defence Production / Research and Development functions. This subset is already in place. The working of this subset and its shortcomings would be elaborated later. To complete PM Nehru's commitment to Parliament in 1953 – what remains, is the commissioning of the *Defence Council*

(DC). The Defence Council chaired by RM and assisted by the respective *Service Boards is* responsible for ensuring the efficient functioning of the Armed Forces, within the charter specified by Parliament and the CCS.

It would be further observed that most of the structures shown are already in place. Several checks and balances are embedded into the system. At one stage, the smaller Services had a genuine fear of losing their identity and their specialised skills - being subsumed under an overwhelming olive green culture. To safeguard this fear - the CDS is to be appointed on rotational basis – as is done presently, in the case of Chairman JCSC. At the same time, to maintain a balance, bearing in mind the sub-continental and ground reality context - the CCS approval stipulates that the VCDS must have a minimum tenure of two years and in cases when the CDS is from the Navy or the IAF – the VCDS has necessarily to be from the Army. The centrality of the Vice Chief of the Defence Staff (VCDS) in the system should also not be missed. To provide for continuity, VCDS is not only the Secretary to JCSC – he is also the head of the JCSC secretariat and coordinates the working of the functional heads e.g. Deputy CDSs (Policy, Planning and Force Development)/ (Doctrine and Training)/ (Intelligence) etc. Deputy CDS (Logistics) has been added here to ensure implementation of Integration of logistics and RML – which is a fundamental necessity not withstanding any option. This would be discussed in greater detail and justified later. VCDS is also the secretary of DAC and a member of the respective Boards. This would maintain the inter-service equation in equilibrium and provide continuity in situations where the tenure of the CDS is inadequate, due to the rotating nature of the chair. In the UK system both the VCDS and the CJO are four star flag officers.

It is also fairly well known that at one stage the CDS was almost appointed. Even the consequential ceremonials that were required to be performed – were rehearsed. But last minute there was a change. That opportunity is not likely to come again.

REVAMPING THE NATIONAL INTELLIGENCE FRAMEWORK

The intelligence subset has been superimposed on the

functional flow chart illustrated at Figure 5.35. This has been further refined by the CCS decision of January 2012. The CCS decision reforms the National Intelligence set up, by creating the National Counter Terrorism Centre (NCTC). The NCTC is dedicated to counter terrorism and has been put under the Home Ministry. It is set to become operational by April 2012. Several State governments have raised objections stating that this is contrary to the Federal structure of the constitution. It offers a single window system dedicated to counter terrorism - receiving all terror related inputs from all agencies. The Director will report to the Director IB and through him to the Home Secretary and Home Minister. It will have no investigative wing under it. The NIA with the help of IB, RAW, NTRU, MI and the State intelligence agencies will be responsible for all investigative action. This is a very similar arrangement to that of US - where the investigative function has been separated from the operational functions.

FORMATION OF INDIAN NATIOINAL DEFENCE UNIVERSITY

In 2002, the GOMs had recommended the creation of the Indian National Defence University (INDU). In 2010, CCNS accorded an in principle approval for the setting up of INDU as a fully autonomous institution to be constituted under an Act of Parliament at an estimated cost of Rs.295 crores. The University is planned to be established at Binula in Gurgaon. The requisite land has already been allotted by the Haryana state government.

It is envisaged that the existing joint services institutions like the NDC, NDA and DSSC etc would be affiliated to the University. New faculties envisaged under the University are:

(a) Institute of Defence Management.

(b) Institute of Advanced Defence Studies.

(c) National Institute of Strategic Studies.

(d) College of National Security Policy. Etc.

In his opening address, at a recent international seminar on Defence Procurement at the IDSA - the RM made a statement propagating the necessity of setting up a National Defence Logistics University on a priority. This was to be on similar lines to the US Defence Logistics University. A suggestion was also made to collocate the same along with the IDSA. It is suggested here that since INDU is already on the anvil - that would be the rightful, rational and logical place to locate the Defence Logistics Institute also.

CONDITIONALITIES BEFORE CDS IS APPOINTED

A list of core issues that would need to be resolved before CDS can now be appointed is given below. It is considered that unless these are addressed earnestly – even those within the establishment, who are fully committed to the restructuring process, would have serious reservations. These concerns may not have been formally verbalised but need to be taken on board, for the success of the venture: -

(a) Pass an Act of Parliament, similar to U.S. Goldwater Nichols Act 1984 – so that the system is not open to manipulation by political/ bureaucratic/ military leadership of the time.

(b) Appoint a high power empowered Task Force with clear-cut charter and commitment to draft the Act, within a stipulated time frame. (Following the GOMs route).

(c) In addition to appropriate provisions, as in the US Act – take care of at least the following concerns in the present system:-

  (i) Introduce the concept of Defence Council headed by the RM (similar to the DAC) and Army/ Navy/ IAF Boards – each headed by a Minister of State (MOS). This would resolve the long outstanding bone of contention over civilian political control vis-a-vis bureaucratic control as exercised presently.

  (ii) Eliminate all ambiguity over chain of military command, over SFC, vis-a-vis National Security Adviser (NSA) – bearing in mind that the NSA has no constitutional / legal authority to exercise operational control over the military.

  (iii) Re-designate Defence Secretary as the Principal Civilian Adviser to RM – in line with his counterpart, the Permanent Under-Secretary (PUS) in UK. His primary responsibility will be on policy, finance, and administration of the Department. In UK, the PUS is the MOD's Accounting Officer and is personally responsible to the Parliament for the expenditure of public money voted for defence purposes.

(iv) The CDS is the professional head of the Armed Forces and the Principal Military Adviser to the RM and the Government. In the case of UK, chain of command for planning and conduct of military operation flows from the Cabinet and Secretary of Defence to the CDS and from him to the Operational Commanders. This is the common practice in all modern democracies – the world over. Implementation of such a scheme would not be practical or appropriate, for India, at this stage, particularly in view of the inherent political inadequacies in the system, as brought out earlier. Also, unlike India, most of the major modern powers have the expeditionary role as the primary thrust. Hence, a phased approach and evolution of an India specific Theatre Command concept would be necessary.

(v) Enunciate clearly, the long, mid and short term role of CDS and the conceptual road map and let him get on with the job.

(vi) Theatre Command concept be implemented only after the CDS is fully in the saddle.

(vii) The protocol situation between the COSs and the Defence Secretary must not be disturbed. This is a very sensitive and non-negotiable issue for the military establishment.

(viii) It is too premature and risky at this stage to contemplate shifting of the operational responsibilities away from the COSs. There are very serious intra-service issues yet to be resolved before contemplating any such move – particularly in the case of the Army. In any case, this is only advisable after the CDS is fully in the saddle and the Theatre Commands become a reality. At that stage the Theatre Commander would also need to be upgraded to the rank of a four star General / equivalent.

(ix) In the Indian context, at this stage, the most workable and acceptable option for CDS would be an adaptation of the Soviet integrated CGS model. This would enable the COSs to continue holding the operational command authority of their respective service through the CDS.

(x) In the first phase, in any case, the CDS was envisaged to be the operational command authority for only the A&N Command, Strategic Force Command and all joint / integrated / functional / unified activities. The Space Command / ABM Command / Special Forces Command and development of Joint / Unified C^3IS, Logistics system network under combined architecture-would be appropriate activities to be brought into the ambit of the CDS.

In the above circumstances - it would seem that the appointment of CDS will take some more time. In such circumstances, without losing any more valuable time, in taking the basic process forward, without compromising on battle readiness of the Armed Forces – it is proposed that the CIDS / VCDS be upgraded to same rank as the three Service Chiefs, on similar basis as the UK VCDS and Joint Force Commander, but with two hats:

(a) Continue as the head of the JCSC secretariat – responsible to CJCS.

(b) Be held directly responsible for the following CDS designated exclusive functions. For these functions he would be accountable to the Defence Council directly and render regular progress reports. In the absence of the CDS such an unconventional step is considered necessary and unavoidable. Lack of any progress on these crucial and urgent issues in the last decade – clearly justifies such an unusual measure:

(i) Operational authority for A & N Command, SFC, Special Forces and Space Commands.

(ii) All development of joint operation capabilities including standardisation / codification / logistics computerisation with a joint architecture and the integrated C^4ISR systems.

(iii) Links with National Disaster Management Authority and National Coastal Security Arrangement.

ACHIEVEMENTS OF CIDS

In spite of the serious constraints imposed on the IDS, due to the absence of CDS - IDS has performed yeoman service promoting the cause of jointmanship between the three services. In the absence of any executive authority - implementation was outside its scope. The following are some of the highlights of its achievement in the recent past..:

(a) Fulfil the role of:

(i) An omnibus Secretariat to CJCSC.

(ii) Coordinating the Long Term Integrated Perspective Plan (LTIPP) under the chairmanship of ACIDS (PP&A).

(iii) Service Capital Acquisition Plan Categorisation Committee (SCAPCC) under the chairmanship of DCIDS (PP&FD).

(iv) Services Capital Acquisition Plan Categorisation Higher Committee (SCAPCHC) under chairmanship of CIDS.

(v) Horizon Core Technical Group under chairmanship of ACIDS (W).

(b) Formulation of:

(i) Long Term Perspective Plan (LTPP) (Navy) / (Army) / (IAF).

(ii) Technology Perspective and Capability Roadmap (TPCR) - capability development for next three plan period.

(iii) Joint Doctrine for Air - Land operations.

(iv) Perception Management and Psychological operations.

(v) Sub-conventional operations.

(vi) Electronic warfare.

(vii) Joint Doctrine for Maritime Air operations.

CHIEF OF DEFENCE MATERIAL

Eventually, the CDM would take on all material and support functional responsibilities for the services from *womb to tomb*. Joint responsibility is shared between the CDS and Defence

Secretary. The Navy in large measures is already well placed to take on the naval part of this mission at short notice. As it stands today, the Defence Acquisition structure is seriously imbalanced. The Special Secretary / DG Acquisition Wing, as structured, is strictly incapable of fulfilling its charter as specified in the DPP. It does not have the wherewithal - except in administrative, commercial and financial aspects. It has all the powers with no responsibilities. Most of the activities assigned to it under the charter are actually being carried out by the respective Service HQs or the IDS organisation. The Service Managers merely serve as an intermediary between the respective Service HQs / IDS / IPMT and DG (ACQ).

In the case of the Navy - the time is ripe now to merge the relevant parts of commercial and financial wing of the Secretary (DP) /DG (ACQ) with COM and empower him with the same authority. As a part of the process of integration of SHQ with the MOD – to begin with, the PSOs concerned in the *staff and support function Divisions* of the integrated MOD should also be designated as Secretaries to the Government and accorded appropriate power and financial authority / responsibilities. Such an arrangement has worked efficiently

Akula II class SSGN (*CHAKRA* II) making waves

in the DRDO. In this context, ATV programme is an excellent example.

CWP&A along with DGND should be put under COM. COM should be re-designated as CDM (Navy) so that the total responsibility from *womb to tomb* becomes part of his ship. Putting a professional in charge would bring accountability to the table. A modified version, incorporating such a proposal is illustrated at Fig. 6.46. Since DPP already caters to a dedicated chapter that deals with war-ship building – accommodation of such a change should not present any great difficulty. Such an action would considerably curtail bureaucratic red-tape delays and improve efficiency. And, unlike a civilian counter part - any financial / contractual irregularity committed by a service incumbent could be promptly brought to books, though a court martial.

The Naval model will serve as a pilot model towards developing the integrated Support Function Division – in conformity with the long-term over-all goal of introducing the division of functions concept, propagated here. In due course, the other services can join the fray, as and when they are ready.

A THEATRE COMMAND OPTION

To meet emerging operational compulsions – formation of Unified Theatre Commands is imperative. Binding together the existing independent Service Geographic Commands into rational groupings - as Service Components of the designated Theatre Commands would be a pragmatic, operationally efficient, cost effective and time saving solution. The collocation demand for the Theatre HQs could be weighed against the dispersion needs in the present scenario. Strong, reliable, secure and inter-operable C^4ISR with video-conferencing facilities are viable and will more than compensate for any collocation advantages.

One Theatre / Regional Command option is presented at Fig. 5:36. The tabulated statement illustrates one possible theatre command option. It shows the existing Service specific Regional commands and its present geographic location. It also indicates the proposed Theatre Command combination along with:

THEATRE COMMAND		LEAD SERVICE		LOCATION
PROPOSED	EXISTING	OPTION	PRESENT	PRESENT
NORTH & WEST	NC/WC/SWC WAC/SWAC	ARMY/ IAF	ARMY IAF	UDHAMPUR/CHANDIMANDIR/JAIPUR. DELHI/GANDINAGAR.
EASTERN	EC EAC	ARMY/ IAF	ARMY IAF	KOLKATA SHILLONG.
CENTRAL	CC CAC	ARMY	ARMY IAF	LUCKNOW ALLAHABAD
SOUTH & PENINSULAR	SC SAC WNC/ENC/SNC A&NC	NAVY	ARMY IAF NAVY JOINT	PUNE TRIVANDRUM MUMBAI/ VIZAG/ KOCHI PORT BLAIR

		REMARKS.
STRATEGIC – COMMAND	UNIFIED	Only NCA can authorise use of Nuclear Weapons.
SFC – STRATEGIC WING NAVY	UNIFIED	CDS-Operation command ; IN – Admin & Tech Authority
SW (IAF)	UNIFIED	CDS- Ops Command; IAF – Administrative & Tech Command
FUNCTIONAL COMMANDS.		
SPACE COMMAND	UNIFIED	CDS – OPS; IAF – Lead Service + Individual Service Components.
SPECIAL FORCE COMMAND.	UNIFIED	CDS – OPS; With Service Components..
AIR-LIFT COMMAND	IAF	CDS – OPS; IAF – Admin & Tech Authority.
LOGISTICS COMMAND.	UNIFIED	CDS – OPS; Army – Lead Service + Individual Service Components.

Abbreviations used: ARMY – NC/WC/SWC/EC/CC/SC – Northern / Western/ South Western/Eastern/ Central/ Southern Commands.
NAVY – WNC / ENC / SNC – Western / Eastern / Southern Commands; JOINT – A&NC – Andaman and Nicobar Command.
IAF – WAC / SWAC / EAC / CAC / SAC - Western / South Western / Eastern / Central / Southern Air Commands.

Fig. 5.36. Theatre Command Option.

(a) The conglomerate of Service Commands that each would comprise of.

(b) Lead role, if any, for a specific Service in each of the commands.

Four Theatre Commands have been proposed - North and Western, Eastern, Central and South and Peninsular. The existing Service specific Commands have been put into four rational groups. The individual Service regional Commands were already focused on actual threat perceptions.

In addition to the existing Strategic Command four functional Commands have also been proposed. Each with a lead Service as a situational head.

This may not be the best or the most optimal option. Some would say that the option presented would result in Commands that would be too large and unwieldy. The focus should be on operational and functional imperatives. Their attention would need to be drawn to the US Northern Command – whose responsibility stretches across the continent, including USA, Canada and Mexico and encompasses homeland security, aid to civil power and disaster management also. The optimum acceptable option would emerge as a consensus among the professionals at JCOSC. However, the option presented, has the following advantages:

(a) Appears rational and could be implemented in shortest period, with least disruption to existing setup. Maximum emphasis, in the initial stages would be in providing requisite networking facilities. This would be unavoidable, in any case, to bring about synergy and jointness. Collocation of the component service HQs element at the Theatre Command HQs could take place in due course.

(b) The option also, essentially retains the existing specialised nature / capacity of forces in the respective regions. These have been built up over the years, on basis of ground reality, environment, type of threat / terrain etc.

(c) Gives due recognition to the unfolding maritime scenario. So far the strategic thinkers were talking about Malacca Strait, Seychelles, Gulf of Aden / Oman as India's Maritime zone of interest. Shri Shyam Saran a former Foreign Secretary in his recent article in the *Indian Express* is already stretching that boundary to Indo-Pacific region. India's horizon is already moving in that direction – substantiating, former foreign secretary's stand. With the commitment of off-shore drilling for Vietnam in the South China Sea and strategic partnership with several nations in the region – it would seem that India is already attempting to convert its *look east* policy into concrete action. Even Hillary Clinton, the US

Secretary of State in her article in the Journal of Foreign Policy is talking about - "The Asia- Pacific having become a key driver of global politics".——— which she in the US context "stretches it from the *Indian sub-continent* to the Western shore of the Americas". These are all pointers to the expanding range of India's maritime interests.

The mind-set problem associated with *turf* concerns would have to be put aside in favour of the compulsions of joint action being the need of the unfolding twenty-first century scenario. The urgency and importance of the requirement is such that it can not be solely left to evolve within the JCOSC without an empowered CDS to impose unpleasant decisions. Meanwhile, CIDS should be designated the authority to steer this programme through the inter-service quagmire. The FC should closely monitor the progress.

SEQUENCE OF IMPLEMENTATION

For a smooth transition, the recommended sequence of implementation is as follows:

(a) At the outset itself, it would be best for the conceptual frame-work, road map (approved by CCS) to be spelt out, along with broad time frame for implementation. The objective should be to establish a three functional divisions in the Armed Force Management structure: Staff / Operation / Support Divisions. The JCOSC be charged with the responsibility of working out the details. CIDS to be the catalyst.

(b) CIDS to be upgraded to same rank as the COS – in line with the VCDS and JOC of the UK system.

(c) Operationalise A&NC and SFC, with the CIDS as administrative, technical and operational authority. Authorise phased build up of full fledged A&NC as a pilot project for Theatre Command concept.

(d) Strategic Wings (Navy) and (IAF) will have Chief of Naval Staff (CNS) and Chief of Air Staff (CAS) respectively as their Administrative / Technical Authority. CIDS being the Operational Authority. Only NCA will have the powers to authorize use of nuclear weapons [NW].

(e) Experience of the above on fast track, be used, to evolve Theatre Command concept – within a set time frame, not exceeding two years.

(f) CIDS be charged with all ongoing and projected Joint / Unified Service activities including: the Space Command / ABM Command / Special Forces Command / Logistics Command and development of Joint / Unified C^4I^2SR system network under combined architecture.

(g) In the interim – the conventional combat forces, gear up in planned stages, not exceeding one year – to adapt the Soviet Union Unified Command model. This would have the following advantages :-

(i) Likely to meet with least resistance from the incumbent COSs.

(ii) Achieve the objective in shortest possible time with least disturbance / dislocations.

(h) Now that IDS has been operational for over a decade – it should be ensured that no CDS or Deputy CDS /CIDS is appointed to IDS unless he has had, at least, one tenure in a Joint Service assignment. Progressively, promotion to all flag rank should also require a tenure in a Joint Service Organisation as a criteria appointment

(i) In the absence of a CDS – such a radical extraordinary measure is considered unavoidable. In any case – the evolutionary experiment with CJCSC at the helm, for the last ten years has failed to deliver against the CCS decision of 2002. Presumably this is attributable to the inherent contradictory demands flowing out of the twin hat situation.

Having had a macro-level view of the proposed over-all HDM interim structure – there is a need now to look at a few of the crucial linked subsets in greater detail. The following important sub-sets will be considered in the next few chapters:

(a) RML sub-set.

(b) National Coastal Security sub-set.

(c) Historical bogey over civil-military relationship.

Replenishment at Sea

Bibliography

1. A.P. Revi "Higher Defence Management". IDR Vol. 21(2). 2006/ p. 91.
2. A.P. Revi "Restructuring Higher Defence Management" Journal of Indian Ocean Studies. Vol. 14 No. 14. December 2006.
3. Admiral. vs. Shekhawat. "Restructuring of Defence Forces including MOD". USI Journal July / September 1999.
4. Anit Mukerjee. "The Absent Dialogue".
5. Anit Mukerjee. "The fuure is now". *TOI*. 17 June 2011.
6. Anit Mukerjee. RUSI Journal. October - November 2011.
7. Brig. Gurmeet Kanwal. "Rebuilding Indian Army".
8. Gen VP. Malik and Brig. Vinod Anand. "Defence Planning Problems and Prospects".
9. Gen. JN. Chaudhury. "India's Problems of National Security in 1970s". USI National Security Lecture 1973.
10. Governement of India Transaction of Business Rules 1961.
11. Hiranandani V. Adm - Transition to Eminence. Part of IN History Series.
12. Jasjit Singh "Air Power and Joint Operation".

13. K. Subrahmanyam. "Higher direction of Defence and its Organisation". ODSA Strategic Analysis. Vol. 11; No. 6. Sept. 1987.

14. Lt. Gen. PC. Katoch "Integrated Theatre Command" SP Year Book 2011 - 2012.

15. Michael C Desch "Civilian Control Over Military".

16. NS Sisodia. DG IDSA - India Strategic July / Aug 2011.

17. Ranjith Pandith "Policy paralysis Hits Submarine Induction" TOI 12 March 2012.

18. Shyam Saran "Mapping the Indo-Pacific" - Indian Express 29 October 2011. <http:/www.indianexpress.com/news/mappng-the-indopacific/867004/0>

19. US Tower Committee Report. NYT. 1986.

20. Wng. Cdr. R. Venkatraman "Indian Higher Defence Organisation and Management? KW Publishers. 2011.

6

Revolution in Military Logistics

Every one on the street today is talking about globalisation. Those in military circles, talk about Revolution in Military Affairs (RMA) and are going ahead full steam on hardware acquisitions. But in the Indian context - when it comes to Revolution in Military Logistics (RML) – particularly in the military circles, we are in a denial mode. Here the intent is to try and bring about a change in the outlook on this very important area – that is taken for granted.

RAISON D'ETRE

The raison d'être for any military logistics system is to ensure that the correct item and service is provided to the end user, at the right time, place and in correct quantity and quality required for the situation.

In the final analysis, most military campaign failures can be attributed to the mismatch between the operational plan and the logistic support capabilities. This could be well illustrated with examples of over stretched logistics, from world military history.

As stated earlier, the contemporary definition of logistics stretches from concept design stage to R&D, prototype production, testing, serial production, induction into service, life-time product support and modernisation, till final disposal. This is further subdivided into two broad categories. The first dealing with acquisition and the other dealing with life-time product support.

A reference to Chapters 1 to 4 will clearly demonstrate that in respect of RML – a common thread that runs across the board, globally, is the integration of logistics within the Armed Forces. Besides improving efficiency and massively reducing the inventory / storage infrastructure – there is a reported over-all saving of over 20 per cent.

In the context of integrated logistics - the weakest chink in the Indian armour today is that of the army. It must first achieve intra-service integration. To enable that - the most essential prerequisite is the computerisation of the logistics. This should be accompanied in parallel by restructuring the overall organisation. This by no account means that the present set up is not delivering. What it means is that by restructuring- the future challenges could be met more effectively, speedily and efficiently - both in material and human terms.

At the same time and in spite of serious handicaps, the most encouraging part, is that the Army, seems to be the most open and willing service to take on this challenge. COAS's *"Transformation Study" report* indicates the way forward. It is considered that this does not go far enough.

In this context, the Navy and the Air force are far ahead of the Army. They have kept pace with each other in bringing about organisational changes linked to RML. The Air force is perhaps a hairbreadth ahead in the conventional logistic management arena. But in the Capital Acquisition and weapon platform development management – the Navy is way ahead.

The need of the hour is to work in unison and share one's experience and expertise to move forward.

HISTORICAL PERSPECTIVE

At the time of independence, the Indian Army, the Navy and the Air Force, inherited a handed down WW II organisational structure from their respective parent service in UK. Since then, the British system has undergone a sea change. Indian armed forces have, however, continued to grow, basically under the same original framework.

In view of above and the NSC directive of 2000 – the UK model is considered first.

THE BRITISH SYSTEM

In the last fifty years the British system has undergone a series of changes in the following sequence:-

(a) Introduction of computerised logistics management.

(b) Integration of all intra-service activities on conventional logistics.

(c) Corporatisation of repair infrastructure – till then, an in-house service.

(d) Privatisation of repair infrastructure followed by outsourcing of other support infrastructure.

(e) Integration of all inter-service logistics, under broad heads of Defence Logistics Organisation (DLO) and Defence Procurement Agency (DPA).

(f) Finally, merger of DPA + DLO + Defence Commercial Service Agency (DCSA) into Defence Equipment and Support Agency (DE&SA) – with the Chief of Defence Material (CDM) in charge, as a four star General / equivalent.

The functional chart of CDM is illustrated at Fig. 2.19. This has been discussed in depth at Chapter 2. It would be observed that the organisation has two major Divisions:

(a) One dealing with capital acquisitions. This is subdivided on functional basis into DG Ships, submarine, combat aircraft, land equipment etc. The next level is illustrated, using DG Ships as an example.

(b) The second division - deals with support infrastructure - with the three Chiefs of Material (COMs) in the rank of 3 star generals heading their respective service support division.

The overall MoD (UK) set-up, with the CDM subset incorporated therein, is illustrated at Fig. 2.20. It would be observed here, that the CDM is a four star general - same as the Chiefs of Naval / General/ Air staff / Joint Operational Command / VCDS.

In the Indian context, if adopted – this would essentially mean delegation to the CDM (I), the responsibility and empowerment of the following existing authorities. As a part of the Service HQ / MOD integration process priority need to be given to designating the CDM (*a Flag Officer*) as a full fledged Secretary to the Government with same financial power and authority as the Secretary (DP&S): -

(a) Master General of Ordinance (MGO) + Quartermaster General (QMG) + E in C + Part of Adjutant General (AG).

(b) Air Officer in Charge Maintenance (AOM).

(c) Chief of Material (COM) + Controller of Warship Production and Acquisition of the Navy + Director General of Naval Design (DGND).

(d) Special Secretary / DG. Acquisition – MoD.

(e) Department of Defence Production (DDP) of MoD.

Though desirable and pragmatic - in the Indian context, this does not appear to be feasible in the near future, mainly because of the heavy historical baggage being carried by the Army. In any case - there is a need to work deliberately and forcefully towards that end.

Since the Naval structure is mature enough to take on this function – the pilot model at Fig. 6.46 should be launched at the earliest. Experience gained would be useful at the stage of implementing the full-fledged integrated Support Division.

Indian military is perhaps the only modern Armed Force in the world, which has the distinction of not believing in a joint logistics organisation.

INDIAN ARMY

In the case of the army, the support Services are responsible to provide the requisite logistics to the Combat Arms. Today, their command and control is split between four different Principal Staff Officers (PSO). In conformity with the *"Transformation Study"* report - the COAS has directed rationalisation of this structure, in a strict time bound frame work. This however does not go far enough

Instances indicate serious disconnect between the combat arm leadership and the logisticians in the field. The crux of the issue boils down to the absence of a credible institutional mechanism for interactive, operation cum logistics process –

especially at operational and tactical level. A classic flow chart illustrating the process needed to be incorporated is at Fig.6.37. This realisation has presumably led to the induction of DG Operational Logistics Organisation (DGOL) at Army HQs. He is currently under the Vice Chief of Army Staff (VCOAS). CIDS also has a Joint Operation Division with a dedicated DDG (Operational Logistics). These, no doubt, are important and urgent requirements. They however skirt the core issue – which has a mind set barrier. In order to achieve a break-through, an out of the box solution has to be found.

Presumably, the above arrangement is an interim one – till such time as appropriate reorientaticn takes place and logistics become fully integrated. Ideally, emulating the British Army model would serve the purpose. This would be the most difficult step to take – bearing in mind the large momentum and deep historical baggage, requiring a change in direction.

A cursory glance at the honours - list board in MGO's office is a revelation of a kind. It would be observed that ever since the creation of the post of Master General of Ordnance

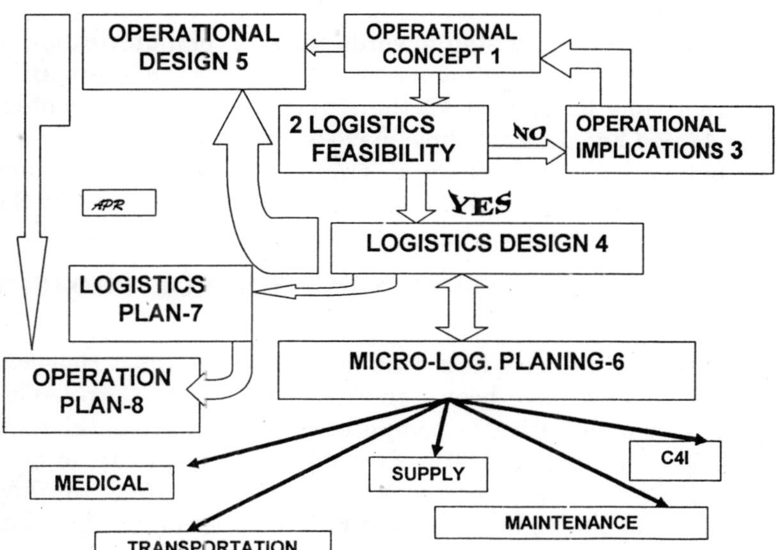

Fig. 6.37. Classic Logistics Planning Cycle.

(MGO) – the PSO heading this Support Service organisation has never been a professional from any element of the Supporting Arm. The feeling of inclusiveness is today considered a basic necessity for the smooth and efficient running of any organisation – even in the corporate Sector. There must have been some legitimate reason for such a situation in the past. This needs to be addressed urgently. In depth knowledge and hands on experience in the multidisciplinary support service is considered an essential prerequisite for showing the way-ahead in this rapidly changing technological environment. One gets the impression that the inordinate delay in setting up of the CICP and an integrated computer logistics management system could be attributed to the poor understanding of the urgency, implications and importance of the facility. As will be discussed later – the absence of such a crucial logistics tool is seriously hampering the operational capability potential of the Army. In recognition of the importance of logistics – many Corporate Houses have started including their logistics chief as a member of their Executive Committee and appointing them as Executive Vice President / Senior Vice President.

COMPUTERISATION

The first logical step towards RML is computerisation of the inventory and creating a network to share the information on real time basis with all the stakeholders. In this context the Armed Forces, as a whole, have failed miserably. No doubt, in penny packets individual groups in each service have achieved sterling success. Some of these are discussed in the following paragraphs.

COMPUTORIZED INVENTORY CONTROL PROJECT (CICP).

CICP in its basic form was formulated in 1994. However belated it may have been - the Army Ordnance Corp (AOC) took a bold initiative to computerize and finally obtained a sanction for CICP in 2001 - at a total estimated cost of over Rs. 460 crores. The project was set in motion in 2002. Initially it was meant to be implemented in five phases but later, that was modified to following three phases:

(a) Phase I was to be primarily devoted to Central Ordnance Depot (COD) Delhi with connectivity to AHQ.

(b) Phase II was required to extend to one Regional Ordnance Depot (ROD), four to five sub-depots and one sample at unit level.

(c) Phase III was required to cover the rest of the system

AOC's initial attempt was to have a customised system of CICP. That basically meant, converting the existing ledger / voucher system into an electronic format – retaining the outmoded procedures embedded there in. Experience in Phase I brought out the rigidity of the system – retaining all the cumbersome, time-consuming procedures. Early in 2007, it was decided to change course and proceed, unlike the Navy and the IAF – to a decentralised solution, adopting commercially available Enterprise Resource Planning (ERP) route. The system had a modular architecture and could have been built up, as one went along. And with experience, the system could be easily upgraded, in line with the technology of the time. The Request for Proposal (RFP) / contract for this was finalised in 2007 /2008 and were projected for expeditious implementation, thereafter. The expected date of completion (EDC) for Phase II / III was set for 2010 / 2012 respectively. Unfortunately, it seems that procedural delays and unfavourable organisational momentum has prevented this vital forward movement - till mid 2010. This was not the end of the story. The contract was finally awarded to Siemens (India) Ltd. In the meantime, the company was taken over by its parent unit abroad – leading to cancellation of the contract, on security grounds. This was followed by further prolonged bureaucratic delays. The whole issue got reopened again – including a debate on ERP / COTs route etc. Fresh RFP has again been floated in September 2011.This is a serious set back. In spite of a CCS approval for such a crucial project – as far back as 2001, the implementation has been held up due to force of circumstances and bureaucratic delays. There were very high expectations from this project not only for the Ordnance Corp but the fall out in other areas of intra-service and inter-service Logistics is incalculable. The linked fall out in connection with codification will be discussed later.

The ASC's Stores Monitoring and Control System (ASMACS) and EME's Reliability Availability Delivery System (EMERELD) operate independently.

COMMAND and CONTROL (C^2) NETWORK

Multifarious, individual service oriented, Command, Control and Communication networks / grids are in place and in the pipe line. The Army field formations and Command / Corp / Brigade HQs reportedly, have a comparatively well developed computerised system. These are likely to become available in the near future. Some of these are listed below:

(a) BMS – Battlefield Management System at Battalion and below level – with links to the Brigade and integrated with ASCON.

(b) Project Samvahak – is to provide BMS link to Corp and Div also.

(c) Project Sanjay – BSS – is a Battlefield Surveillance System.

(d) ACCS Shakti – is an Artillery Combat C^2 System.

(e) ADC&R – is an Air Defence Control and Reporting Systems.

(f) F-INSAS – Future Infantry Soldier as a System Project – its sub-system comprises of:

  (i) TCS – Tactical Communication Systems. – 2014.

  (ii) MCCS – Mobile Cellular Communication System.

  (iii) Wi Max system – will interface with CIDSS, ASCON and BMS.

(g) Project Asteroid – CIDSS – provides - Command Information and Decision Support System at the Corp level and:

  (i) Links together all automated systems e.g. BSS, ACCS, ADC&R and BMS – giving a holistic picture.

  (ii) In the future - will link communication systems at strategic, operation and tactical level.

(h) ASCON Phase II – has stabilised and provides data links between static HQs and those at peace locations.

(i) ASCON Phase I –lacks ISDN capabilities for real time transmission of maps streaming videos and its capabilities to provide data link is limited.

It would appear that in most of these systems, one critical component seems to be out of the loop. As brought out earlier, in the case of the AOC's CICP – the integrated logistics management system can today just about feed the online logistic input, on real time, basis to Army HQs. The situation on codification is yet another story – which will be discussed separately. Till such time as the CICP phase III is implemented - it is not possible to make such inputs available to lower formations. The field formations will have to wait till then to be able to get on line logistics information on real time basis. Hence, the necessity for a dedicated Deputy CIDS (Logistics) with HQIDS - to give the necessary impetus to a closely coordinated, integrated approach and speedy implementation at the inter / intra service and DOS (MOD) levels. This aspect will be elaborated later.

Ware housing system would also need modernisation – adoption of universal bar-coding and RF Identifying Device (RFID) systems etc are necessary, to facilitate prompt response to all demands including online tracing of items in transit.

These are critical issues affecting operational capability and needs to be addressed urgently and with extra-ordinary determination. It is considered an important enough issue to be singled out for close monitoring by CIDS and DC.

In the above context, till the formalisation of the Indo-Afghan Strategic Partnership Agreement, concluded on 5 Oct. 2011 – preparations for an *Out of Area* Joint / Unified operations for India was merely an academic exercise. Those undertaken earlier - were aberrations. There is an urgent need now to give serious consideration for such possibilities and make determined contingency planning and realistic preparations.

INDIAN AIR FORCE

In the case of the Air Force - single point responsibility for conventional logistics management lies with the Air Officer in Charge Maintenance (AOM) at Air HQs. The material management and physical distribution function is performed by the Logistics Branch. Maintenance of aircraft and equipment is the responsibility of Air Engineering Branch (Mechanical Electrical). The overall responsibility rests with the AOM.

In Command HQs – logistics and maintenance branches are responsible to the Senior Maintenance Staff Officer (SMSO). The Command Logistics and Maintenance Officer (CLMO) is responsible to the SMSO for all logistics activity of the Wings/ Units within the Command.

INTEGRATED MATERIAL MANAGEMENT ON LINE SYSTEM (IMMOLS)

To facilitate logistics activity – IAF made an investment of over Rs. 50 crores to develop a customised IMMOLS. Audit compatibility was built into the system. The unfortunate part is that, in this day and age, the system was customised exclusively for the IAF and the chances of compatibility and the possible need for exchange of data with the Navy / Army was perhaps not even considered. In the initial stages the emphasis of the prime user of IMMOLS seems to have been more towards central control. The fundamental RML requirement of total asset visibility / transparency across the board, at least within the service - in an open, on-line real time basis, was put on the backburner. This could perhaps have been attributed to the fear of misuse by competing demands from multifarious users of scarce resources.

In an environment of shortages – centralised control is inevitable. It is considered that the advantages of transparency and allowing on line data access to lower formations on real time basis - far outweighs the perceived disadvantages. Such perceived apprehensions have now apparently been taken care of - by resorting to *stove- piping* data release on a selective, *need to know* basis.

AIR FORCE NET (AFNET)

In exchange for spectrum being released by the Defence Forces – the Memorandum of Understanding (MOU) signed between MOD and Department of Telecommunication (DOT) agreed to set up dedicated network for use of defence forces. This calls for DOT – laying of about 40,000 route kilometres of optical fibre cable connecting 290 army stations, 32 naval stations and 162 points for the IAF. The estimated overall cost of implementing the "Network for Spectrum" project is about Rs. 10,000 crores.

IAF Mother Tanker Breast Feeding Navy's MIG29a/c

The IAF AFNET has been developed in collaboration with HCL and BSNL, at an estimated cost of Rs. 1,000 crores. The facility was inaugurated by RM on 14 Sept 2010. AFNET will be connected and extended to a Unified Digital Grid, encompassing all the legs of the Armed Forces. This has been a great blessing in disguise.

AFNET incorporates the latest traffic transportation technology in the form of:

(a) IP (Internet Protocol) Integrated Air Command and Control System (IACCS).

(b) An automated command and control system for Air Defence (AD) operations - integrating all ground-based and airborne sensors, AD weapon systems and C^2 nodes.

(c) Subsequent integration with other services networks and civil radars will provide an integrated Air Situation Picture to operators to carry out Air Defence role.

AFNET is planned to be an effective force multiplier for - intelligence analysis, mission planning and control, post-mission feedback and related activities. This includes maintenance, logistics and administration. The network is secured with a host of advanced state-of-the-art encryption technologies. It is designed for high reliability with redundancy built into the network design itself.

The AFNET is also capable of transmitting video from Unmanned Surveillance Aircraft (UAV), pictures from Airborne Warning and Control Systems (AWACS) to decision makers on the ground and providing intelligence inputs from remote areas.

It would seem that AFNET is compatible with both IACCS and IMMOLS.

Past experience on joint operations during IPKF / Maldives actions and recent amphibious exercises have thrown up serious lacunae - especially in the intercommunication and data transfer role among the Army / Navy / IAF units participating. These need to be addressed urgently. Embedded service units trying to operate as relaying stations is not a satisfactory solution.

INDIAN NAVY

The US Navy (USN) and the Indian Navy (IN) cadre structure are poles apart. In the USN, the *line-officer*, heads all departments on board a ship. One day he could be an Engineer Officer and on another, he could be a Navigator / Gunnery / Communications / TAS / Executive / Commanding officer etc. They are, however, highly dependent on the day to day running of the Engineering Department onboard, to enlisted technical sailors, NCOs / JCOs.

In the case of the IN, on the other hand - the departments are headed by specialist officers. Onboard ships, there are no horizontal movements possible between the Executive and the Engineer officer. The sailors on board are divided into three categories – the highly skilled Artificer / Mechanician, the semi-skilled Mechanic and the Seaman. This situation is likely to continue even after the intake, of sailors is raised to 10+2 level and that of the Executive officers upgraded to B.Tech level. Improvement can only come about, when Engineering and Electrical (E and L) branches are merged, the logistics function is restructured and *user maintainer* concept is implemented in letter and spirit. Alternatively, the US Navy's "line officer" system would need to be adopted, along with their logistics concept.

The Controller of Logistics (COL) is responsible, through the Chief of Material (COM), for most of conventional logistic activity for the Navy. The COM is overall responsible for the material state of all ships, submarines (s/m), infrastructure and equipment. Induction of any equipment / technology into the Navy has to have COMs endorsement. He is also the technical authority for all the Dockyards and Base Repair Organisations. Controller of Warship Production and Acquisition (CWP&A) under VCNS is responsible for all warship production in India and acquisition from abroad.

In the area of Design, Development and Production - the Navy has had distinct advantages over the other two services. The indigenisation orientation was the hallmark of all the Chief of Naval Staffs (CNSs) since independence. The ships and submarines being an integrated fighting machine, with multidisciplinary functions incorporated within - further facilitate this.

The Navy has evolved in stages from designing and building small ships and sophisticated Destroyers to an aircraft carrier and a nuclear powered submarine. It has designed in house, over seventeen class of ships and built beyond eighty ships indigenously. The nuclear powered ballistic missile s/m (SSBN) INS Arihant has been designed and built in India. It is presently undergoing basin and harbour trials. More capable SSBNs are in the pipe line. The indigenously designed a/c carrier at CSL is well under way. In addition to two HDW SSK s/ms - MDL is presently building the scorpene class of SSK s/m under licence from DCN of France. The Navy is getting ready to take on the next challenge of designing and building the next generation of conventional s/m under Project 75(I). To achieve this end - the Navy started training naval designers abroad from the early 1950s. An in-house, multidisciplinary, Design Bureau was also set up. The Navy was fortunate, for having chosen the model of in-house design, not only because - there were no takers in the industry, at the time. But also, because this had the intrinsic advantage of the Navy (as the user), being fully involved and committed in the design choice - from concept stage to delivery and induction into the service. All the stakeholders had full opportunity to have their say, at each stage. Backing out of any project mid-stream was out of question as every step was a corporate decision, supported with requisite funding. Any delay in freezing the design or thereafter, requiring changes in equipment / weapon package would naturally result in cost / time over runs. Today, the order books of all PSU shipyards are full. To make up for their poor productivity – there is an urgent need for adopting modern modular construction methodology and multi-skilled workforce. Also, emerging private sector shipyards need to be encouraged to provide the much needed competition. A beginning has already been made by off-loading construction of five "Sukhania" class of Off-shore Patrol Vessels (OPV) to Pipov Shipyard and some critical s/m hull fabrication work to Larson and Tubro Ltd etc. Also, Pipov Shipyard has gone into Public Private Partnership (PPP) with Mazagon Dock Ltd. Unfortunately this has been put on hold, in view of strong objections from other Private Sector Ship Building Yards.

Due to lack of such long term commitments, vision and frame of mind - the Army and the IAF are still struggling to induct their first indigenous Main Battle Tank (MBT) / Combat Aircraft into the service.

INTEGRATED LOGISTICS ON LINE MANAGEMENT SYSTEM (ILMS)

Like the IAF, the Navy has also developed a customised logistics management system. Integrated Logistics Management on Line System (ILMS) was formally launched in December 1997. ILMS is also audit compatible. But unlike the IMMOLS – it is all encompassing. And has provision for on line data access, on real time basis, across the board, at all levels - from on board ships to Command HQs, ware-house Depots, issue-centres and to NHQ etc. On board connectivity has been facilitated by ship's Logistics Management System (SLMS). ILMOS (Air) deals with naval aviation spares. Weapons Equipment Depots and Armament Stores Depots work outside the ILMOS system. All these systems need to be brought to work - under one frame work.

COMPUTER-AIDED ACQUISITION AND LOGISTICS SUPPORT (CALS) POTENTIAL

As stated earlier, the Navy already has a wide-area network with Integrated Logistics Support and Integrated Management software in place. This creates the data environment required, in its basic form. Electronic commerce solutions are under implementation. Design work undertaken, at the Design Bureau at NHQ and Design Office at the Shipyards are already in digital format. Design drawings / data are exchanged on a daily basis through secure inter-linkages. They currently use the two most widely used STEP and CALS compliant ship design and construction software package – *Tribon* and *Catia*. The *scorpene* s/m package at Mazagon Dock Ltd (MDL) is under validation.

This needs to be carried forward to develop into a full fledged CALS frame-work.

CADRE RATIONALISATION PROGRAMME

In course of time, some substantial reforms have been affected by the Navy, in reducing the disparity between branches. In the early 1980s, posts of Naval Attaches abroad, in important maritime capitals, were opened up to non-executive officers. These have proved to be very productive. Similarly, in recent times, the posts of Controller of Warship Production and Acquisition and Controller of Personnel Services (CPS), both at Vice Admirals rank and Senior Directing Staff (Navy) at National Defence College have been filled up by technical officers. Hopefully, in the near future, other non-operational but responsible assignments like the Chief of Personnel (COP) and ACNS (P&P) etc. would also become open to suitable technical officers.

The Navy has made several serious attempts at restructuring, in other spheres also. Rationalising the personnel structure, to meet the changing demands from the revolution in technology, was another such area. This was also, in line with the practices in vogue, in most modern navies. Two broad alternatives were considered. One pertained to the *"user-maintainer"* concept – linked to the USN's line officer structure. The other, pertained to the limited *"maintainer-operator"* philosophy – linked to the French, Soviet and the British Navies.

As part of the above exercise, a Navy Order (N.O) was promulgated in 1969 – requiring the transfer of responsibility, of power generation and distribution (PGD) on board "Kamorta" class of ships (Project 159AE) to the Engineering Branch. This N.O was kept alive till late 1980s. Similarly, in 1975, under a formal CNS directive, the decision for introducing "*operator-maintainer*" concept on board the remaining ships of soviet origin was also promulgated. Accordingly, the infrastructure requirements and training / manning programmes were put in place. The training programme of the original crew in USSR was also dovetailed into the policy. Over seventy crew (of Projects I641K, 159AE, 205, 877EKM, 61ME, 205ER, 1241RE, 277ME) were trained in USSR – each for a period of about twelve months – based on a *user-maintainer* concept. In spite of all that – such a progressive venture was not allowed to succeed, due to undermining of these efforts, by vested parties from within the service. Lack of will, on the part of the naval hierarchy to see the proposals through to its conclusion, was the final '*nail in the coffin*'. The earlier efforts of amalgamation of Engineering and Electrical (E/L) Branches, as a process of rationalisation (which was implemented in the RN over half a century ago) – also did not see the light of day.

By the time, the 2010 entry of Executive officers at the Naval Academy (NAVAC) graduate – all executive officers there after, would be B.Tech degree holder. This should greatly facilitate the transition into the *user-maintainer regime* - which has evaded the Navy since 1969. To ensure success and facilitate a smooth transition – the Navy must from the very beginning clearly spell out, up-front, its intentions along with a road map:

(a) The original blue print of the 1975 master plan be resurrected and updated.

(b) Transfer *power generation and distribution* responsibilities across the board - as a follow up from the Navy Order (NO) of 1969 on Power Generation and Distribution (PG&D).

(c) Implement the E&L merger, giving the existing young electrical officers, who can earn their Engine Room Watch Keeping (ERWK) / Deck WK tickets, the option between Executive and Engineering Branches.

(d) At the time of bifurcation of Branches, for professional courses, at NAVAC – the electrical officer designates be given the option to volunteer for Engineering / Executive branch duties. Thereafter, they be streamed according to their choice towards Engine Room Watch Keeping (ERWK) / Deck WK duties.

When it comes to implementing the UK DE&S HDM model - the Navy and the Air Force are well placed to take off at a short notice. In the case of the Navy - all that is required is for CWP&A's and DGND's organisations to be shifted from Staff Branch to Material Branch under COM. At the same time, COM would need to be empowered to the extent of the Secretary DP along with integral financial, commercial / contracting staff. Such models are already working well in the DRDO. DGATV is a typical example. They have further refined and streamlined the process through innovative means. Creation of the institution of a financial sub-committee of the Apex Board with the SA, DGATV and FADS as members has greatly facilitated the process.

In any case, due to its special nature, the DPP already has an exclusive category dealing with ship building and a dedicated chapter dealing with such matters. A service incumbent would be professionally competent and accountable in all respects. Additionally, unlike the bureaucrat counter part – in case of any irregularity, the service incumbent could be promptly taken to task under a court martial procedure. As illustrated earlier at Chapter 2 – in the case of UK, the CDM a four star General from the Royal Corp of Engineers performed this role in respect of all three services for last four years.

STANDARDISATION AND CODIFICATION

Standardisation and codification is the key to efficient and effective logistic management. Right from the outset, the Soviet Union had, to a great extent, universalised their standardisation process. Even in late 1960s, one could find the same prime mover, being used in different warships and ashore - for power generation. And same being employed for driving heavy duty specialised commercial / military vehicles and common tractors for ploughing in the fields. Also, HP air compressors, common motors, pumps and communication equipment were used across the board, for multifarious uses.

DIRECTORATE OF STANDARDISATION

In India, the Directorate of Standardisation was established, within the Ministry of Defence (MoD), about forty eight years ago. They are also charged with the responsibility of codification. Today, they have about three hundred personnel with them. Phenomenal amount of work has been put in. But with very little results to show - in the area of practical utility to the service customer. It would seem that their efforts were out of *sync*, with the immediate needs of the users. The user often categorised their work – as academic. Also, due to the service preoccupation with their day to day fire-fighting – standardisation and codification had perforce to be put on the back-burner. Hardly any cooperation was forthcoming, on this count.

At Battle Creek in Michigan – USA has over one thousand dedicated personnel working on codification. They claim to have codified over sixteen million items and over one million companies have contributed towards compiling the data required. They use the NATO codification system (NCS). All of Europe including Russia, erstwhile Warsaw Pact Countries, Canada, Australia, Scandinavia, Israel and most of S America also now use the new NCS format for codification.

The 9th June 2008 Memorandum of Understanding (MOU) with Allied Countries (AC) 135, in Brussels, had the potential of revolutionising the Indian scenario. As far as codification is concerned – the operationalisation of Tier I agreement on NCS had the possibility of bringing all the three services and DOS on to the same grid. This would also make it possible to remove all the technical hurdles in the way of sharing data between the inter-service and intra-service computerised logistic management systems (ILMS / IMMOL/ CICP / ASMACS/ ILMS (AIR) / EMERELD etc.) This could serve as the first step for establishing inter-linkages – and hopefully eventually, leading to an integrated system. However, to convert this into reality- a mind set change would be essential.

The Fig. 6.38. illustrates a simple commercial codification concept. Understanding the basics of this concept becomes necessary here - due to the need for the acceptance of the simplicity in its introduction. More than half the battle against acceptance of a unified codification system would be won – if a jointly acceptable formula could be worked out.

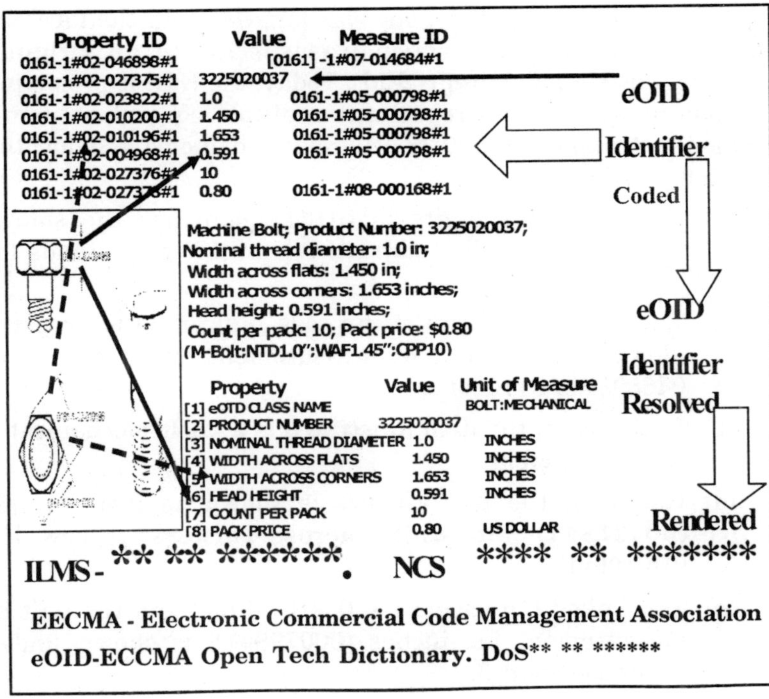

Fig. 6.38. Codification concept.

First, it must be understood that for the computer - digital format is a must. Hence, all information must be provided in a digital form. And a system devised to convert all information, including item description, dimensions, material specification etc. into digital form is essential. The item illustrated is a simple mechanical bolt and given a product No: 3225020037. The codification system originator is Electronic Commercial Code Management Association (ECCMA) and it uses the ECCMA - Open Technical Dictionary (eOTD) for codification purposes. The illustrations shows that the eOTD *class name* for the item works out to – *Bolt Mechanical* at the rendered resolution statement. The illustration also shows how the digitally coded *property identification particulars, value / dimension and unit / measurement identification particulars* for the item translates into item description.

Up to the 20th century, one was familiar with the Part No/ Pattern No system – which was specific to an Original Equipment Manufacturer (OEM). Today, the NCS is promoting a generic system and represents multiple equivalent items. This illustration at Fig. 6.38 attempts to demonstrate how the system works:

(a) The first four digits in (0161) identifies the source responsible for the codification – in this case stands for (eOTD).

(b) The last eight digits of the code indicates the property identification / unit of measurement, respectively i.e. 046898#1 / 014684#1.

(c) In this case, the item illustrated is a <bolt-mechanical>-serial [1] refers.

(d) Height of the bolt <head> is shown against row [6] (004968#1) and width across corners at row [5] (010196#1).

(e) The linked dimension i.e. 0.591 / 1.653 and the unit of measurement i.e. inches (000798#1), is shown under columns 2 and 3.

(f) Similarly, other dimensional properties are also clearly defined.

(g) The linked <product number> i.e. 3225020037 fully identifies the item.

(h) It would also be observed here that this item is not being linked to any specific manufacturer. The master data base also provides the known vendors, globally.

The present codification format in use by the respective service and the proposed *format* under the new NCS dispensation is illustrated at Fig. 6.39. For the last 48 years - DoS has been trying to implement the original version of NCS system. The rate of compliance has been very discouraging especially from the Navy and the IAF. This situation arose mainly not because the respective service - do not wish to cooperate but because of their preoccupation with operational matters and fire-fighting in their own back yards. And they consider this work as an academic exercise. Without a solution to this issue, no amount of macro level decisions, on logistics

		(Group)	(Class)	(Serial No)
DOS –	existing.	**	**	******
CICP –	existing.	**	**	******
		(Group)	(OEM)	(Part No)
ILMS –	existing.	**	**	******
IMMOLS-	existing.	**	**	******
NCS -	new format.	****	**	*******
		(Commodity Class)	(Country Design Source)	(Serial No)

Fig. 6.39. Structure of Codification Format.

reforms - would bring forth any success on the ground. This can not be over emphasised.

The golden opportunity offered under the provision of India having signed the Memorandum of Understanding (MoU) with AC135 in June 2008 remains unutilised. In the case of the Air-force and the Navy more than ninety percent of the imported equipment, ships, submarines and aircraft are acquired from RF, France, USA, UK and now Israel. All these countries are members of AC135. And are committed to use of NCS format for their codification. This should greatly facilitate India - in expeditiously transiting to the NCS format. In the bargain, inter-service benefits would also accrue as a result of commonality between the IAF and the Navy (e.g. MIG29/ MIG29K, Hawk Trainers, LCA, LCH, Brahmos etc). Both the DoS and the respective service must give priority to codify such acquisition projects. Also, the DPP should now stipulate that, to begin with, all future contracts should clearly specify that all catalogues must indicate the NCS Part Numbers in addition to data already being included. Separate contract could be signed with them in respect of earlier supplies. A serious impetus would be given to this process if CIDS is charged with this responsibility and given the means to see it through by appointing a dedicated Deputy CIDS (Logistics).

Experience of the western world military in adopting an integrated and computerised logistics system has confirmed following advantages:

(a) Joint evolution of operation cum logistic plan at – strategic, operational and tactical levels.

(b) Efficient and effective logistics system.

(c) Higher customer satisfaction.

(d) Prompt response to flexible operational demands.

(e) Large reduction in stock holdings.

(f) Fifteen percent savings in inventory costs.

(g) Better sourcing contracting – leading to further twenty percent savings.

Everything now seems to be converging towards a solution. Only the three Services, DOS, AHSP and DGQA have to put their acts together. Since, on this count, DOS under MOD has not been able to deliver in the last half a century – it is better to give CIDS the responsibility as a nodal agency to provide over-sight as a part of an integrated MOD set up. An urgent solution must be found. This issue can not be looked at in isolation – as has been done in the past. The importance of an on-line net-work, providing logistics inputs on a real time basis, on demand, to the field formations cannot be over-emphasised – particularly in the context of out of area operation contingencies.

DEFENCE CAPITAL ACQUISITION (INDIA)

DEFENCE PROCUREMENT PROCEDURE

Looking at it holistically - Capital Acquisition forms an important part of the overall logistics activity. To deal with this vast subject - the Ministry of Defence (MoD) has promulgated the Defence Procurement Procedure (DPP) document. These are a series of documents promulgated by MoD, since 2002. These form a near comprehensive set of documents – covering all feasible options available in defence capital acquisition process, along with the linked procedures. These are regularly revised every alternate year. Urgent, amendments / alterations are incorporated on an as required basis.

CATEGORY NOMENCLATURE.	ACQUISITION PARTICULARS.
1. BUY & MAKE - (B&M)	Tank-T90, Su 30, Hawk (AJT), MRCA /MMRCA,Towed Gun, Ultra Light Howitzer
2. BUY GLOBAL - (BG)	*Jalasho / Trent*, C130J- Super Hercules, Tanker- IL78, MIG29K, Goroshkov / *Vikramaditya, Boeng* P8I- LRMR a/c, Barakh I & II.C17 - *Globe MasterIII, Sea King UH-3, FleetTanker.*
3. DESIGN COLLABORATION & MANUFACTURE. (DC&M) –	IAC, FGFA, Brahmos, Barakh IV.
4. BUY & JOINT DEVELOPMENT (B&JD). -	AWAC IL76.
5. DESIGN & MANUFACTURE (Indian) -D&M (I) –	LCA, LCH, AEW&C a/c, ALH.
6. DESIGN & MANUFACTURE (Strategic) – D&M (S) –	AGNI, PRITHVI, ARIHANT
7. DESIGN & MANUFACTURE (Navy). – D&M (N) –	Proj. 15A, 16A, 17, 25A etc.
8. MAKE under LICENCE – M (L).	SCORPENE. Projects -P75; P75I etc.
- Private Sector – Mohindra & Mohindra Ltd - In collaboration with IAI (RAMTA)/ (ELTA) of Israel.	Light Armoured Multi-role vehicle, border surveillance vehicle, GPS & communication equipment
9. BUY INDIAN – B (I) –	>30% indigenous – if systems are being integrated by Indian vendor.
10. BUY & MAKE Indian – B&M (I)	Purchase from Indian vendor followed by license production / indigenous production.
11. MAKE Indian – M (I) APR	-High Tech complex system design, development and production indigenous. -Proven or matured technology w/o fundamental research. -Level playing field for Public / Pvt players. -Time bound. - OPV – at Pipov Ship-yard. - PPP between Pipov ship-yard & MDL for building warships.
12. BUY INDIAN	Low Tech Mature System > 50% indigenous content.
13. FAST TRACK (FT).	- To meet OPS / unforeseen urgent requirements.

ABBREVIATIONS: MRCA / MMRCA – Medium Multi-role Combat A/C; IAC – Indigenous A/c Carrier; AWAC – Airborne Warning & Control A/C; AEW&C – Airborne Early Warning & Control A/C; FGFA – Fifth Generation Fighter A/C; LCA – Light Combat A/C; LCH – Light Combat Helicopter; ALH – Advanced Light Helicopter; OPV – Off-shore Patrol Vessel; PPP – Public Private Partnership; MDL – Mazagon Shipyard Ltd.

Fig. 6.40. Categories of Acquisition – DPP 2008.

DPP 2008 gave some clarifications on issues that were not clear earlier and essentially provided further breakdown of the *"Make"* category. A typical list of the capital acquisition process has been divided into categories as shown at Fig. 6.40. This is not an up-to-date comprehensive list. It is only an indicative list of categories involved. For purpose of clarity – each category has been identified with specific projects also. An amendment was issued on 29 Sept 2009 - basically introducing a few new *"MAKE"* categories and increasing the ceiling on delegated financial powers etc. The last version DPP2011 was published in December 2010. In essence, DPP2011 introduces a policy that extends the:

(a) Ship-building section to include private participation.

(b) Off-set policy to include aerospace, internal security and training within the gambit of eligible product and services.

As an example, the process involved in executing a typical *"Make"* category of acquisition is functionally illustrated in the flow charts at Figs. 6.41, 6.42 and 6.43. This clearly indicates the demarcation of responsibility between the major players involved. The role of the respective SHQ, HQIDS and Acquisition Wing are also illustrated. Details are available in the DPP 2008 document.

Financial powers, for capital acquisition, have been delegated as follows. These are reviewed periodically:

(a) Vice Chiefs - upto Rs. 30 crores.

(b) Secretary DP. - upto Rs. 50 crores.

(c) RM. - upto Rs. 100 crores.

(d) RM + FM. - upto Rs. 200 crores.

(e) CCS. > Rs. 200 crores.

The DPP document has progressively evolved into a realistic and workable concept. Main weakness, however, lies in the highly inadequate wherewithal being provided to the designated organisations. The activities in flow chart at Fig. 6.41 are primarily those to be handled by HQIDS. After obtaining *Approval of Necessity* (AON) from the Defence Acquisition Council (DAC), shown at serial 18 – the baton is passed on to the Acquisition Wing. Acquisition Plan Categorisation Committee (APCC) at serial 8 of the flow chart is chaired by the Deputy

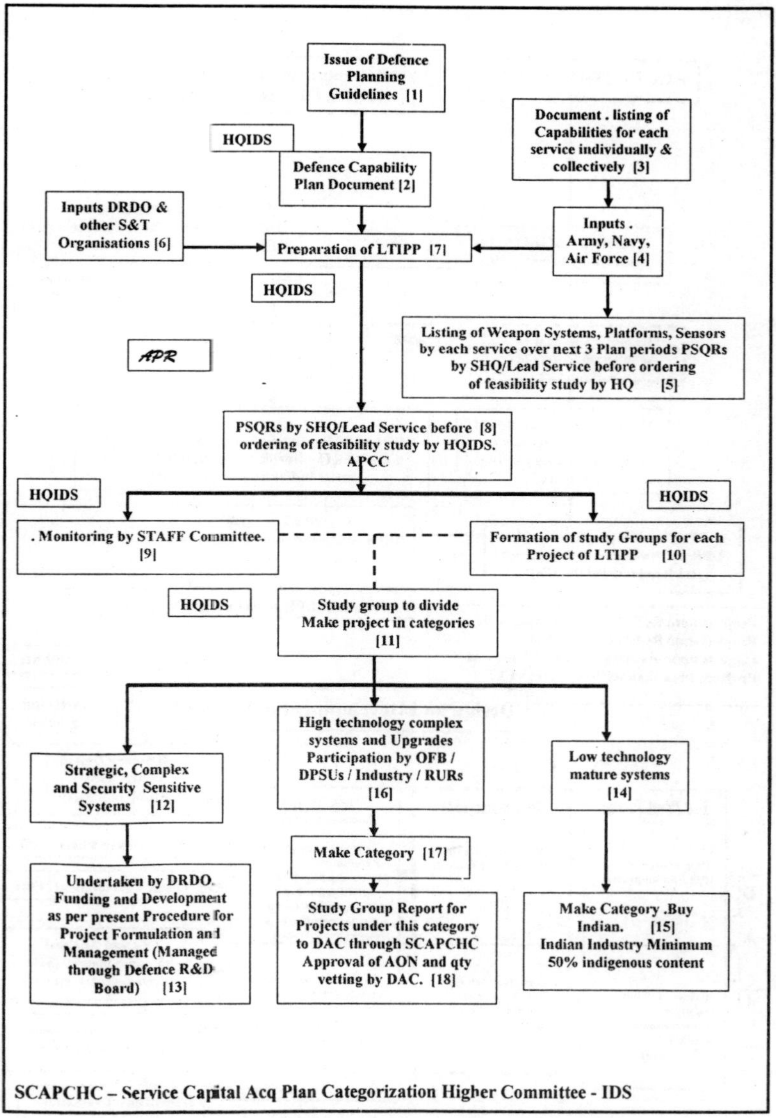

Fig. 6.41. Make Category Flow Chart.

CIDS (Policy, Plan and Force Development) i.e. DCIDS (PP&FD) and has members at the Joint Secretary level from the relevant Departments. The Service Capital Acquisition Plan Categorisation Higher Committee (SCAPCHC) is charged with

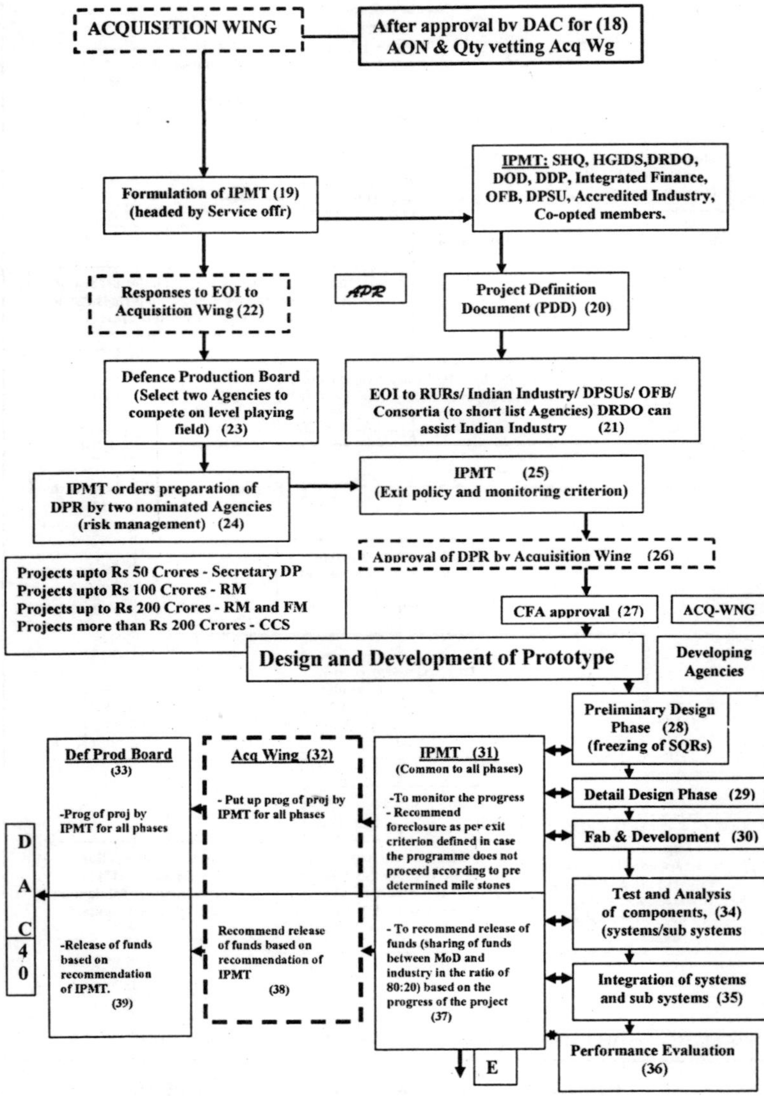

Fig. 6.42. Make Cat Flow Chart II.

the responsibility to recommend increase in off-set percentages / waiver, in very special cases. This committee is chaired by the Chief of Integrated Defence Staff (CIDS). Vice Chiefs are

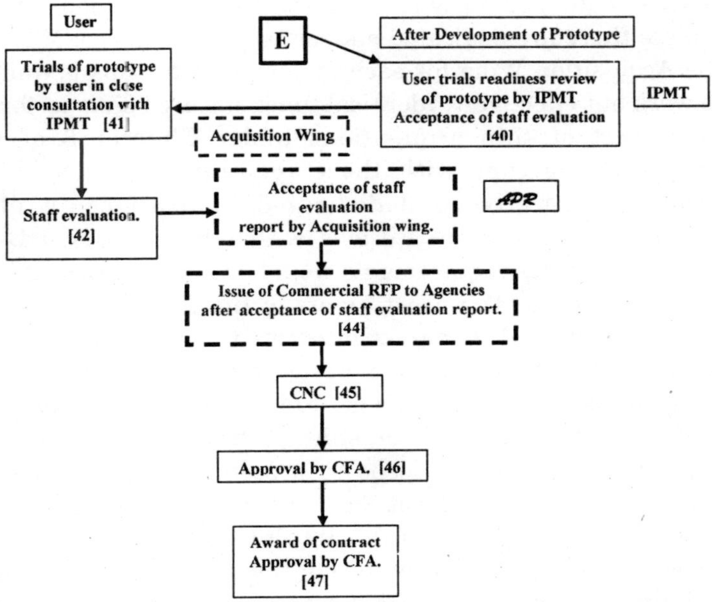

Fig. 6.43. Make Cat Flow Chart III.

members, with equivalent representation from DRDO, Department of Defence Production (DDP), DG Acquisition etc. The Deputy CIDS (PP&FD) acts as the secretary. This is shown as activity number 18. The Defence Offset Facilitating Agency (DOFA) has the responsibility to advice on areas where off-set would be preferred. Neither of them seems to be empowered to stretch the off-set provisions to include some of the strategically important areas, as would be discussed later. The DPP must necessarily be extended to incorporate the same in one form or the other.

All the activities from serial 19 through to serial 40 on Fig. 6.42 are meant to be steered through by the Acquisition Wing. The Integrated Project Management Team (IPMT) is convened by the Acquisition Wing and comprise representatives from SHQ, HQIDS, DRDO, Department of Defence (DoD), DDP, Finance, Ordinance Factory Board (OFB), Defence Public Service Unit (DPSU) and DG Quality Assurance (DGQA). IPMT has been assigned the most crucial role at every step. Conceptually, the process is viable. But IPMT, as constituted, is least equipped to deal with the massive responsibilities. Unless there are dedicated supporting core teams (PMT) with the Acquisition Wing for each major project – this is unlikely to work out effectively. Identical functions are being performed in respect of ship acquisitions under Chapter 3 of DPP document. To cope with these requirements – NHQ has elaborate, effective and dedicated institutions in place. Replication of such institutions with other Service HQs, to deal with similar requirements would go a long way to streamline the process. The constituents of the IPMT could remain the same but SHQ, as part of integrated MOD, should be made the convener. It would be more appropriate for such Project teams under SHQ to handle all support responsibilities to the IPMT. There is a need for shifting from the present mere *procedural irregularity* focus to a *value for money* oriented approach. The flow chart at Fig. 6.43 demonstrates the process involved after successful completion of the prototype development phase. Acceptance of the staff evaluation report, leading to commercial request for proposal (RFP), final approval by CFA and award of contract follows.

OVERSIGHT REQUIREMENTS

In addition to the institutionalised internal technical audit superimposed by the MOD (Finance) systems - Parliamentary over-sight requirements are catered for by the Controller and Auditor General (CAG), Central Vigilance Commissioner (CVC) and Parliamentary Standing Committee for Defence (PSCD). The CAG undertakes a mandatory audit of all projects costing over Rs. 75 crores and a sample audit on all others. The CAG's report is laid on the table of the House. Public Accounts Committee (PAC) of Parliaments, thereafter, follows up with a deeper scrutiny and submit their recommendations to Parliament for appropriate action. The CVC exercises both preventive and punitive role. The PSCD provides additional over-sight.

SHIP BUILDING

Naval involvement with shipbuilding, as brought out earlier, has been so extensive that a dedicated chapter had to

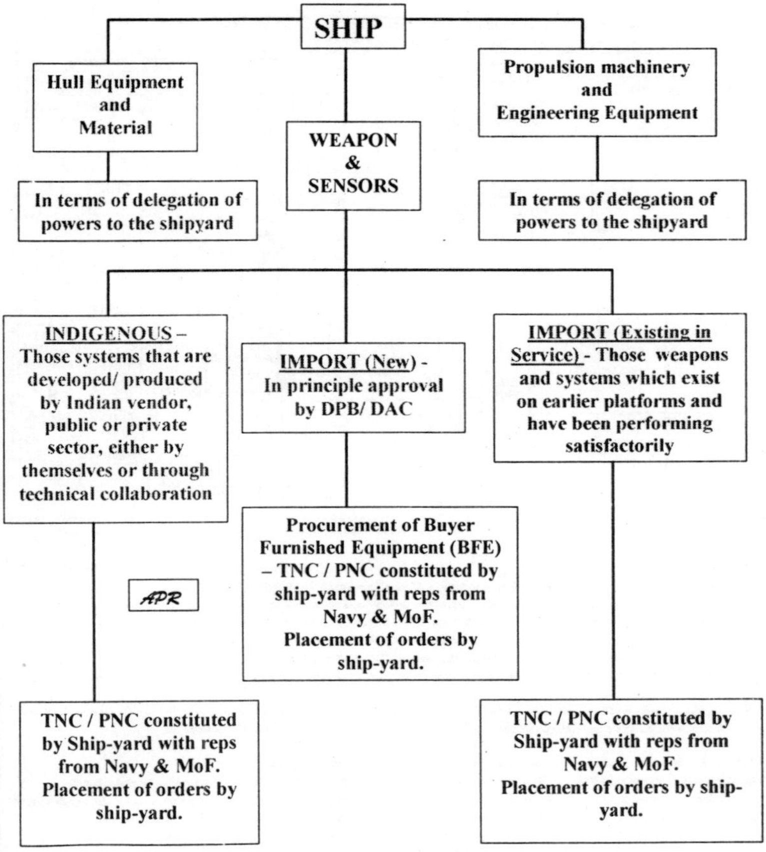

Fig. 6.44. DPP 2011 – Flow Chart Ships.

be devoted in the DPP, on this exclusive category. The ship acquisition model is illustrated at Fig. 6.44. For better understanding of the ship acquisition process – this should be read along with the flow chart at Fig. 6.45. The naval model has reached such a mature stage that with not too great an effort – this model is almost ready to be dovetailed into a DE&S (UK) model illustrated at Fig. 2.19. The naval model has already graduated to accepting private sector participation in competition with DPSU /PSUs and Public Private Partnership in warship building activities for the Navy and Coast Guard.

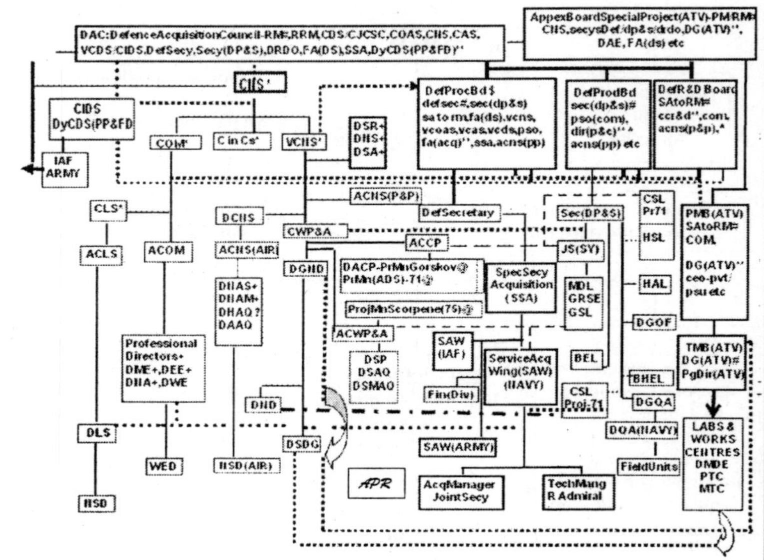

ABBREVIATIONS: RM-RakshaManthry,CNS-ChiefofNavalStaff,VCNS-ViceCNS,COM-ChiefofMaterial, DEE-DirElectricalEngineering;DWE-DirWeaponEngineering;DNA-DirNavalArchitecture;DNAS-DirNavalAirStaffDivision ACWP&A- AsstChief of WarshipProduction&Acquisition;SpSecyAcq-SpecialSecretaryAcquisition;DRDO-DefenceR&D Organisation; DNAM-DirNavalAirMaterial;DHAQ-DirHarrierAcquisition:DSP-DirShipProduction;DAAQ-DirAircraftAcquisition;DoD-Dept of Defence DSAQ-DirShipAcquisition; NSD-NavalStoresDepot; WED-WeaponsEquipmentDepot; NASD-Naval Armament Supply Depot DLS-DirLogisticSupport; ProMan-ProjectManager; Secy(DP&S)-SecretaryDefenceProduction&Supply; DGOF-Director General DGQA-DirGenQualityAssurance;SAtoRM-ScientificAdvisot toRM;CIDS-Chief of IntegratedDefenceStaff;DOD-Department ofDefence ;

DQA(N)-DirQualityAssurance(Navy);MDL-MazagonDockLtd;GRSE-GardenReachShipYard;GSL-GoaShipyard Ltd; DCNS – Dy Chief of Naval Staff CSL- CochinShipbuildingYard Ltd; HAL-HindustanAircraft Ltd; BDL- BharathDynamic LTD; BEL-BharathElectronic Ltd

DSMAQ-DirSubmarineAcquisition; DND-DirectorNavalDesignBureau.;ATV – Advanced Technology Vessel; ACNS(AIR)-AsstChiefNavalStaff(Air);HSL-HindustanShipYard; SAW – Service Acquisition Wing;PMB – Programme Management Board. DSA-DirSubmarineArm;DSDG-Dir s/mDesignGroup;JS(SY)-JS Shipyard;PSO-PrincipleStaffOff coopted as concerned JS(SY)-JS shipyard; CDS-ChiefDefenceStaff,CJCSC-ChairJointChiefStaffCommittee,FA(DS)-FinancialAdviser(DefServices),PMB-ProgrManagementBd coas-ch of ArmyStaff;cas-Ch AirStaff;vcoas-vice coas;vcas-vice cas;cwp&a-ControllerWarshipProduction&Acquisition. DyCDS(PP&FD) - DeputyChief of Defence Staff(Policy Planning & ForceDevelopment); TMB – Technical Management Board; DMDE- Defence Machnery Development Establishment; MTC - Machinery Trial Centre; PTC - Prototype Test Centre; CLS-Controller of Logistics Services; ACLS- Assistant CLS; ACOM- Assistant Chief of Materials; DME- DirectorMarine Engineering.

Fig. 6.45. Functional Organisation Chart Naval Acqisition.

The illustration at Fig. 6.45 identifies and further elaborates, as follows, the linkages involved in the acquisition process:

(a) The role of major players involved in the ship acquisition process.

(b) The chain of inter-linkages between the important stake holders at NHQ and institutions involved with Defence Procurement / Production and DRDO.

(c) Dedicated project teams specific to each mega-naval projects (e.g. Scorpene, Vikramaditya / Goroshkov, indigenous Aircraft Carrier [IAC] and Arihant etc).

Project monitoring is normally undertaken at the:

(a) Apex level with Secretary of Defence Production in the chair – every six months.

(b) Second echelon level – CWP&A chairs the review every quarter with members participating from the Acquisition Wing, DP, Finance Defence, DGQA, CDA (N) and Ship Yard concerned.

As the next step forward - it is recommended that a support function Division for the Navy be set up as a pilot project. This would require some reorganisation of the existing structure and putting CWP&A and DGND under COM along with the Naval Acquisition Wing. This arrangement is illustrated at Fig. 6.46. Such a measure would facilitate eventual formation of an integrated support division.

The illustration at Fig. 6.46 is a subset of the overall organisational structure at Fig. 5.35 and a modification of the existing Naval Acquisition matrix shown at Fig. 6.45. All Naval support elements of NHQ and MOD have been integrated and put under the COM - to provide a comprehensive womb to tomb support to all naval assets. This would entail shifting of CWP&A, the DGND organisation and the Naval Acquisition Wing (which is presently under DG Acquisition / Special Secretary Acquisition) and integrating them with the Material Branch. This will ensure a single window comprehensive service provider for the Navy, with full accountability.

In the new dispensation - the illustration also shows the cross linkages between NHQ and the Defence Procurement / Production / R&D Boards. The horizontal linkages between the following entities are also shown:

(a) DSDG with DMDE / SBC / TMB.

(b) DND with the Shipyards.

(c) COM with the Defence Procurement / Production / R&D Boards.

(d) CIDS with the Defence Procurement / Production / R&D Boards.

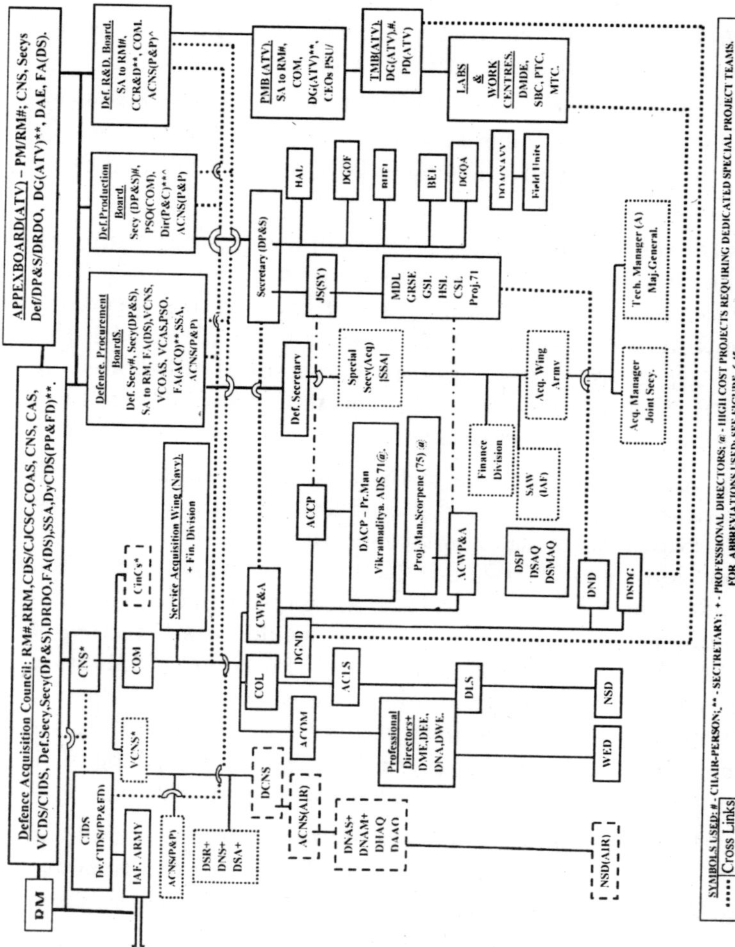

Fig. 6.46. Projected Organisational Chart Naval Acqusition.

(e) ACNS (P&P) with the Defence Procurement / Production / R&D Boards.

(f) VCNS with the Defence Procurement Board.

(g) CNS with Defence Acquisition Council.

The Chief of Material (COM) as a PSO to CNS will be fully accountable to CNS for the total support function of the Navy. At the same time - COM being a member of the Navy Board, the Defence Procurement / Production / R&D Boards and the DAC will, to that extent, take the organisation one stride forward towards achieving functional integration of NHQ and the MOD. In due course, this model could be adapted and emulated by the other services, in a manner best suited to them. In the context of ship-building and acquisition the Navy has already demonstrated an effective workable model. This step would only enable taking that process to its logical conclusion.

Such an arrangement with a pilot project – would in no way curtail / impinge on the legitimate prerogative of the Naval Staff Branch in the following areas of policy matters and issues of strategic concern to the Naval Staff:

(a) Formulation of capability requirements.

(b) Allocation of priorities to Naval Projects.

(c) Naval budget allocation and control within the service.

(d) Corporate role in:

  (i) Evaluation of SQRs.

  (ii) SEPC.

  (iii) Concept design formulation.

  (iv) Preparation of Statement of case.

  (v) TEC recommendation.

  (vi) Staff evaluation report.

  (vii) Proceedings of the Defence Procurement / Production / R&D Boards.

As part of the over-all integration plan of SHQ with MOD – designate COM as a Secretary to the Government and empower him with linked financial power and authority.

Fig. 6.47 illustrates the flow chart in respect of the *Buy* option of the acquisition procedure. It would be observed that out of thirty three activities listed – the Acquisition Wing has

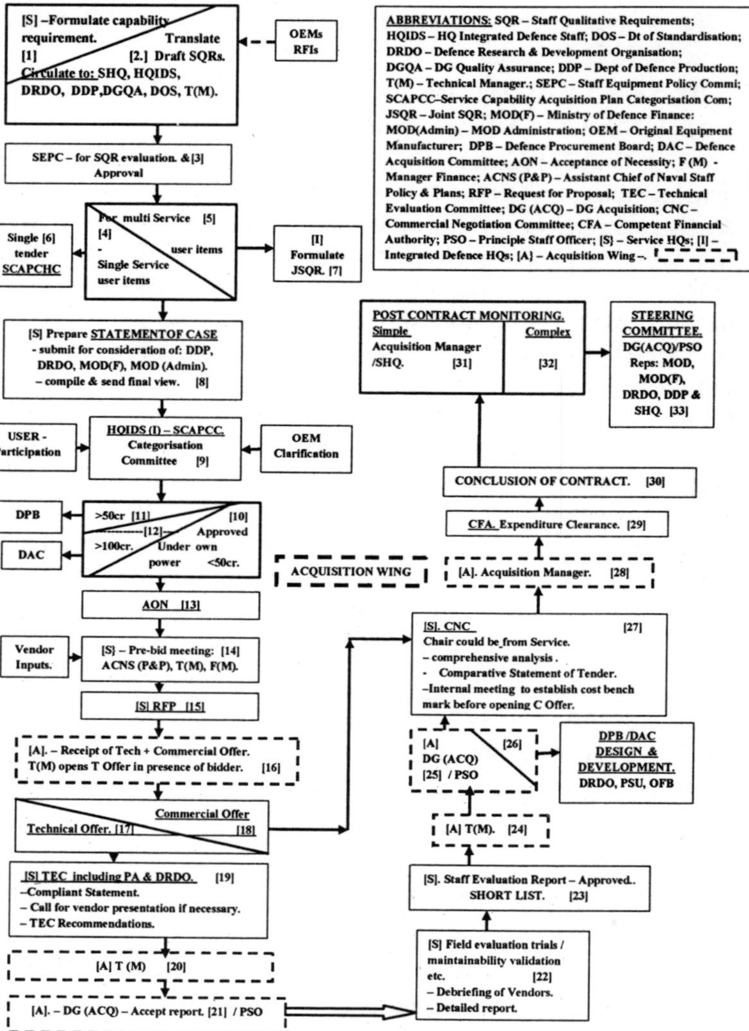

Fig. 6.47. Analysis of DPP 2011 – buy option.

only an administrative clearance role in respect of six activities (i.e. at serials 16, 20, 21, 24, 25/26, and 28). DGAQ has no professional expertise to stand on judgement over the TEC recommendations or the Staff evaluation Report. He can only check out on the conformity of the technical document presented to the format prescribed. In respect of the Navy - these functions would be more effectively and efficiently performed if COM was empowered to under take the same and he could be justifiably held responsible and accountable for any impropriety committed. CIDS could perform the oversight role.

UK's CDM structure at Fig. 219 and 2.20 has been further rationalised in 2012. This new entity – in the form of DG (Resources) has also been introduced, as CDM Board Member. He provides financial and commercial support at the corporate level. This has been achieved by resorting to re-appropriation from existing entities within the CDM establishment.

Defence procurement Manual (DPM) 2009 deals with procurements through the revenue budget.

OFF-SET OPTIONS

The off-set option offered in DPP2008 and extended further in DPP2011- opens up many new possibilities. DPP 2011 opens the door to include civil aerospace, internal security and training, within the scope of offset discharge obligations. This must be intelligently exploited. The DPP in its present form does not go far enough. Some of the possible avenues for improving the offset obligation advantages, in India's context, are briefly discussed below:

(a) It is estimated that in the next ten years (up to 2022), India is likely to spend about $235bn towards defence acquisitions. On the basis of the present dispensation of thirty percent off-set - this gives an opportunity of extracting transfer of know- how and cutting edge technology benefits - worth at least $70bn. The DPP is however still very restrictive on this count.

(b) Empirical studies of the global scenario have shown a cost escalation factor of up to 30% of actual value of the product - towards the offset provisions.

(c) Against an offset demand of 100% in the case of Europe - India has restricted itself to 30%.

(d) In the case of MMRCA - media report indicated that the cap on the offset provision has been raised to 50%. The CMD HAL in an interview in the March 2012 addition of the India Strategic has defined the cap, at 50% of the foreign exchange element of the contract. Hence - what all this means is not yet in the public domain

(e) India could easily increase the offset obligation limit - provided it puts in place the requisite mechanism to absorb the same, efficiently. This would entail revamping of the existing Defence Offset Facilitating Agency and the SCAPCC. India could increase the obligation limit to nearer the European demands. In which case - it would be advisable for India to reallocate only 40% of that to direct obligations as opposed to 100% today. The remainder being absorbed under indirect obligations. This should however, be only resorted to after clearly identifying specific priority area of interest and putting in place an efficient institutional arrangement to ensure implementation.

(f) In context of its offset policy -India has so far refrained from using the multiplier factor concept. Most countries use this to their advantage. There is no reason why India should not take advantage of the same.

(g) Some countries have assigned a multiplier factor of up to ten for TOT - particularly in activities related to R&D in cutting edge regime.

(h) Multiplier factors could be used to considerable advantage - to fill critical gaps in existing technology. Some glaring examples relevant to India are listed below for illustrative purpose. The unique s/m case is elaborated in greater detail later:

  (i) Engine for Army's Main Battle Tank. This has been the main bugbear holding up the project for several decades.

  (ii) Design and development of a/c propulsion system for future generation combat a/c. The Kavari GT engine project has remained ongoing for the last half a century.

  (iii) Fire control system for ships.

  (iv) Towed array sonar.

  (v) Single hull conventional s/m design.

  (vi) FGFA design and development.

  (vii) Air Independent Propulsion System (AIPS) for s/m.

(i) The existing arrangement fore-closes options for off-sets, in respect of R&D transfer of technology (TOT). The problems in costing, seems to be the main deterrent to even opening a dialogue on the matter.

(j) There should be no reservation in seeking transfer of design know-how / know-why against off-sets. It is a misnomer to think that there is no scope or that costing such transfers are not feasible. These are much better options than to striking it off against tasks which are labour intensive and call for low technical skills - already available in the country. The much publicised export of airframe panels and manual grinding of casting and forgings etc. are some classic examples of tasks to be avoided as part of off-set. Similarly, sourcing defence related software from India is yet another soft option that the vendors often resort to. Most Corporate giants are, in any case, without any institutional prompting - already out sourcing their IT functions to Indian entities. Allocation of additional share under the offset clause would be of no advantage to India.

(k) The above issues in relation to acquiring design know how transfers are not considered - insurmountable problems. It is of national importance and needs to be pursued vigorously. Some of the past instances that indicate some of the possible avenues for getting over these hurdles are listed below:

(i) Precedence exists within the core Defence sector itself. They only need to be unearthed from the archives and used in the new incarnation - in a new format.

(ii) The Submarine to Submarine Killer (SSK) acquisition project with Howaldswerke Deutsche Werft (HDW) - envisaged transfer of design know-how and know-whys for s/m hull and system design. A multi-disciplinary design team comprising of about twenty five design specialists received design training under Professor Aben Gobbler's unit at Kiel / Lubek in Germany, for over twenty months. They were given full access to relevant software, design data, empirical formulae and linked values of design coefficients etc. To earn their diploma - the team had to prepare a concept design of a s/m, to a given Qualitative Requirement (QR) and take it up to and submit a complete -preliminary design. This team has been the back-bone of other s/m design groups (SDG) with the Navy. These went by the board-due to the fall-out from the alleged Bofor / HDW scam.

(iii) The conventional Transfer of Technology (TOT) in respect of s/m production / operation/ maintenance and repair formed altogether a separate entity.

(iv) Full exploitation of the acquired design know-how transfer against the HDW project on other assignments was hampered due to:

- A mismatch between the type of know-how received and what was the need of the hour.
- Due to suspension of the HDW contract - validation option for any other indigenous design was no more open.

(v) Such a contingency could not have been foreseen. In that context, the western expertise was in the area of single-hull s/m. Where as, India's immediate requirement, at the time, due to compulsions of its own - were for a double-hull design. The know-how acquired is not redundant. It will be required for later designs.

(vi) It is heartening to note that, in this case, measures were taken to keep the knowledge alive and kicking for future use and not allowed to fall by the way-side as happened in the case of MDL building skills. The Naval Design Bureau has had an institutionalised system in place to archive all such design know-how imbibed by the individuals and the establishment. Though the original design team is no more available to the Bureau - the where with all is not lost and can be retrieved and built up on, at any time needed.

(vii) Any deficiency observed, on hind-sight, from the HDW project - should have been taken care of in the follow-on s/m acquisition project (i.e. the scorpene project with Direction des Construction Navale (DCN) France. It seems, however, that opportunity has not been made use of - to the extent that it ought to have been.

(viii) Similar to the HDW s/m contract - the scorpene contract also provided for transfer of a comprehensive set of design know-how documents. This package was considered adequate to enable our designers to undertake any modifications and even venture into design of the next generation of single hull s/m. The catch is believed to be on account of being denied access to the linked compendium of s/m equipment and component data /specifications, along with its vendor particulars. This is considered a crucial element needed in systems design. A separate Government to Government Agreement was being insisted upon for any such transfer. The Government failed to appreciate the importance of such an input and did not pursue it aggressively enough. Bearing in mind the national interest in attaining and perfecting an indigenous s/m design capability - this should have been included as a strategic objective of the project. This could have been obtained as a part of the contract or even against an offset obligation. The advice, in this context, of the professional members was discounted by the acquisition bureaucrats of the Board.

(ix) In the circumstances - instead of waiting for another opportunity to open up against the Project 75I (which may not go in favour of France) - an out of the box solution should be found by making a piggy-back attempt against an on going negotiation of a mega project with France. A part of the 50% offset obligation clause attached to the rafale MMRCA project should be exploited to meet this strategic objective. The Navy is at present on the threshold of a break-through in acquiring this capability but for the want of this specific know-how.

(x) Further opening, on this count, will become available again with Project. 75.I on the horizon. In case the option suggested against rafale acquisition does not workout, then - this opportunity must not be allowed to slip by. All deficiencies in design know-how transfer must be clearly identified. All avenues must be pursued, inclusive of exploiting the off-set provision and making full use of the multiplier factor. In this case it should be a full bore Joint Venture (JV) design, development and production contract. Validation of the indigenous design and tank test etc should form part of the deal.

(xi) Another source that may be tapped for finding precedence and means of getting over such hurdles could be discovered, if one looks into DRDO's archives also.

(xii) Similarly, India has the experience of design collaboration, in the case of Brahmos missile project with the RF. There is, hence, no dearth of models available to draw on. Only information needs to be shared between the Defence Departments itself.

(xiii) The so called joint design, development and production Agreement with RF on FGFA - could have been yet another golden opportunity in respect of a combat aircraft This opportunity could have enabled a technological leap-frog effect in acquiring design know-how for a FGFA. The past record of HAL in this context since HF24 does not give much confidence in their capability and determination to extract and imbibe the design know-how opportunity. DRDO /ADA / NAL /HAL/ IAF combination with IAF / DRDO in the driving seat would have had a better chance to deliver.

(xiv) Since it is public knowledge now that the basic Russian a/c proto-type already exists in the form of PAK-FA. - it seems more and more likely, that the FGFA JV is confined to a development / production Agreement only. In which case, the choice of HAL as the lead organisation could be considered rational - since they have the basic requisite expertise of preparing working / production drawings etc.

MISSED OPPORTUNITY - INDEGENOUS DEVELOPMENT OF SUBMARINE ANCILLARIES

As seen from above - the absence of an industrial complex capable of delivering conventional s/m ancillaries and non-inclusion of critical documentation for the same, as part of the original contracts for HDW and DCN s/m - has rendered a well strategized naval plan, for developing a design and development capability, to a naught. The onus for which can once again be squarely laid on the narrow minded approach of the bureaucrats in the Acquisition Department.

This brings to the fore, another parallel attempt made earlier - which could have partly compensated for the deficiency highlighted:

(a) In the mid 1980s - DRDO had established Defence Machinery Development Establishment (DMDE) and Machinery Test Centre (MTC). These establishments were tasked to develop and test machinery and systems for an indigenous special s/m programme. The task included - all s/m parts pertaining to the secondary propulsion, ventilation, air-condition, hydraulic, pneumatic, steering, stabiliser, diving and surfacing system etc. Most of the s/m system parts required, would have been functionally identical to the parts of s/m in service - except that size and power ratings would be different

(b) In the late 1980s - the author had recommended extending the scope of DMDE and MTC to include development of all engineering equipment and ancillaries required for the s/ms in commission also. This was not conceded to on - security considerations.

(c) At the time - USSR was committed to supply Repair Technical Document (RTD)s including manufacturing drawings and detailed material specifications for all engineering machinery and system components for projects I641K and 877EKM s/m. Majority of documents for I641K were already in place.

(d) The concept of patents and proprietary rights was almost non existent in the Soviet jargon. Resorting to reverse engineering with parts available on the shelf and RTD documents - would have raised no eye-brows. In any case - the soviet practice required the ship yards to produce its own spare parts.

(e) Had DMDE started a parallel line with development and production of specialised s/m part for I641K and 877EKM - then three decades later a flourishing industry would have been available to take on all s/m requirements for the existing and future conventional and nuclear s/m. Hundreds of crores could have been saved against import of Current Repairs (CR) and Medium Repairs (MR) spares kit also.

(f) As brought out earlier - along with the HDW contract for SSK - a compendium of documents listing the range of equipment, machinery and parts that form the s/m system were provided along with specification and vendor details for each. Similar documents have been provided for the scorpene s/m also. These data should have been sourced to develop a range of industrial complex. The CCP approved long term s/m building / acquisition plan - could have been used as a bait to attract full private sector participation.

(g) The growth of the Indian automobile auxiliary industry illustrates the possible advantages in taking this route.

(h) Working in closed water tight vertical silos has prevented exploitation of the commercial / industrial potential of the country. And have left the s/m design and development programme in a limbo. This is the price one will continue to pay for demolishing an established institutional professional arrangement for small parochial sectarian gains.

(i) The status of the in-house professional institutions must be restored. Give these institutions - total over all responsibility for managing their respective technologies including.:

  (i) R&D.

  (ii) Technology induction and life time management.

  (iii) Professional Training & HRD plans.

  (iv) Authority Holding Sealed Particulars (AHSP).

DEFENCE OFF-SET FACILITATING AGENCY (DOFA)

DOFA, today works under MOD (Department of Defence Production). Director (Planning and Coordination) functioning under Joint Secretary (Exports) - acts as the interface with the Industry and the Acquisition Wing. The monitoring of the execution has been left to the Acquisition Wing. This is to be based on the vendor's quarterly report. Neither the DOFA nor the Acquisition Wing has the where withal to do justice to this important function.

In the existing global scenario - the off-set provision is not confined to defence transactions only. It is an issue of national concern. In the Indian context - the lion's share of the off-set provision may, for the present, be largely confined to defence. As per global practice - rationally, there should be a broad based National Commission preferably under the Commerce Ministry, empowered to formulate, regulate and monitor execution of the National Policy on off-set management. All the stake holders should be duly represented in the Commission.

Till an inter-ministerial consensus can be built on the issue and defence continues to dominate the arena - DOFA could carry on handling the subject. For this purpose DOFA would need to be nominated the nodal coordinating Agency for policy formulation and implementation of the off-set provision. It would need to be restructured as follows:

(a) Comprise of a dedicated and integrated specialist cadre to provide continuity and comprise of experts in foreign trade, national economic priories, technology, industrial and military affairs.

(b) Take policy directive from and report / coordinate monitoring progress of off-set implementation to DAC.

(c) Instead of duplicating efforts in DOFA and Acquisition Wings - the respective PMTs with SHQ be delegated the responsibility of monitoring and reporting the implementation of off-sets to DOFA through CIDS.

(d) Similarly, the SCAPCC to fulfil its linked obligations through CIDS.

FOREIGN DIRECT INVESTMENT (FDI)

FDI is yet another issue of deep concern. In 2002 - the defence sector was opened up to private sector participation by Indian Firms and allowed up to 26% in FDI. The Indian policy seems to expect the foreign investor to put in his money into a venture devoid of any control over the partner and accept an unfair advantage in favour of the public sector. Unless such a policy is liberalised - there is little hope of any substantial change in enthusiasm among the potential FDI investors on off-sets.

The Ministry of Finance in its Economic Survey (2008-09) had suggested an increase in FDI to 49% across the board with 100% on a case to case basis. Ministry of Commerce and Industry later recommended raising of the cap on FDI to 74%.

The Brahmos and the Multi Role Transport a/c (MTA) projects have accepted a 50:50 equity participation.

The reported French proposal to go into a Joint Venture with Reliance India Ltd (RIL) on implementation of the off-set provision, against the rafale MMRAC accord, is an encouraging sign. What incentives have been offered / accepted is not yet in the public domain.

DEFENCE OUTSOURCING

Defence *out-sourcing*, as a phenomenon, is not a new one. It predates the medieval period. Kings, then, did not consider it economical to maintain large standing armies. When requirements arose, the kings commandeered their chieftains to undertake such tasks on their behalf. US have been formally practicing *out-sourcing* even during their Revolutionary War. They continued that through the Korean and Vietnam wars too.

In the corporate world – outsourcing has become the single most significant development of the period. There has been an outcry, on this count, in the developed countries. Many states in USA and the federal government are putting laws in place, to discourage /curtail *out- sourcing*.

On the other hand, in the Armed Forces of advanced nations – *out-sourcing*, in the non-core sections, has now become a rule rather than an exception. It is estimated that defence contractors in Iraq and Afghanistan consumed nearly a third of the US budget for the region. UK claims a cost saving, in the range of thirty percent on this count. This has mainly been brought about due to constant pressure put on the Defence Forces, by the respective governments, to bring down the over-all defence expenditure and impose of combat man-power ceilings.

Most commonly *out-sourced* service today – include catering, transportation, security, hospitalisation, training and life cycle management of major systems. New Zealand *out- sources* even conventional logistics and all depot level maintenance functions. Australia has extended this further – to include recruitment as a joint venture.

INDIAN PERSPECTIVE

India has yet to seriously begin *out-sourcing*. The pressure is mounting - due to the manpower ceilings in place and new combat units being raised having to take the *teeth to tail* ratio seriously. In a phased and calculated manner - India could also eventually follow the global pattern. This is, however, not considered a priority issue for India. In this context India should follow an accelerated step by step UK approach to RML as discussed at Chapter 2 earlier. Some of the areas, where outsourcing is already in vogue are listed below:

(a) Standing transport contract at local station level.

(b) Internal / external area maintenance in Hospitals and Defence establishments e.g. R & R Hospital in Delhi.

(c) Annual servicing contracts with reputed OEMs on equipment and machinery in non combat areas.

(d) IAF is seriously considering signing AMC with foreign OEMs in respect of aircraft and weapon packages acquired in small scales.

SUPPLEMENTARY NAVAL ISSUES

SUBMARINE ACQUISITION MANAGEMENT

A lacuna encountered with the HDW SSK s/m project, was the watertight nature of the Project management set up, adopted at the time, in Naval Head Quarters (NHQ). The choice of personnel for the project team was near ideal. The best and the most talented in each specialisation of the s/m arm were made available. Structured programmed engagement with the professional institutions at NHQ was however not catered for. Presence of the Principal Staff Officer (PSO) involved, at the apex review level was considered adequate. This led to the situation in which - the first of the class of submarine was received ceremoniously at the homeport, on arrival. But, every one ashore other than the s/m operating authority (SM9) washed their hands off. They were least prepared to provide the requisite shore / dockyard support. The matter, of course, got further complicated later, due to the fall-out after the alleged 'kick-back' exposè. Hopefully, the 'scorpene' project has not repeated the same mistakes, in not maintaining the requisite embedded horizontal linkages with professional naval institutions at NHQ. This time, having put the Project Manager (75) under CWP&A as shown in Fig. 6.45 obviate any such contingency. Once the proposal illustrated at Fig. 6.46 is implemented – there would be a dramatic improvement in the performance, in respect of over-all ship-acquisition, production and life-time product support functions.

The idea of a stand alone and self contained Submarine Arm is neither a practicable, desirable nor an affordable proposition. Neither the hard-ware nor the human resource involved can be sustained in a *stove pipe*.

Professional institutions already exist within the Navy with knowledge / expertise / technology, along with supporting infrastructure for all disciplines involved in s/m design / development / production / maintenance / repairs. These have considerable commonality with the surface ships. Support infrastructure is also largely inter-linked with it. It is conceded that operational and tactical skills are specialised. Developing, nurturing and honing these skills need a dedicated institutional approach. Exclusive training establishments, Directorate of Submarine Arms (DSA) and Submarine Authority (SMA)s already exist for this purpose. Building up and sustaining a *esprit de corp* is, no doubt, an essential factor also. But, *stove –piping* is not the answer. It is considered detrimental to Submarine Arm's over-all well being. The existing multi-disciplinary professional institutions must be fully exploited and whereover necessary augmented to cope with induction of new technology, weapon systems and types of weapon platforms. Otherwise, submarine arm could even claim exclusive right over nuclear propulsion. What happens then – when induction of nuclear powered carrier or cruiser becomes a reality?

INDUCTION OF NUCLEAR PROPULSION

The introduction of INS Chakra II and Arihant into the Indian Navy brings with it a new form of energy source for propulsion. Every thing else fundamentally remains the same - including the rest of the propulsion package. The introduction of this technology into the Navy should be treated as an evolutionary process in the development of propulsion system - same as:

(a) Oars.

(b) Sails.

(c) Coal fired boiler with reciprocating steam engines.

(d) Oil fired boilers with steam turbine.

(e) Diesel powered ICEs.

(f) Gas turbine propulsion.

(g) Electric propulsion.

(h) Nuclear reactor and steam generator as the primary source of energy for propulsion.

The training and support infrastructure should be dovetailed into existing system. Only specific type training and support infrastructure linked to primary regime needs to be created. The technology management structure should be built around and part of the existing Marine engineering frame work - in all its manifestation. As stated earlier, it must be borne in mind that use of nuclear propulsion in the IN - is not likely to be restricted to s/m only - cruisers and a/c carriers are likely to follow suite.

It must also not be forgotten that nuclear propulsion was born out of DME's initiative in the 1970s and has been nurtured up to this stage under its benign eyes.

The temptation to create a new cadre should be avoided. It should be treated as a super specialised stream within the marine engineering cadre. All infrastructures must be dovetailed into the concept.

R&D DOMAIN

Similarly, another area of serious concern - is the absence of institutionalised, independent technical audit system on highly classified DRDO projects. This is especially so, in respect of complex, multidisciplinary, high value, design and development projects. One may try and explain away, the absence of such a crucial system, on grounds of security concerns. And such shortcomings could claim to be offset by including the COS concerned at the Apex level reviews and the PSO concerned at the Programme Management Board reviews. Not allowing them, the benefit of institutionalised consultations, even with their own professional watchdogs - would in fact nullify any benefit of their participation. In 1988/89, it is believed that the CNS and Chief of Material (COM) had informally instituted such an in-house mechanism to deal with this lacuna in context of a special project. Subsequently, however, this had to be dismantled, in spite of CNS's personal intervention. Being the ultimate end user, surely the CNS and his concerned PSO should be entitled to seek independent professional assessment from their in-house institutions. As a result, in the case of one such project - what was originally slated to be delivered in 6 to 7 years, has now taken more than 20 years. Yet there is no guarantee that the product would come up to the nation's expectations, as and when it fructifies. Security concerns could have been suitably dealt with - without sacrificing the basic tenets of project management.

Now that the programme has gone past the launching stage – greater institutional naval participation is being permitted. After all, the Navy will have to have the infrastructure to induct and sustain the platform for its life time. Abin-i-ti-o, all these have to be now dove-tailed into the existing and planned naval infrastructure.

A structured independent technical audit system, with service institutional participation, should be the order of the day, for all future programmes of this magnitude – how ever classified.

Bibliography

1. A.K. Sharma Cdr. IN. - ILMS case study.
2. A.P. Revi. "Revolution in Military Logistics". IDR. Vol. 23(2). July 2008. p. 49.

3. Air Marshal. BD Jayal. "Offset Challenges and opportunity". IDR Vol. 23 Jan. 2008.
4. Annuradha Mitra. "Survey of Successful off-sets. Experience the world over". IDSA Seminar July 2011.
5. Chopra, Sunil, Meindl, Peter – Supply Chain Management – Strategy planning and operation. Dorling Kindersley (India) Pvt. Ltd.
6. Col. Bradley E Smith. "Mandate to revolutionize Military Logistics". Air and Space Power Journal. Summer 2007. p. 92.
7. Col. Karen. E. Ledoux – "LOGCAO – 102: An operational planner's guide". Army Logistician. July 2007. p. 24.
8. David A Payne. "Chinese Logistics Modernisation" Army Logistician. Vol. 140. Issue 4. Aug. 2008.
9. Deba R Mohaashy. "Indian Defence Procurement Policy: An Evaluation". S Asia Defence and Strategic Review. July 2010.
10. Defence Logistics – Better Management and oversight of Prepositioning Programs needed to reduce risk and improve future programs – GAO US Publication.
11. Defence Procurement Procedure 2003/2006 / 2008. Government of India. MoD Publication.
12. Dennis J Blasko "Chinese Military Logistics: The GLD System". April 2011.
13. Detra R Mohasty. "India's Defence procurement policy: an Evaluation". South Asia Defence and Strategic Review July. 2010.
14. "DLA 1977 – 1990" – http://en.wikipedia.org/wiki/Def.LogAg.
15. Dr. Milan Vego."Modern Naval Logistics". Naval Force 1/2010.
16. Ganesh Mahadevan Cmde. now V. Adm – "Continuous Acquisition and Life-time Support – A new paradigm in Military system development and acquisition." NDC Thesis. 2002.
17. Gp. Capt. TP. Srivastava "Defence procurement – muddling along" Defence and Technology. Mar. 2008. p. 10.
18. http://mod.nic.in/dpm/DPP2008.pdf.
19. http://mod.nic.in/dpm/DPP2011.pdf
20. Introducing the Logistics Branch "Army Logistician" July. 2007.
21. J. Ronald Fox – US Defence Management Challenges – Weapon Acquisition. 1988.
22. J.V. Singh. Gp. Capt. – Transformation in Defence Logistics: Trends and Pointers. KW Publications. 2010.

23. John Schank, Santa Monica – Acquisition and Competition Strategy Options for DD(X) – USN's 21st century Destroyer. 2006.
24. Joint Publication 4-0 "Joint Logistics" US Publication July 2008.
25. JV Singh. Gp. Capt. "Transformation of Defence Logistics".
26. K. Subrhamanium. "India Defence Acquisition System; Improving oversight and system". IDSA International Seminar on Defence Acquisition. July 2011.
27. "Logistic Officers Corps" Army Logistician. Oct. 2006. p. 2.
28. Lt. Gen. CV. Christianson "Joint Logistics – shaping our future: A Personal perspective" Army Logistician July. 2008.
29. Lt. Gen. CV.Christanson "Joint Logistics – shaping our future" Army Logistician Aug 2006. p. 2.
30. M Suman. "Protecting PSU Ship Yards".
31. Maj. Gen. SB Asthana "Transformation of PLA Logistics System : An Analysis". USI Journal Vol. CXLI No. 586. December 2011.
32. Maj. David R Gibson. "An 8 step process for improving Logistic Activity" Army Logistician. Oct 2005. p. 30.
33. Maj. Gen. AK Mehra "Pitfalls in Arms Procurement" IDR. Vol. 25(1) Jan. 2010.
34. Maj. Gen. Mrinal Suman. "Indian Defence Offset Regime – needs reforms" IDR. Vol. 23 Jan 2008. p.38.
35. Maj. Gen. S Sunda ADG(WE). "Implementation of off-set policy in Defence contracts – Indian Army Perspective".
36. Maj. Gen. Julian Thomson "Life blood of war- Logistics in Armed Conflict".
37. Maj. Vickie D Stenffos "Logistics officer Corp : Growing Logistics Pentathetes for the 21st century" Army Logistician Sept. 2006 p. 2.
38. Mark McTagne and Roger Honeck. Army Logistician July. 2005.
39. Mark W Akin and George L Topic "Transformation Joint Operational Level logistics" JFQ IVth Qr. 2007.
40. Martin Whil Maj. Gen – Logistics Blackadder's War.
41. Moshe Kreis – Operational Logistics – The Art and Science of sustaining Military Operations.
42. Mrinal Suman "Defence Off-sets" – IDR Jan 20109. Vol. 25.

43. Mrinal Suman "Off-Sets in US Military sales". IDR. Vol. 23. Jan. 2008.

44. Mrinal Suman "The new Make Procedure – a retrograde step". IDR. Vol. 22. Oct. 2007.

45. Mrinal Suman. "Defence Procurement – time for radical reforms" IDR Vol.25. July.2010.

46. Mrinal Suman. "Defence Purchases – time India asserts itself". IDR Vol. 24(4). Oct 2009.

47. Mrinal Suman. "Demisting the new B&M(I) procedure". IDR. Vol. 25. Jan 2010.

48. Mrinal Suman. "Doing business with Indian Defence Regime". IDR Vol. 23. Jun. 2008.

49. Mrinal Suman. "Import of Key Technology need to revisit policy". IDR Vol. 26(2). Apr /Jun 2011.

50. Mrinal Suman. "India's Defence Off-set Regime". IDR Vol. 23(11). 2008.

51. Mrinal Suman. "Outsourcing of Defence Logistics in Indian Military". Strategic Analysis Vol. 31 (4). July 2002.

52. Mrinan Suman. :DPP 2011". SP's Military Year Book 2011 - 2012.

53. National Seminar on Defence Offsets" 24 October 2008.

54. NATO CALS Handbook 2000. (www.dcincn.com/ncmb)

55. Parmod Sarin Brig.– Military Logistics – The third Dimension. Manas Publication. 2000.

56. Procedings of IDSA International Seminar on Defence Acquisition. 12 - 14 July 2011

57. R. Adm. A.P. Revi IN(Retd) "Naval Acquisition Matrix" IDR Vol. 21 (4). Oct. 2006 p. 82.

58. Randy. S Kendrick "Joint Logistics EUCOM AOR" Army Logistician. Dec. 2005.

59. Robert D Paulus "Combined Army Support Command reorganisation for the future" Army Logistician. Oct. 2005.

60. Robert Mckay & Kathy Flemin. "Transformation in Army Logistics". Military Review. Oct 2000. p. 45.

61. Sandra I Errwin. "Pentagon reviewing proposals to create LOCOM"

62. SN Misra. "Impact of Off-sets policy". IDR Vol26(3). July / Sept 2011.

63. Sujeet Samadhar .Cmde. "Off-set absorption road map for IN adding Arsenal to Armament". IDSA seminar July 2011.
64. Supply Chain Management – Strategic Planning and Cooperation – Case Study.
65. Thomas Mathew Dr. " Essential Elements of India's Defence off-set policy – a critique."
66. Thomas Mathew. "Review of International Off-set Experience". IDSA International Seminar on Defence Acquisition July 2011.
67. Thomas Withington. "Supply and Demand" Military Technology. 12/2010.
68. US Defence Logistics Support Chain Manual. JSP. 886 Vol. 1 Parts 1&4. July /Sept 2007.
69. US GAO – "Defence Logistics – Better Management" – Sept 2005.
70. Vinod Anand .Brig. "Joint and Integrated Logistics system for Defence Services". Strategic Analysis. IDSA Apr. 2001. Vol. XXV No.1.
71. VK. Mishra former Secretary (Defence – Finance) – India Strategic. July / Aug. 2011.

INS JALASHO on Amphibious Mission.

7

Coastal Security Architecture

There was a public outcry / outrage after each of the following major tragic events / incidents along the Maharashtra – Gujarat coast. On each occasion, the public perception pointed a finger at the Navy. Notwithstanding the clear jurisdictional demarcation of responsibilities – the media also, without any hesitation, held the Navy guilty of dereliction of duties. Conveniently, the government also did not make any attempt to correct the impression:

(a) The 1993 Serial Blasts in Mumbai.

(b) The 26/XI terrorist attack on Taj Hotel at Mumbai.

(c) The beaching of MVs Wisdom and Pavit on to Juhu beach and sinking of MV Rak off Mumbai coast.

An attempt will be made here, to take stock of the coastal security architecture and make a reality check. To begin with – the vastness of the domain involved must be appreciated. Seeking for a rogue ship / craft in the middle of an ocean is worse than looking for a needle in a hay stack. To keep abreast of the situation in a defined area of interest in say Iraq / Afghanistan – the US had to deploy an array of surveillance satellites. Even then 24 × 7 coverage could not be provided. In addition, land based Airborne Warning and Control System (AWACS) a/c, carrier based surveillance aircraft and Unmanned Airborne Vehicles (UAV) were also extensively used along with SF troops on the ground.

India has a vast coast line of over 7500 kilometres. This is spread out between nine coastal states and four union territories. Security of twelve major ports and almost two hundred minor ports in the country are of concern. The conventional security of the major ports is the responsibility of Central Industrial Security Force (CISF). The minor ports are the responsibility of the State Maritime Board / State Government. Additionally, the twelve major ports, fifty three minor ports and five shipyards conform to International Ship and Port Facility Security (ISPFS) requirements.

On the sea-ward side -the traditional peacetime jurisdictional responsibility between the Indian Navy (IN) and Coast Guard (CG) was simple. Responsibility of CG was up to EEZ and the Navy's extended beyond that. The port authorities, DG Light House, customs, police, immigration and narcotic control agencies had their respective roles cut out for them along the coast, ports and harbour regions. Demarcation of responsibilities, in respect of sea front security of coastal, industrial, military, Department of Atomic Energy (DAE) and off-shore establishments, were also clearly stipulated.

Truth of the matter is that none of the above incidents would have happened -had the institutions, designated for each task and zones, been geared up, alert and net-worked. The serious lacuna that existed at the time of 26/XI would be clear from the fact that since then – over Rs. 2000 cr approval has been accorded by the Cabinet Committee on National Security (CCS) for capital expenditure towards creating / upgrading infrastructure dedicated for coastal security. The systemic inadequacies interdepartmental coordination were crippling. These would take, over a decade, to overcome – provided the establishment has the will and determination to evolve and implement an out of the box solution. Most of these will be elaborated later.

Many agencies, including the Central Government Ministries / Departments, the respective State Governments and linked local administrative / law enforcement / intelligence agencies are deeply involved in affairs of coastal security. The Navy should focus on its primary role and only be expected to provide overall guidance and maritime expertise in creating the necessary infrastructure including coastal Command, Control, Communication, Intelligence and Surveillance (C^3IS) network and provide training skills in preparing the personnel concerned for working in a maritime environment. Also the coastal information network should be closely integrated into Navy's and Coast Guard's C4ISR network – so that a central picture is always available. To the extent of maintaining a network, capable of receiving inputs from the multifarious sensors/ sources and facilitating access to such information, on real time basis, to the concerned agencies is a responsibility the Navy could take on. Constabulary role and coordination between the civil agencies is totally outside the scope and capability of the Navy. Navy should not even consider venturing into those domains. The Navy is already over-stretched with enhanced expectations from the developing scenario in the Indian Ocean and South China Sea regions. Dealing with sea piracy is yet another urgent issue. The case of the entire international maritime community, with all its resources – not being able to suppress the piracy menace originating from Somalia is a pointer to the dilemma. Long term solution can only be found on the main land after establishing a viable / stable government which can address the law and order / economic hard-ship issues of the local population. Having said that – an over view, of the measures taken by the government since the Mumbai serial blast in 1993, on coastal security is discussed briefly in the following paragraphs.

Following the serial blast in Mumbai – *operation swan* was launched with the limited objective of preventing landing of contrabands and infiltration, along the Maharashtra – Gujarat coast. This among other things - authorised CG an expenditure of over Rs. 340 cr for acquisition of fifteen fast interceptor boats and setting up of three CG Stations at Dhanu, Murad Janjune and Verawal.

In the year 2000 - the issue of coastal security was once again high-lighted by the *Task Force on Border Management* as part of the *Kargil Review Committee* recommendations. The recommendations included:

(a) Setting up of a specialised marine police force in the form of coastal police stations.

(b) Augmentation of the strength of the Coast Guard.

(c) Formation of fisherman watch groups.

(d) Establishment of an Apex body for the management of maritime affairs.

As a follow up from above, an Apex body - National *Committee on Strengthening Maritime and Coastal Security (NCSMCS)* against threats from the sea was constituted. The Body is chaired by the Cabinet Secretary and all stakeholders are members e.g. IN, CG, Ministry of Home Affairs (MHA) / Fisheries / Shipping / Surface Transport / Agriculture, DG Light House / Ships and Chief Secretaries of Coastal States. The first meeting was held on 04 September 2009. The NCSMCS, unlike many other such bodies, meets quite regularly.

The present status of the assets of the CG could be summarised as follows:

(a) Platform holdings – ninety three surface crafts and forty six aircraft including:

  (i) Ten OPVS, six Advanced OPVs, fifteen Fast Patrol Vessels (FPV), thirteen Inshore Patrol Vessels (IPV), and nineteen Interceptor Boats.

  (ii) Eighteen Chethak Helicopters, four Dhruv Helicopters, six Multi-roles Surveillance a/c.

(b) CGs future plans include two hundred ships / small craft and ninety a/c.

(c) Also, thirty percent increase in manpower has already been approved.

(d) By the end of present eleventh plan period - CG will have forty two CG Stations including:

  (i) Existing four + seven at – Ratnagiri, Minicoy, Karwar, Gandhinagar, Verawal, Hutbay and Murad-Janjira + three at Mundra, Kolkata and Dahami.

  (ii) And additional nine at Pipavav, Androth, Karasikkal, Krishnapatnam, Nizamapatnam, Gopllpur, Frazergunj, Kamorta Mayabunder etc. are in the pipe-line.

(e) CG has set up four Regional / Joint Operation Centres (ROC) net-worked to customs and IB at – Mumbai, Vishakhapatnam, Kochi and Port Blair. Each Coastal District is to have District Operation Centre

In 2005 – the Coastal Security Scheme 2005 (CSS2005) was sanctioned by the Cabinet Committee on Security (CCS).

S. No.	Name of State/ UT	Costal Police Stations	Vesse-ls	Jeeps	Motor Cycles	Check post	Out-post	Barracks	Rubber Inflated Boats
1	Gujarat	10	30	20	101	25	46	-	-
2	Maharashtra	12	28	25	57	32	-	24	-
3	Goa	3	9	6	9	-	-	-	10
4	Karnataka	5	15	9	4	-	-	-	-
5	Kerala	8	24	16	24	-	-	-	-
6	Tamil Nadu	12	24	12	36	40	12	-	-
7	AP	6	18	12	18	-	-	-	-
8	Orissa	5	15	10	15	-	-	-	-
9	West Bengal	6	18	12	12	-	-	6	-
10	Pondicherry	1	3	2	3	-	-	-	-
11	Lakshadweep	4	6	8	8	-	-	-	-
12	Daman & Diu	1	4	3	5	-	-	-	-
13	A&N Islands	-	10	18	20	-	-	-	-
	Total	**73**	**204**	**153**	**312**	**97**	**58**	**30**	**10**

* A lump sum assistance of Rs.10 lakh **per police station** is also given for equipment. computers and furniture

The approved five year outlay for the scheme is Rs400 crores for non-recurring expenditure and Rs.151/= crores for recurring expenditure on fuel, maintenance / repairs of vessels and training of personnel.

Fig. 7.48. CSS Phase I regional infrastructure allocation.

CSS2005 introduced the concept of a three layered coastal patrol system between IN, CG and the Coastal Police. The CSS2005 provided for a comprehensive five year plan with an allocation of Rs. 400 cr for non-recurring and Rs.150cr as annual recurring expenditure for Phase I.

The breakdown of the type of infrastructure sanctioned against CSS Phase I is listed at Fig. 7.48. And a statement of the status of the infrastructure sanctioned, as of early 2011, is indicated at Fig. 7.49. It would be observed from the tabulated statement at Fig. 7.50 that as per MHA report for 2010 – 2011 – the national statistics shows that over 92% of the 73 Coastal Police Stations (CPS) sanctioned for the Phase I had become *operational* by January 2011. At the same time, the statement indicates that in 19% of the cases - construction work was yet to begin. Performance of Gujarat is no doubt exemplary. Similarly, on examining the status of Maharashtra, the state most affected – it indicates that out of twelve CPS sanctioned – no construction work had commenced in the case of eight of them. There is also a serious doubt on the interpretation of the terminology *operationalised* used in the report. It probably, in this case - only stands for CPSs launched. The normal understanding of the terminology *operationalised* would entail:

(a) Personnel of all specialisation recruited, trained, worked-up and effective in the role assigned.

(b) Infrastructure completed and working, including:

  (i) Buildings.

  (ii) Furniture.

  (iii) Computers.

  (iv) Secure communication network.

  (v) Transportation system – over-land and water ways.

(c) Efficient and effective command and control system established inclusive of inter-linkages with local police, civil administration, custom / revenue intelligence authorities and other concerned agencies.

In mid 2011, when several incidents of ships drifting on to Mumbai beach took place – media reports indicated that the CPSs in Mumbai were no where near ready. They reported boats tied up along side – unable to undertake any patrolling

State/UT	Sanctioned buildings		Made operational	Construction complete	Construction in progress	Construction not yet started
Gujarat	Coastal PS	10	10	10	-	-
	Check-posts	25	25	25	-	-
	Out-posts	46	44	44	2	-
Maharashtra	Coastal PS	12	12	2	2	8
	Check-posts	32	32	19	-	13
	Barracks	24	24	18	-	6
Goa	CPS	3	3	-	2	1
Karnataka	CPS	5	5	5	-	-
Kerala	CPS	8	6	6	2	-
Tamil Nadu	Coastal PS	12	12	12	-	-
	Check-posts	40	35	31	9	-
	Out-posts	12	10	10	-	2
AP	CPS	6	6	6	-	-
Orissa	CPS	5	5	2	1	2
West Bengal	Coastal PS	6	6	3	1	2
	Barracks	6	4	4	-	2
Puducherry	CPS	1	1	-	1	-
Lakshadweep	CPS	4	4	1	2	1
Daman & Diu	CPS	1	1	1	-	-
A&N Islands	-		-	-	-	-
Total	Coastal PS	73	71	48	11	14
	Check-post	97	92	75	9	13
	Out-posts	58	54	54	2	2
	Barracks	30	28	22	-	8

Fig. 7.49. CSS Phase I infrastructure status report 2011.

Sl. No.	Name of State	Costal Police Stations	Boats/Vessels		Number of jetties	Four-wheelers	Motor Cycles	Remarks
			12 Ton	Others				
1	Gujarat	12	31		5	12	24	
2	Maharashtra	7	14		3	7	14	
3	Goa	4	4		2	4	8	
4	Karnataka	4	12		2	4	8	
5	Kerala	10	20		4	10	20	
6	Tamil Nadu	30	20		12	30	60	
7	AP	15	30		7	15	30	
8	Orissa	13	26		5	13	26	
9	West Bengal	8	7		4	8	16	
10	Daman & Diu	2	4		2	2	4	
11	Lakshadweep	3	6	12 *	2	3	6	RIBs
12	Pondicherry	3	6		2	3	6	
13	A&N Islands	20		10* 23**	10	20	20	*LV ** RIBs ***10 MOCs
	Total	131	180		60	131	242	

Fig. 7.50. CSS Phase II Regional Allocation.

due to lack of fuel supply and inadequate technical manpower. In spite of all the public outrage at the time of the series of episodes – when that is considered along with the MHA report above clearly illustrates the apathy displayed by the state authorities.

The present demarcation of zonal responsibility is as follows:

(a) Marine Police - up to 12 nautical miles.

(b) Coast Guard - from 12 to 200 nM.

(c) Indian Navy - beyond 200 nM.

Activities in respect of following are also well under way:

(a) Arrangement for issue of ID Cards / Universal Identity Cards (UID) in over three thousand coastal villages, by National Population Registrar. *[53% data collected; 45.44% digital data compiled].*

(b) Introduction of Automatic Identification System (AIS), Electronic Tracking Device (ETD) and compulsory registration of vessels. Eighty four AIS stations have been contracted for in September 2011 at a cost of Rs. 132 crore with ELCOM MARINE (INDIA) / SAAB.

(c) Fitment of AIS on fishing vessels above twenty meters in length has already been made compulsory. Resistance is expected in making AIS compulsory for smaller vessels – due to financial constraints of the individuals. Ways and means of giving incentives in the form of compensation packages would have to be considered.

(d) Distribution and status of Sensor Stations in Phase I are as follows:

(i) Coast Guard in high threat areas has forty six electro – optical sensor Stations.

(ii) Twelve Remote Operation Sensors / Station (ROS) are fed into - one of the four Regional Operation Centres (ROC) at Mumbai, Kochi, Chennai and Vishakhapatnam.

(iii) All will be networked, on real time basis, to the Apex Control Centre at Gurgaon, NC^3I complex.

(iv) And inter-linked to Navy's Combat Management Centre.

(v) BEL Project cost for developing software for CSS is estimated to be about Rs. 700 crore.

(vi) ROS will have the means to remotely manipulate coastal radars and cameras through a Camera Management System. Integral health monitoring and alarm system has also been catered for.

(vii) Infra red (IR) cameras are being procured from Israel; daylight cameras from Canada and coastal surveillance radars from Denmark.

(viii) DG Light House / Ships has contracted with SAAB for 12.2 million Euros for an integrated coastal surveillance system. The system comprises seventy four sensor stations linked to six Regional Control (RCC) Centres and three National control Centres (NCC). These are to be connected through broad band satellite links.

(ix) Coastal Radar chain plan comprises 46 Coastal Radars. This was contracted in September 2011 for Rs. 601.77 crore with BEL. Deliveries are planned to materialise within 6 to 12 months. It is reported that the existing Light Houses with DGLH will be responsible for operation / maintenance of the Radar and Electro Optics Sensors. Thirteen towers will be set up ashore in Phase I and thirty seven more in Phase II.

THE CONCEPT OF MARITIME DOMAIN AWARENESS

In Apr 2010 – NCSMCS approved the concept of National Maritime Domain Awareness (NMDA) for an integrated information grid for sea farers. Detailed Project Report (DPR) for this programme has been prepared by the Navy. Basically, this *revolves around Navy's National Command, Control, Communication and Intelligence (NC³IN) system at the* centre of the hub and will generate a "common operational picture" (COP) through an institutionalised mechanism of collection, fusing and analysing information, involving:

(a) Coastal Surveillance network of Radar.

(b) Space based automatic identification system.

(c) Vessel Traffic Management System (VTSM).

(d) Registration of Fishing Vessels.

(e) Fishermen biometric identity data base etc.

The concept of MDA is not new to the Navy. In its traditional domain, whether in the strategic, operational or tactical roles – the Navy has been in this business all along. When ship / fleet is at sea- whether in the role of exercising sea control / sea denial or just passage or even in the process of leaving / entering harbour – the MDA process is deeply embedded in to the system and mind set of the sailor. Also, aerial surveillance of the maritime area of concern to the Navy is maintained on a regular basis – through Tu 142, Dornier 228 and IL 38 a/c. The Boeing P8I Long Range Maritime (LRMR) aircraft when inducted will further augment this effort. This is part of its SOP in all four domains – sea, sub-sea, and air and cyber space. Since 26/XI, this concept is now required to be carried forward and stretched to include coastal security and strategic maritime concerns, in a holistic manner.

MDA focused on coastal security could be broken down into four basic subsets. All these need to be networked into Regional and National Maritime Centres:

(a) IN domain.

(b) CG domain.

(c) CPS / Local domain.

(d) Central Intelligence domain.

(e) DGLH domain

MDA is only one element of the coastal security architecture – which receives, collates, analyses and makes the information/ intelligence accessible to all stake holders for action. To that extent the Navy, as a facilitator, can be nominated as the *situational head* in the form of the Nodal Agency. Each domain stake holder must be held responsible for converting this domain awareness capability empowerment into pre-emptive / proactive / reactive actions.

The MDA architecture must provide for networked inputs from and out puts to - all stakeholders including National Intelligence Agencies, on real time basis. The Regional and National Maritime Operation Centres must be manned by professionals with domain knowledge and capability to sift out actionable information from raw intelligence inputs from multifarious technical and human sources and create a realistic comprehensive Common Operation Picture (COP). To assist in handling this task speedily and efficiently – computerised data integration and automated algorithms to assist in handling such vast and disparate data stream would be essential. Embedding of an intelligence agency element here would enrich and enhance the effectiveness of the system

It would be seen from MHA's report that in hardware terms – considerable stress has been laid on putting in place technological wherewithal to meet the requirements of surveillance. The HUMINT gathering capability with respective stake holders is at present very weak. Sufficient attention has not been paid in evolving an overall C^2 mechanism down to grass-root level. Having an apex-body at the national level is not sufficient. C^2 structure at all levels must be formulated, promulgated and implemented. *Situational Heads* for each domain must be identified and notified – so that accountability is not in doubt.

In Sept 2010 – Cabinet Committee on National Security approved the CSS Phase II with an outlay of Rs.1100 crore for the five years (2011 – 2015). CSS Phase II regional allocation is tabulated at Fig. 7.50. Summary of the additional allocation is as follows:

(a) Coastal Police Stations – 131; 12 ton Boats – 180; Jetties – 60; Rigid Inflatable Boats – 35; Four Wheelers – 131; motor-cycles – 242; Large Vessels – 10 for Andaman &Nicobar and 12 for Lakshadweep islands.

(b) Lump sum grant of Rs.15 lakhs per CPS for surveillance equipment, night vision devices, computers, furniture and POL expenditure for first year after supply of one hundred and eighty boats materialises.

(c) Separate allocation for annual maintenance contracts for boats and training of Marine Police Personnel.

The Navy has also been authorised a thousand strong dedicated specialised force - called "*Sagar Prahari Bal*". Their role is to provide security protection to all naval assets and bases on the east / west coasts and the island territories.

The proposal of the creation of a National Maritime Advisory Board with a Maritime Adviser is at present on hold. The Navy seems to have reconciled itself to the idea that NCSMCS with CNS as a member adequately meets the need. The issue of lack of coordination between various agencies involved in coastal security still persists and most of the governments in the coastal states continue to remain indifferent to coastal security.

THE COASTAL POLICE FORCE

The main issue remains unresolved. No amount of technical surveillance hardware can compensate for the lack of human intelligence capability and efficient intelligence coordination, investigation and constabulary capabilities. A dedicated coastal agency responsible for intelligence coordination, analysis and requisite powers to act is essential. They need to work closely with the respective state civil administration.

The recruitment policy for the Marine Police Force (MPF) needs to be reconsidered. The scheme of inducting volunteers from the local police has not worked out. Since there are only few volunteers - most of the undesirables have been palmed off to MPF. Most are land lubbers – prone to sea sickness and disgruntled. It seems that granting of an incentive of fifty percent of the basic pay as additional allowance is inadequate. Unless there are enough motivated, dedicated and capable boots on the ground as beat constables both ashore and afloat – this scheme is not likely to work out.

The Maritime Police Force has to be an elite force - hand picked, with specific expertise for each category of personnel. They must be dully trained and well compensated to attract the best human resources. Those on the beat and in the Police Stations must not only be competent but must be sensitised and have the confidence of the local population. Those manning the patrol vessels should be drawn from the local sea-faring population and retired naval personnel.

Maharashtra, Gujarat, Tamil Nadu and Andaman and Nicobar Islands which took the brunt of recent coastal tragedies – are at present in the fore front of pro-active action. As brought out earlier, in spite of having taken the brunt of most of the coastal assaults – Maharashtra has not responded adequately. Most of the other coastal states, particularly on the east coast have been dragging their feet also.

The coastal security arrangement that originally emerged in Maharashtra and Tamil Nadu were driven by different motivating forces. In Maharashtra after the Mumbai multiple bomb blast case – the thrust was on preventing landing of contraband and narcotic substances. Where as, in the case of Tamil Nadu (TN) - the emphasis was to prevent landing of illegal immigrants from war torn Sri Lanka. Accordingly, the Joint Coastal Patrol (JPT) team in Maharashtra comprised eight personnel including one Sub-Inspector of Police, three armed constables, four naval personnel and two custom inspectors. Due to the thrust of the proposed action – the custom inspector was nominated as the leader of the team.

In this context, Tamil Nadu had a lead over the others due to its having raised a Coastal Security Group (CSG) for preventing illegal migration from war torn Sri Lanka. An Additional DG of police was the head of the CSG. He was responsible for coordinating with almost four hundred and fifty Village Vigilance Committees, IN, CG, local police, fishery department and Custom / Revenue intelligence authorities. The Additional DG was also responsible for creating the infrastructure and building the requisite cadre including *quick reaction teams etc.*

The role of the CSF and CPS has since been substantially enhanced.

The National Coastal Security System is a complex, multi-agency organisational set up - which is still in its infancy. As illustrated earlier, the CSS structure is based on a *hub and spokes* principle. The set-up has five basic levels and each spoke works in its own *stove-pipe. T*he CSF / CSPS are at the first echelon in one of the stove-pipes. The raw information / intelligence and data collected at the grass root, both from the *Humint* and *Techint* sources are transmitted to the Area Coastal Security Operation Centres (ACSOC) at the second echelon level. After sifting through the inputs from all sources – the relevant ones are forwarded to the State Coastal Security Operation Centres (SCSOC). The SCSOCs are collocated at CG District HQs. This is the third echelon. The next level is at the Regional Operation Centres (ROC) – which are collocated at the CGROCs. The next echelon is at the four Joint Operation Centres (JOC) in Mumbai, Visakhapatnam, Chennai and Calcutta. This gives an integrated picture at the four Naval Commands. Finally, a Combined Operation Picture (COP) is generated at the National level in the National Maritime Operation Centre (NMOC).

DGLH, Customs, IB etc operate independently in their respective stove pipes and feed the inputs generated within its domain, in a similar manner, to the ROC and then on to the respective JOC and finally to the NMOC to create an overall Maritime Domain Awareness picture.

Action within the domain of each entity is to be taken at the respective zonal level. CG's assistance can be sought at the discretion of CPF to deal with any situation outside the capacity of the CPF. Similarly, when called upon, the CinCs of respective Naval Commands would provide assistance to CG. The onus of responsibility for action in the respective zones would squarely rest with the designated zonal agency.

Unfortunately, the system being created in the twenty-first century is still geared to work in stove pipes. Each subset is working independently and is only responsible to its own hierarchy. There is no structured single entity in place that is responsible and has the authority to oversee the functioning of all the stove-pipes at each level in the entire system.

The system logic is that – each Agency in the stove-pipe is expected to effectively fulfil their respective designated role, on their own. That is considered sufficient, for appropriate action to be taken by the Operation Centres at the hub. Periodic coordination meetings between the stakeholders and regular structured exercises are considered adequate to ensure performance.

Each of the agency identified here, is venturing into unchartered waters - where they have little or no experience or expertise. The Navy, the CG and Original Equipment Manufacturers (OEM)s responsible for providing the sensors and the integrated network systems are being called upon to train their personnel. It seems that the Indian ethos / mind-set do not permit the concept of *situational heads* being given authority and responsibility over the whole network.

In the circumstances, designating the Navy as a nodal agency and DGCG as the Commander of the Coastal Command seems a futile exercise. Firstly, there is no such entity as a Coastal Command. Also, in this context, the questions that beg answers to are:

(a) As a nodal Agency – what is expected of the Navy?

(b) Is the Navy just a whistle blower?

(c) If so – does that entail bearing sole responsibility for providing actionable info to all the CSS Operation Centres?

(d) Is that possible, with the Navy having no say on / control over – how, when and what type of information each

Agency has to focus on – particularly in the present dynamic situation?

(e) Is it restricted to the management of the integrated MDA communication net-work only?

(f) As a service provider to the stakeholders in the CSS – is the Navy just a recipient / custodian of the inputs received from the designated sources, with the responsibility as a facilitator to the subscribers, to make the means of access available to them, on demand - on line, on real time basis?

(g) Or is the Navy responsible for the entire CS system?

If results are to be expected from this initiative –it would be more appropriate to give DGCG additional charge of the over all coastal security arrangement and formally designate him as the *situational head* for the entire coastal security system, duly empowered.

It was encouraging to note that in this context, the RM is a realist. He has reserved his judgment on piecemeal announcement of fulfilment of task at each milestone. He would rather wait till such time as he can see at least one complete system commissioned (hub to spoke) and perform to his satisfaction.

On the question of mind-set block and turf considerations coming in the way of progressive reforms – one needs to take a good look at post 9/XI scenario in USA, especially at the salutary changes brought about in the US intelligence structure. Suffice is to draw attention here, to the way CIA has accepted the idea of embedding their operatives under the Special Forces with the US Central Command in Iraq and Afghanistan. And how the entire US Intelligence setup has been revamped to :

(a) Put together all analytical talents residing in CIA, FBI, and DIA into a conglomerate.

(b) Emulate the military in separating the organisation, training and equipping function from operational deployment functions.

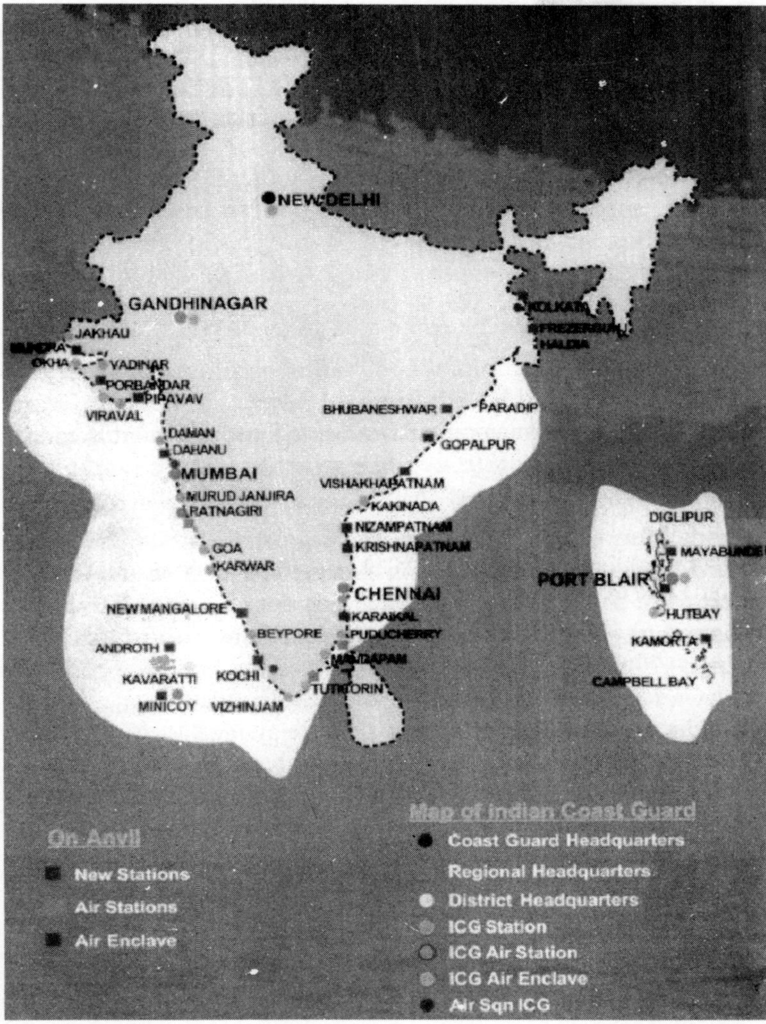

Fig. 7.51. Coast Guard Station Locations

Bibliography

1. "National intel grid to thwart maritime threat from Jan?" TOI 06 Dec 2010.
2. http://ajaishukla.blogspot.com/search?q=coastal.
3. http://www.sanctuaryasia.com/resources/environlaw/crz.doc.
4. Maritime Domain Awareness www.globalsecurity.org/intell/system/mda-htm.
5. PK Gosh "Coastal Security arrangement in Maharashtra: An Assessment". IDSA.
6. PK Gosh "India's Coastal Security - Challenges and Policy Recommendations" www.orfonline.org.
7. Ranjit Pandit "3yrs after 26/11. Govt OKs coastal radar chain" TOI 12 Sept 2011.
8. www.brahmand.com/news/india-to-set-up-National-MDA-grid-for-coastal- security/5687/3/13html.
9. www.dhs.gov/xlibrary/assets/x.
10. www.idsa.in/idsacomments/WitherCoastalSecurity_ pdas_ 261109.
11. www.marinebuzz.com/2010/03/31/india-coastal-security-scheme-update.
12. www.mha.nic.in/pdfs/AR(E)1011.pdf./ Annual report MHA 2010-2011.
13. www.observerindia.com/cms/or/online/modules/issuebrief/attachment/Ib_22_ 1283150948708.pdf.
14. www.security-risk.com/security-trends-south-asia/india-defence/india's-coastal-secirity-profile-the officialview.

8

Civilian Control Over Military

Ever since independence, in spite of the impeccable record of service to the nation, unquestionable loyalty and supreme sacrifice made by the military fraternity – it would seem that the political leadership abetted by the bureaucracy still has reservations on the professional integrity and loyalty of the military leadership. One reason is perhaps the fear of a coup or imposition of military dictatorship as in many of the neighbouring countries. Such conclusions cannot be drawn in isolation to the Indian democracy, culture, ethos and the historical record of the military itself. Carriapa, Thimmaya and Manekshaw – the most professional military leaders of our time – have for some motivated reasons been tarnished with this brush. In this context, side line portion of Lord Louis Mountbatten's letter at Annexure 1 also refers to such issues. Such a myth must be put to rest : earlier the better. At least now, on hind sight, one must be pragmatic and draw a lesson and nail those who keep calling wolf.

Michael C Desch in his book "Civilian control over the Military" has carried out an extensive study at a global scale. He has examined in detail, various factors that effect civilian control over military. Eventually, he came to the conclusion that the external / internal threat to any country are the two predominant factors that effect civilian control over the military. He has supported his arguments with sufficient historical data. His hypothesis is summarised in the graphic illustrated at Fig. 8.52. The matrix has been drawn depicting the effect of internal

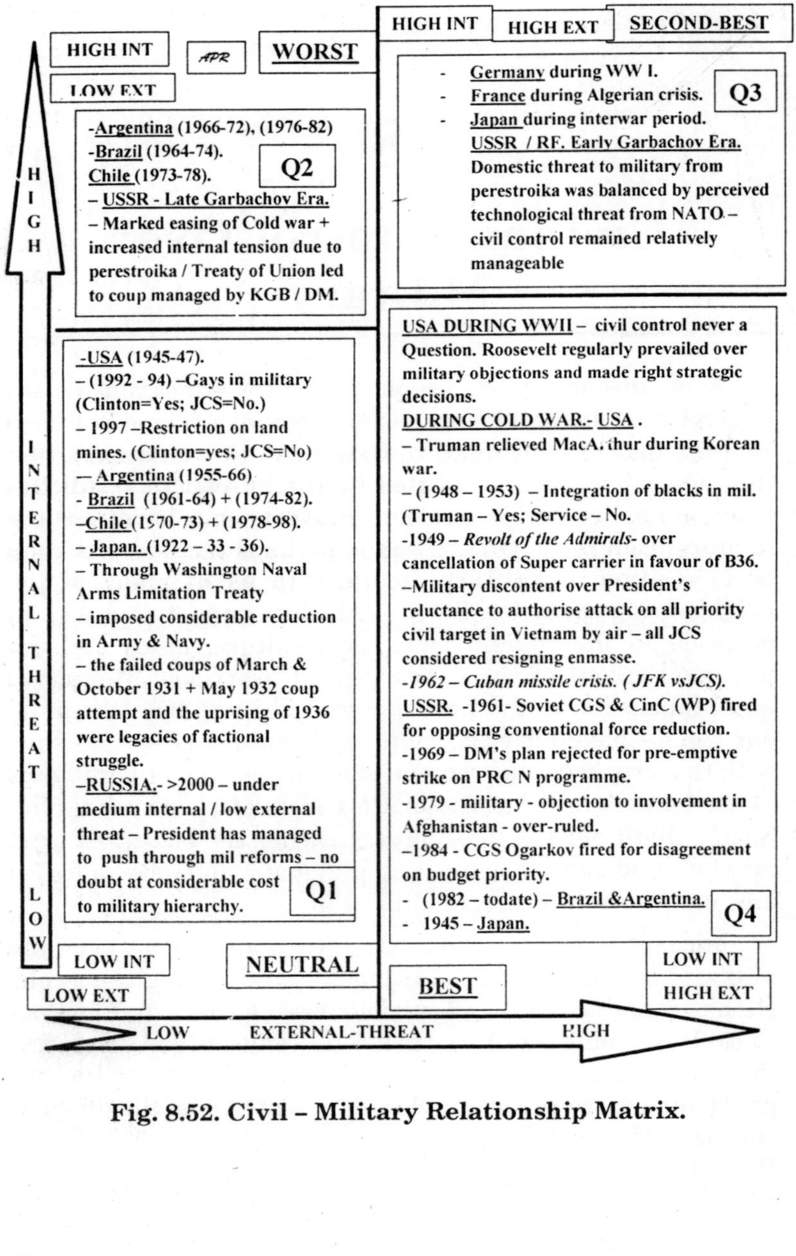

Fig. 8.52. Civil – Military Relationship Matrix.

/ external threat to a country and its relationship with the effectiveness of civilian control over military. His conclusions are predicated by the statement that the military's perception of which threat is more predominant will be the deciding factor.

The matrix has been divided into four quadrangles. The horizontal axis represents external threat – escalating from left to right. The vertical axis represents internal threat to the country – ascending from bottom to top. The graphic shows that:

(a) Quadrangle [Q1] represents a neutral category. There both the internal and the external threats are minimal. In such circumstances the threat to civil military control hovers in the uncertain regime. A typical example that falls in that category is USA immediately after the WWII. (1945 – 1947).

    During the last decade – under medium internal threat with low external threat situation and in a neutral environment – the RF President has managed to determinedly push through military reforms - admittedly at considerable cost to the military hierarchy.

(b) Quadrangle [Q2] falls during a period when for any specific country – the internal threats are high and the external threats are minimal. The worst scenario for civil control over the military is likely to occur in such circumstances. This is typically represented by:

    (i) The situation that prevailed during the early portion of Garbachov's Presidency in USSR. Marked easing of cold war tensions and enhanced internal tensions due to the introduction of perestroika / glasnost and the thrust towards a Treaty of Union caused serious uneasiness amongst the existing power centres. Finally that led to the coup - primarily engineered and executed by the KGB chief, supported by the DM and the Ground Force Chief who felt threatened by the reforms.

    (ii) Argentina, Brazil and Chile also - during the periods indicated.

(c) The quadrangle [Q3] encompasses a period where-in both

the internal and external threats are perceived to be high. This is a state during which the civilian control over military can be expected to be reasonably under check. During the early stages of perestroika in USSR – the domestic threat to the military was duly balanced by the perceived external threat from NATO due to their marked lead in military high technology. Civilian control over the military remained reasonably manageable.

(d) Quadrangle [Q4] covers a period when the internal threats are minimal and external threats are high. This is the most favourable regime where civilian control over the military is expected to flourish. The WWII and cold war periods are typical examples.

The above hypothesis is generally valid for the sub-continental situations also. Only, the historical, religious / cultural ethos and local conditions need to be super-imposed to get a realistic assessment. Pakistan's is a complex case – mixed with an identity crisis born out of partition and the artificial creation of a state. There the landed gentry and the military nexus got a strangle hold over the country's governance in its infancy before the political leadership could get a firm grip and provide a democratic frame-work. Since then, the military has managed to retain power, in one form or the other, by sustaining an existential external threat phobia conjoined with the projection of a high internal insecurity situation due to an ineffective and fractured political establishment. Such manipulation has superficially created a Q3 environment. In reality, most of the time, Pakistan actually has been in the Q2 regime.

The unfolding situation, at the end of 2011, in Pakistan need to be carefully watched. The internal situation is serious and the actual external threat is minimal. In these circumstances, the executive has been trying to assert its will. Logically, the situation falls into Category 1. In such an environment, an assertive President could take advantage and get away with it. To turn the tables – the military would have to once again create a situation to escalate the external threat factor and project a fractured politics.

Under Fig. 8.52 categorisation – India would fall in the Q4 regime most of the time. China and Pakistan have been a persistent and unpredictable serious threat most of the time. On some occasions – it may have drifted into Q3 regime for a short time. Many of the internal threats are also externally fuelled. In spite of the nuanced bureaucratic overtones – the situation has been favourably inclined towards a stable civilian control over military.

Professionalism, dedication and loyalty have been the hallmark of the military leadership. Without batting an eye lid - the Indian soldier is willing to lay down his life for his country and honour of his Regiment. His soft spot is his Regimental honour and *Izzath*. Any perceived threat in that domain could lead to serious consequences. If mobilised - there is a huge organised veteran population that could take up the cause

The insecurity felt in the political hierarchy is unfounded. Adoption of the interim, medium and long term measures suggested in Chapter 4 would address most of their apprehensions at the macro level. As discussed earlier –there is a need to exercise some discreet political oversight in the HRD policy jurisdiction without appearing to be interfering.

COMMENTARY ON RECENTS EVENTS ON THE INDIAN SCENARIO

Dissent as an embedded phenomena, is a part of all democratic institutions. Military dissent is, however, usually considered not acceptable. The nuanced difference between professional dissent and other wise - is not generally understood, especially in India. A strong ethical environment that discriminates between the pliant / sycophant and the conscientious professional dissenter could make the difference between victory and defeat. Michael Desch further adds that "Civilians meddling in matters of military expertise is almost as bad as the military involving itself in politics".

History is abounding with instances that reinforce the above hypothesis. A few of the glaring examples are sited below as a reminder:

(a) India's debacle in 1962 against China.

(b) The Chinese Cultural Revolution and PLA's diversion into political and commercial affairs earning them a bloody nose at the hands of Vietnam.

(c) The commitment of US ground forces in Vietnam and in Iraq is attributed to the capitulation of the professional military dissent to the civilian hawks.

As a rebound from the Vietnam-war - Collin Powel and his colleagues went so far as to vow that when their time comes to call the shots - they would not quietly acquiesce to a half-hearted warfare for half baked reasons.

At the first look, the issues thrown up recently in India regarding the apparent fissure between the COAS and the RM - raise some serious questions on the civilian military relationship. Deeper reflection, however, shows that the two are not so closely related, as being made out. The assessment made earlier, in respect of India, on the basis of the empirical matrix is considered still valid.

The civil military relationship has deteriorated more due to inaction caused by:

(a) The political leadership being seriously handicapped due to reasons enumerated at Chapter. 5 under inherent inadequacies in the Indian environment.

(b) Total dependence of the political leadership on bureaucrats-who have their own agenda.

In the case under discussion - there is no personality clash involved. Also, both of them have an unimpeachable record on honesty and integrity.

None of the restructuring proposals made in the book are affected by the current development. The situation only emphasises the urgency of implementing the exercise. No cosmetic changes would do. There is no doubt that in addition to the restructuring proposed here - serious introspection is called for, within the military. Internally, the system is out of synch with the realities of today. The situation needs to be thoroughly investigated and root causes clearly identified. Most of the reality is known in house. The establishment is in a denial mode and does not have the courage of its conviction and the will to implement such hard decisions. There has been strong resistance to even the COAS's implementation plan on 'Transformation Study report.

As brought out earlier, much wider restructuring is called for. Resistance to change is normal and is to be expected. Its scope and ramifications must however be clearly understood and factored in. The need for reforms is indisputable. Unless at least three successive COASs are agreed on the template and are determined to see the case through with imagination, vigour and perseverance – not much can be expected to come out of any such bold initiative. For success – they will also need whole hearted support and understanding of the government and the public.

In this context, Navy's expeprience in their attempt to implement the restructuring programme would be a good indicator to the hurdles that are likely to arise. The care rationalisation programme initiated in the late 1960s and vigorously followed up in the mid 1970s has yet to take root. This has been the case – in spite of there being near unanimity of views on the subject between the successive CNSs.

Case study of the military perestroika attempted by Russia, after the collapse of USSR – should serve as an eye opener too. Several Defence Ministers, Chief of General Staff and innumerable Generals were relieved from their duties – for perceived obstructions to the ordained process of *perestroika*. They are still far away from achieving their objective.

None of this, however, should deter the Army from working out a pragmatic and phased restructuring programme with vision and foresight.

Compared to the Navy and the Air Force – the Army procedures are more complex because of the enormity of its size and due to numerous line directorates involved in the capital acquisition process. Multilayered processing at each stage leads to further delays. These need to be rationalised too.

Bibliography

1. Andrew Cockburn. "Rumsfield: His Rise, Fall and Catastrophic Legacy".
2. Charles. A. Stevenson. "Warrior and Politician".

3. Col. Raj Shukla. "Civil Military Relations". IDSA research paper.
4. Colin. L. Powel. "The American Journey".
5. Dale. R. Herspring. "The Pentagon and the Presidency".
6. Eliot. E. Cohen. "Supreme Command - Soldier, Statesman and Leadership in war-time".
7. Michael C Desch. "Bush and the Generals". Foreign Affairs. June 2002.
8. Michael Desch. "Civilian Control of the Military".
9. Samuel. P. Huntington. "The soldier and the State".
10. Yoram Peri. "Generals in the Cabinet".

9

National Disasater Management

The Armed Forces are meant to be called in to assist civil administration only as a last means of resort – when the situation is beyond their capacity. In practice, however, the Armed Forces have historically played a major role in emergency support functions. Rather than taking over every thing that nobody is willing to take on – the military should be channelling their vast expertise, experience, and organizational / managerial skills and resources – to push the civil authorities both in the state and the centre to gear themselves up to deal with disasters. The military should only be the fall back agency, as a means of last resort – when speedy response is critical. The military should provide all training / managerial assistance, storage and logistics back-up for heavy duty and specialized equipment - positioned at strategic locations. And be prepared in peacetime to provide rescue, relief and immediate rehabilitation measures, when called upon. This principle equally applies in the case of coastal security arrangements discussed in the last chapter.

The political hierarchy finds it much easier to call in the army than to put the appropriate civil machinery in place. The dilemma faced in dealing with the naxalite menace typifies the situation. In the absence of any long term civil arrangement to deal with such situations - the Army is caught in the quagmire of dealing with internal security situation on a permanent basis. The army has to intervene even in such mundane issue as rescuing a child fallen into an open manhole to flood and earthquake relief work. This has been possible in peace time without any apparent loss of efficiency / effectiveness in its primary role. What if such a situation arises during a time when the military is preoccupied with its assigned role? It is encouraging to see that the present HM is trying to prepare for such contingencies

A beginning has been made now by enacting the National Disaster Management Act (NDMA) 2005. The NDMA is a comprehensive document dealing with all aspects of disaster management – both at the macro and the micro levels. The Act rightly envisages the Armed Forces as a means of last resort. It lays down the organisational set up from the grass root level to the apex body at the centre.

The NDM Authority has been designated as the Apex body – with the PM in the chair assisted by nine other members. Since 2009 – the former COAS General NC Vij has been the Vice Chairman. The Act also transferred the responsibility of coordination of all NDM activities from the Ministry of Agriculture to Ministry of Home Affairs (MHA). Accordingly, the Home Secretary has been designated as the chair person of the National Executive committee (NEC) of the NDMA. The CIDS has been made a member of the NEC. The COAS is a member of the High Powered Disaster Management Committee. The CIDS also heads the Defence Crisis Management Group.

The chain of command runs from the NEC to the State Executive Committees (SEC) with the Chief Secretary in the chair. The District Disaster Management Authority (DDMA) is at the next echelon.

The NEC comprise of the Home Secretary, Secretaries of Agriculture, AEC, Defence, Drinking Water Supply, Environment & Forest, Finance (Expenditure), Health, Power, Rural Development, S&T, Space, Telecom, Urban Development, Water resources and CIDS. Additionally, the Secretaries of MEA, HRD, Mines, Shipping, and Road Transportation and Highways are special invitees.

The State Disaster Management Authority (SDMA) for Delhi is chaired by the Lieutenant Governor. The Chief Minister is the Vice Chairperson. The SEC is headed by the state Chief Secretary. The District DMA is headed by the District

Magistrate / Collector / Deputy Commissioner with an elected representative of the local authority as a co-chairperson. The local authority includes the Panchayath Raj Institution, Municipal Corporation, District and Cantonment Boards.

For the purpose of handling disaster management crisis – disasters have been categorised into four broad groups:

(a) Natural: Earth quake, Flood, Draught, Tsunami, Avalanche, Global warming etc.

(b) Accidental: Industrial, Chemical, Nuclear, Petrochemical etc.

(c) Social: Discrimination, Female, Caste, Social economic deprivation etc.

(d) Terrorist.

The disaster management handling process has been divided into five levels:

(a) L0 – Ground Zero.

(b) L2 – District level.

(c) L3 – State level.

(d) L4 – National level.

A project team lead by Aromar Revi has, after extensive survey and research, developed a Gujarat Hazard Risk & Vulnerability Atlas. This is one of the most comprehensive disaster and risk assessment initiative in India. It conveys risk assessment for the twenty five districts and two hundred and twenty six taluks of Gujarat in respect of six natural and man made hazards. It undertakes quantification of physical, socio-economic and economic vulnerability. It also estimates – the separate and combined risks to population, infrastructure, capital assets and economy of the state. Other States must emulate the example set. The Ministry of Urban Development has been given the responsibility for generating the vulnerability Atlas of India.

The onus of disaster management is squarely left on the respective states. To cope with disaster management at the national level a dedicated National Disaster Response Force (NDRF) has been sanctioned. The NDRF comprises of eight battalion of Central Para Military Force (two each from BSF,

CRPF, CISF and ITBF). Each battalion will provide eighteen self contained specialist search and rescue teams of forty-five personnel each. These include doctors, paramedics, structural engineers, technician, electricians and dog squads. Each battalion comprises of about 1,200 personnel. Raising of two additional battalions has also been approved. These battalions are spread out and located across the country. They are available for augmentation of the state means. Presently four of them have been equipped and trained to respond to any Chemical Biological Radiological & Nuclear (CBRN) emergencies. The present location of the NPMF is indicated in the map at Fig. 9.53.

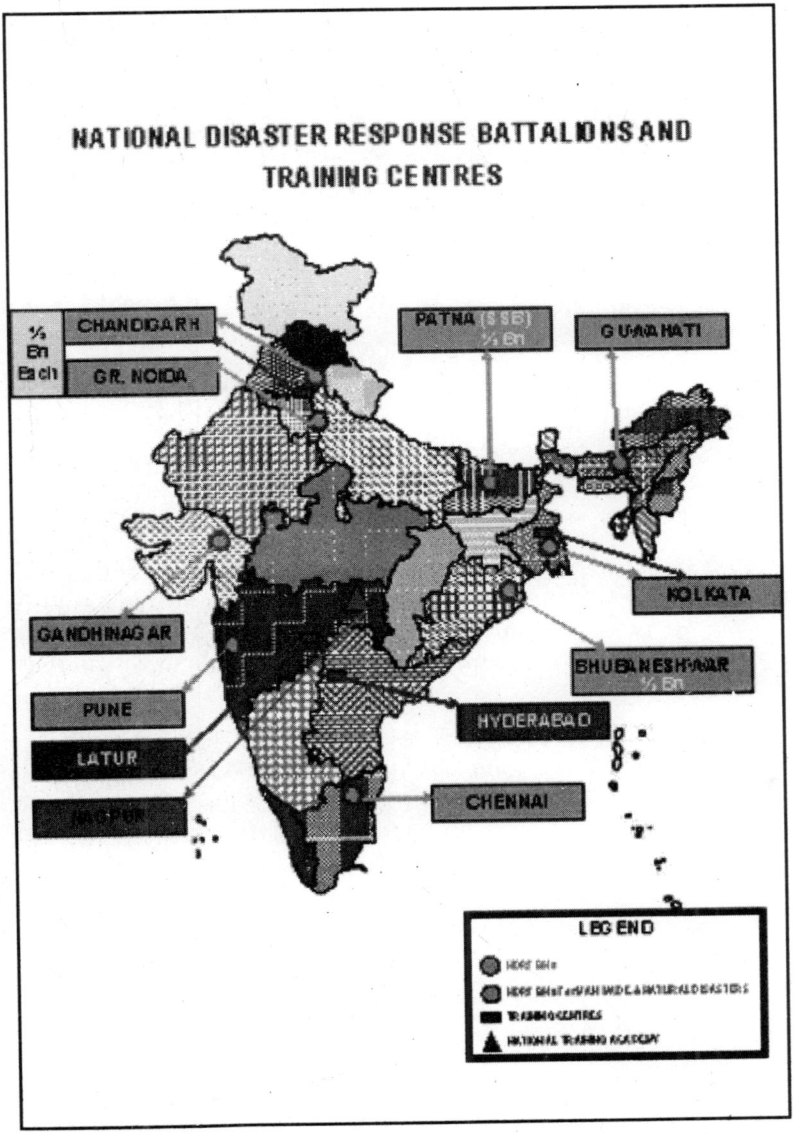

Fig. 9.53. Map showing location of disaster response battalions and training centres.

10

Resume of Conclusion and Recommended Course of Action

CHECK-OFF LIST ACTION PLAN

In conclusion, a summary of the recommended course of action is listed in the succeeding paragraphs. All time-frames projected here, are with a view to being prepared to take on the perceived China's pace of Defence build up. Their Defence white papers indicate that by 2015 they would be prepared for out of area projection of power – even out of South China Sea.

PRINCIPAL THRUST OF PROPOSED REFORMS

CCS approval for following course of action be taken:

(a) Accept the long term objective of developing an Indian HDM option akin to the current UK model illustrated at Fig. 2.20. This would need to be brought into force within five years. This would entail acceptance of breaking up the military organisational structure into three functional Divisions: Staff, Operation and Support.

(b) Accept some further delay in the appointment of the CDS.

(c) Initiate expeditious action to mitigate the *conditionality* issue raised in Chapter 5. To be implemented within one year.

(d) As an interim, stop gap measure, accept the HDM model illustrated at Fig. 5.35, for immediate implementation.

Fundamentally, it conforms, in spirit to CCS decision given in 2002. Some minor variations have been incorporated to accommodate some important lacunae, thrown up since. It should also put to rest the serious observation raised by the PSCD.

(e) During the last decade there has been a stale mate in the restructuring process. This is largely attributable to the absence of a CDS. What is required at this point of time is to put in place, a leader, empowered to execute the core restructuring objectives without any impairment.

(f) In the circumstances, CIDS could break the impasse and take the perestroika exercise forward. To empower him – CIDS would need to be upgraded to same ranks as the COSs. This would be analogous to the VCDS and CJO (UK). In this capacity CIDS will be required to render quarterly progress review statement to DC on the reform / restructuring front. This will obviate the need to set up a special task force after ten years of inaction.

(g) Introduction of the concept of Defence Council chaired by RM and Army / Navy / IAF Boards, each under the charge of a Minister of State. This would be in conformity with assurance given by PM Nehru to Parliament in 1953. And will also meet the requirement of enhancing Political control over the military. Both the DC and the Service Boards would be chaired by the RM. The Executive Council of the Service Board will be chaired by the respective COS.

(h) Elimination of all ambiguity in the chain of military command vis-à-vis the NSA. In conformity with modern democratic practices and to ensure that orders are not struck down on legal grounds.

(i) Eradication of the perception of bureaucratic imposition over the military, as opposed to civilian political control.

(j) Re-designation of Defence Secretary as the Principal Civilian Adviser to the RM.

(k) Revisit the *MOD rules of business* and incorporate appropriate amendments.

(l) Pass a comprehensive Act of Parliament , similar to the US Goldwater Nichols Act of 1986 – so that the system is not open to manipulation by political / bureaucratic / military leadership of the time.

(m) Appoint a high powered Task Force with clear cut charter and commitment to draft the above Act within a stipulated time frame. (Following the empowered GOMs route).

IMMEDIATE AND SHORT TERM REFORMS

MACRO LEVEL REFORMS

(a) To ensure speedy and phased execution of the much needed Logistics reforms – JCSC, to immediately appoint a dedicated Deputy CIDS (Logistics). To steer through this important programme – if need be, CJCSC may consider appointing the Deputy CIDS (Log) from internal resources. Absence of such an arrangement will have serious implications on operational effectiveness of the field formations.

(b) The concept of unified theatre command seems to have been put on the backburner. This needs to be rejuvenated, as a mid-term objective – with a clear cut-off period, not exceeding three years. The option illustrated at Figure 5.36 is quite pragmatic, workable and reasonable. And could be considered by the JCOSC for implementation, as a serious model for adoption.

(c) Over ten years ago, the Andaman & Nicobar (A&N) and the Strategic Force (SF) Commands were launched, to form the pilot project for the ultimate theatre command concept. This was then considered a stepping stone and confidence building measure – to generate the requisite ethos for a unified theatre command concept to take root. The A&N command had existed as a joint command of sorts, under the Fortress Commander (A&N) for many years before. The joint-ness at work however does not seem to have yet jelled. In the absence of a CDS - the only way, the A&N Command can achieve its potential and show the way ahead, would be to give CIDS this, as a direct responsibility. This will give it the requisite stimulus, priority and direction that it deserves. For this task he would be directly responsible to CJCSC. Regular quarterly stock being taken of the progress by the DC

(d) JCOSC to workout on priority – a fast track build up plan for A&NC. The A&NC should be built on a unified command basis and programmed to reach a full fledged theatre command status within two years. Mile-stones to achieve this goal must be clearly defined and monitored. CIDS to render quarterly progress review report to DC.

(e) Next, a crucial policy decision must be taken regarding the direction in which the restructuring of the combat forces is to proceed.

  (i) Is the plan to divest, the incumbent COSs of their operational responsibilities – in line with the US and UK formulation?

  (ii) OR –Should India plan to go the USSR Unified General Staff way?

(f) This is a call - JCSC must take urgently.

(g) Splitting the military on functional basis, as practised in most modern countries now, is a neat and rational scheme. Such an arrangement is justifiable on purely good management principles. General JN Choudhury, a former COAS, had in his National Security address to the USI, on practical grounds, strongly advocated the splitting of the role of COAS into *staff & operation* functions.

(h) Some may consider adoption of the global model in its entirety as unviable in the Indian circumstances – especially due to the inherent political inadequacy factor, brought out at Chapter.5. Hence, this could be reconsidered after the CDS is fully in the saddle.

(i) To some others, such a solution could also be perceived as a means of preventing development of any undesirable power-centre within the military hierarchy.

(j) To begin with, it is suggested that India adopts a mixed approach. The A&N / SF Commands and the Strategic Wings (Navy)/ (IAF), follow one model. All under the operational command of the CIDS.

(k) In the case of the SWs (IN) / (IAF) - the administrative and technical command authority could continue with the respective service. This could be used as a springboard for achieving the ultimate goal of *unified theatre commands*, as stated earlier.

(l) In the interim, the rest of the combat forces, gear themselves up, in planned stages – to adapt the RF unified General Staff / theatre command model, within a period not exceeding twelve months. This would have the following advantages:

  (i) Likely to meet with least resistance from the incumbent COSs.

  (ii) Would achieve the objective in the shortest possible time – with least disturbance / dislocation to the existing functioning mechanism.

  (iii) The experience of SFC, A&N Commands and SW (IN) / (IAF), which would be on a fast track - would give the feedback, for midcourse corrections, if need be, to the evolving theatre command concept.

(m) As a matter of policy, ensure that all new strategic infrastructure being planned / in the pipe line, including space assets, are set up in the integrated / joint / unified domain under CIDS.

(n) To facilitate eventual formation of an integrated support division – to begin with, set up a support function Division for the Navy as a pilot project. Put CWP&A and DGND under COM and merge the Naval Acquisition Wing with the Material Branch, as illustrated at Figure 6.46.

(o) As a part of the over-all integration plan of SHQ with MOD – designate concerned PSOs as Secretary to the Government and empower them with linked financial power and authority.

(p) In case of high value projects, where dedicated project team, is a must e.g. Project 75 "*scorpene*", Project 75(I) & Project 71 "*Goroshkov*" etc - in addition to the horizontal linkages with the DOD, structured connectivity with the Professional Directorates at NHQ, at all levels, must also be ensured.

(q) This would be greatly facilitated – when CWP&A and DGND are shifted out of the Staff Branch and merged into the Material Branch under COM. The illustration at Figure. 6.46 is relevant.

(r) Next logical step would be to empower COM with adequate financial powers on naval capital acquisitions – with integrated financial / contractual backing. In this context, precedence already exists in that – Rear Admiral Daya Shankar occupied the chair of the Controller General of Defence Production in the capacity of an Additional Secretary from 1960 – 1963. Single point accountability would be clearly established. DGATV is yet another working example. He would continue to follow the basic procedures laid down in the DPP2011 with minor alterations. This would improve efficiency, eliminate most bureaucratic hold-ups and considerably speed-up the acquisition cycle.

(s) IAF should follow suite and the Army in due course.

LOGISTICS REFORMS

(a) An affirmative JCSC decision be taken - on the long-term need for a unified military logistics system. CIDS to steer the case through.

(b) Amongst all the computerised logistics systems in place – the Navy's seems to be the most advanced one. The system-combine caters for all functions of contemporary logistics from womb to tomb and is audit compatible also. Except for the commercial aspects all functions are adequately covered. The Navy needs to carry this forward and develop a full fledged CALS architecture. Under the circumstances, it is only rational that a unified computerised logistics architecture be generated from the Naval model with NCS incorporated.

(c) Deputy CIDS (Log) be appointed to steer through and oversee implementation of following:

(i) The Joint Logistics Committee to evolve and adopt - an integrated codification doctrine – within a quarter.

(ii) Garner all where-withal available in the country, towards rationalization of military codification system.

(iii) Get full mileage out of following opportunities knocking at the door:

- Tier I membership of NSC - 09June 2008.
- Indian membership of ISO.
- Utilize all US FMS transactions - to gain full access to NSN catalogues and their supply chains.
- Russian Federation Protocol offering supply of spare parts catalogue with NSC based part numbers.
- Assistance from local ERP vendors – to integrate logistic soft ware.

(d) DOS to add above to their charter and give priority to implementation. CIDS be designated the nodal coordination agency.

(e) DPP to stipulate inclusion in all contracts with AC (135) compliant countries – of a provision for Illustrated Parts Lists (IPL)s with NCS numbers and vendor particulars incorporated.

(f) The Navy needs to take its logistics restructuring process forward and overhaul the cadre structure to give it technical orientation and make it totally inclusive.

(g) Navy to implement the cadre rationalization programme as discussed at Chapter 6 with determination.

(h) Rationalization of the naval command structure, as applicable to logistics - on the model of the IAF would also be necessary.

(i) The Army to carry forward the DGOL prescription to its logical conclusion, in line with the suggestion in Brigadier Pramod Sarin's book "Military Logistics – the third dimension".

(j) Implement the COAS's *"Transformation Study"* recommendations urgently.

(k) Progressively to restructure logistics function within the service to take on *womb to tomb* role.

(l) The IAF to inter-link the IMMOL's online real time connectivity with field units and other defence aviation establishments. Command & Control will continue to remain with AOM.

(m) The Air force to become more institutionally involved and committed to military aeronautical design and development projects. Utilize the openings becoming available in projects such as Fifth Generation Fighter Aircraft (FGFA) , Multi Role Transport a/c (MRTAC) etc.

(n) For maximum benefit to accrue, from the so called Joint Design Development and Production Agreement on FGFA and MRTAC – the LCA model with DRDO / ADA / NAL / IAF in the inner loop would have been ideal. HAL is not reputed to have the design capability / superstructure / culture to imbibe / absorb the design know how necessary to carry forward the capability built up by the LCA team. HAL's record for carrying forward a/c design capability is clear from the history of HF24.

(o) Unless the so called Joint Design / Development collaboration Agreement on FGFA is confined to joint collaboration from detail design / production / manufacturing / assembly drawing stage onwards only? This seems to be the case – since the basic a/c PAK-FA already exists in Russia.

(p) CICP has lost too much ground. It must be put on fast track and adopt the NCS route. CIDS be tasked to ensure speedy implementation and integration with the operational net-work.

(q) In due course, the Navy & IAF must also follow suit – the earlier the better.

(r) Adopt modern ware-housing technology, supply-chain management system. Provisioning of improved mobility, mechanical handling facilities and universal use of bar-coding system etc would go a long way in achieving higher efficiency and productivity.

(s) CIDS to use Andaman & Nicobar command to develop on priority, a pilot project to implement an exclusive unified command logistic system.

(t) Navy to undertake – commensurate cadre structure review. And implement E&L merger of Branches and introduce *User Maintainer* Concept on board ships.

Note: In conclusion, it may be added that- as far as the integration of Military Logistics is concerned – intra-service integration, to a large extent, already exists in the cases of IN & IAF. Also, Army Medical Corp (AMC), Military Postal Service, Movement Control Organization, Military Engineering Service (MES), Canteen Service and to a limited extend, even the ASC are already part of a unified service.

(u) The urgency is such, that the immediate and short term logistics reform plans need not wait – either for the appointment of the CDS or the JCSC to arrive at a decision on adopting a unified military logistics system. This is considered to be well within the scope of the uniformed fraternity. Only joint *will* and perseverance is needed.

(v) If one can come to an amicable agreement within the JCSC on such contentious an issue as the Unified / Joint Space Command Concept – then such mundane issues as above could also be resolved by mutual discussions.

COASTAL SECURITY IMPERATIVES

At the macro level, from the centre, serious attempts have been made towards harnessing all possible resources towards achieving better coastal security, expeditiously. The NCSMCS initiative is great. CSS2005 and CSS Phase II sanctions are commendable.

The idea of designating the Navy as a nodal Agency for coastal security and DGCG as the Commander of a non-existing Coastal Command is very suspect.

The Navy should certainly have a central role in formulating the coastal security architecture. Specially, bearing mind:

(a) The over all perspective in a wartime scenario.

(b) Generational maritime expertise and experience.

Designating the Navy as a nodal agency can be very misleading. Pin-pointing true accountability will become impossible.

It would be more appropriate for DGCG to be given additional charge of the overall coastal security arrangement.

To a limited extent - he already plays a constabulary role and has close interaction on a daily basis with DGLH, customs, revenue intelligence, narcotic control agencies, Port Authorities and local civil administration etc. He needs to be empowered accordingly and given operational control over:

(a) CSF.

(b) DGLH control centres – over all coastal surveillance facilities.

The Navy may be designated as the nodal agency for MDA and held responsible for:

(a) Maintaining a network capable of receiving inputs from multifarious sensors / sources and facilitate access to such data, on real time basis, to all the concerned subscriber agencies.

(b) Provide overall guidance and maritime expertise in creating the necessary infrastructure including coastal command, control, communication, intelligence and surveillance network and provide training skills in preparing the personnel for working in a maritime environment.

MEDIUM AND LONG TERM PERSPECTIVE PLAN

(a) The Army to establish an integrated intra-service logistics system / organization – from Corporate / Command HQs and Central Depots to field units.

(b) Evolve a unified / integrated logistics management architecture for the three services.

(c) Great deal of spadework is required to be undertaken, before considering formation of a Unified Functional Logistic Command. The services must first set their own house in order and bring about an atmosphere of professional convergence.

(d) CIDS to be tasked to implement all the above speedily under a unified concept. Quarterly progress report to be rendered to DC.

(e) The naval model of a captive Design Bureau, along with its embedded horizontal linkages, has delivered the goods.

What remains to be achieved, is a marked improvement in shipyard productivity and efficiency. They should also encourage synergy with private sector and resort to greater public / private partnership and outsourcing.

(f) The other services should consider emulating the naval model, in a way best suited to them. The way forward, for the Air force would be to capitalise on:

(i) The JV with Russia on FGFA and MRTAC projects.

(ii) The MMRCA project.

(g) Institutionalised independent technical audit for all high value R&D projects, with long gestation periods, irrespective of its security classification, must be made mandatory.

(h) Fully commission a unified functional Division for Defence Acquisition and life time product support. Progressively evolve, within five years, a structure akin to UK's DSES as illustrated as figures 2.19 and 2.20 - to take on the total logistics responsibilities.

(i) Nowhere in the world has the HDM restructuring process been implemented – sans any pain. The political leadership, in all cases has had to 'bite the bullet' and assert them-selves – even if it meant, that in the bargain a few heads had to roll. Only great care needs to be exercised in the process, to ensure that a fair and level field has been provided to all the stake holders, devoid of any parochial / partisan undertones.

(j) When it comes to in-house restructuring within the services – all the above arguments are equally applicable to the service hierarchy.

(k) It has been shown in Chapter 1 and 2 that both the USA and UK have an institutionalised system of SDR. UK conducted their last one in 2011 and USA in January 2012. In the Indian context, no such statement has been forthcoming as a policy guide-line document for the IDSHQ to generate the requisite joint strategy.

(l) In 2002, RM's operational directive was issued. There is an urgent necessity for NSC in consultation with the DC and the CJCSC to formulate and promulgate a National Security Strategic (NSS) document. This could be in two parts. One a classified portion. The other an unclassified part for public consumption.

(m) The classic process of evolving a Military doctrine involves the following stages. Formulation of:

(i) National Aims.

(ii) National Interest.

(iii) National Grand Strategy.

(iv) National Security Objectives.

(v) National Security Policy.

(vi) National Military Objectives (NMO).

(vii) National Military Doctrine.

(m) The DC should promulgate the NMO to the SHQs so that IDSHQ could formulate the joint military doctrine and put it up to NSC for approval. These could there after be promulgated in two parts – the classified and the unclassified part.

(n) Institutionalised SDR must also be introduced on a regular basis – to update the same with changed environment. The MOD had committed to the 14th Lok Sabha PSC on defence that a NSS would be evolved by 2009. After two years – this does not even find a mention in the 15th LSPSC of defence report.

(o) To inculate a joint services ethos – institute a criterea system, requiring.

(i) All officers in initial posting to SHQ – be given a six month assignment at IDSHQ.

(ii) One appointment with a Joint Services Organisation / Institution as a prerequisite for promotion to Lt. Gen. / Vice Admiral / Air Marshal.

Annexure

BROADLANDS.
ROMSEY.
HAMPSHIRE.
SO5 9ZD

TELEPHONE
ROMSEY (0794)

27th September 1977

Dear Chib,

Thank you so much for your letter of the 20th September which I have read with the greatest of interest.

It is nice to see a Subaltern from the days when you mounted guard at Viceroy's House now a Major General and Director of Military Operations. Many congratulations.

To answer your questions in your paragraph 6:-

(a) The main reason for not urging an immediate appointment of a CDS was precisely that it would be a number of years before a naval or air force officer would be senior enough to be considered for the appointm The tragic death of the most senior air force officer, Air Marshal Mukerji, in Japan, put back the date at least a couple of years.

But there was also another reason and that was although Prime Minister Nehru agreed with me in principle he said it would be difficult at thi moment to get through the appointment of a CDS as it would give to the Indiar politians the idea of perpetuating the idea of the great "Commander in Chief in India" of whom the last one, of course, was Field Marshal Auchinleck. He did, however, agree to reconsider later.

(b) Lord Ismay and I worked hand in hand on these proposals but I thought it would come better from him than from the Constitutional Governor General as I then had become. He also tried to negotiate a CDS but met wi the same opposition from Nehru and for the same reasons.

(c) I have never had any doubt that the time would come when India should have a CDS. It is more important now than ever in my opinion as India is about the only major country that does not have a CDS or at least a Chairman of the Chiefs of Staff's ~~system~~ Committee.

I should perhaps add that the last time Nehru stayed with me here at Broadlands before the Chinese invasion on the North East Frontier, I urged him to appoint General Thimayya to be the CDS right away as I could see trouble brewing up. He liked Thimayya immensely and was no longer opposed to the idea of a CDS provided it could be got through the Minister of Defence, at that time our mutual friend, Krishna Menon. He said ~~M~~ Krishna was so bitterly opposed to Thimayya and, indeed, all the really intelligent independent senior officers such as Muchoo Chaudhuri, that he was sure he could never get Krishna to agree.

I told him that the real danger was that Krishna was appointing people like Thapar as CGS who was a good administrator but had no command experience and worse still, Kaul who appeared to be a political appointment, though he had been a personal friend.

I warned him that if war came the Indian Army would suffer a quick defeat. He said there was no question of there being a war as India wished to be at peace with everybody. To this I replied that it took two sides to decide whether there would be a war or not and if either China or Pakistan were to invade they would have a war on their hands.

He replied that he relied on his agreement with Chou en Lai and the Chinese would never invade. I questioned this and then I said "If you are so certain you are going to have no war, why don't you cut down your armed forces and save money?"

This, however, he was unwilling to do as Krishna was against it.

I then said "Well, when you do get involved in a war I will do everything I can to come to your help."

When the Chinese invaded the first thing I did was to send out Field Marshal Sir Richard Hull, then the CGS, in a Britannia ~~with~~ which I had loaded to the very brim with self-loading rifles, as I knew the Indian Army had no up-to-date small arms.

The next thing I did was to send out my two Intelligence officers who were extremely high-class and did co-ordination with other Intelligence Services, to try and re-organise the Military Intelligence branch which had faded right away under the influence of the remarkable Sikh whose name I forget, who ran the Government Intelligence Service.

I came out myself a bit later on and met the Defence Council and Senior Officers and if you can find the Minutes of that meeting I think you will find I urged once more that they should immediately appoint a Chief of the Defence Staff and suggested that it should be General Thimayya.

It is just possible I made this remark out of Committee because of the well-known opposition of Krishna Menon, but I certainly made the suggestion to Nehru and I am afraid it wasn't adopted, I think again through Krishna Menon's hostility.

You have correctly noted that I managed to get a very considerabl degree of unification in command and administration in the British Services. In those days we had overseas commands and I appointed ~~many~~ Supreme Commanders under the title of "Unified Commanders-in-Chief" for the near East, middle East and far East. All this went very well, particularly during the confrontation in Borneo with Soekino.

However, I have always made a great point of saying that we would not follow that ludicrous Canadian example whereby they put the Army, Navy and Air Force into green uniforms and gave them the same titles.

My elder daughter, Patricia, is Colonel-in-Chief of Princess Patricia's Canadian Light Infantry and I have been three times with her when she visited her Regiment and each year I notice that they are returning more and more to their own mess dress, their own ranks and their own uniforms. I think they will soon return to having the prestige and esprit de corps of their own Service while still having the benefit of unification at the top.

Great care is needed to avoid destroying esprit de corps of any Service by putting them all into a green uniform!

Be careful how you use this letter as it is probably irregular for a former Viceroy-Governor-General to communicate direct with the Director of Military Operations.

For this reason I have marked the letter "Confidential".

You can show it to the CGS if you like on a strictly confidential basis for advice as to how to proceed if you want to follow up these ideas.

I wouldn't in the least mind writing to the new Prime Minister as Morarji Desai is an old friend and would probably take some note of what I wrote, but I don't want to intervene at this moment when he has so many other problems on his plate.

Yours sincerely

Mountbatten of Burma

Index